Carnival, Canboulay and Calypso
Traditions in the making

JOHN COWLEY

CAMBRIDGE
UNIVERSITY PRESS

Published by the Press Syndicate of the University of Cambridge
The Pitt Building, Trumpington Street, Cambridge CB2 1RP
40 West 20th Street, New York, NY 10011–4211, USA
10 Stamford Road, Oakleigh, Melbourne 3166, Australia

© Cambridge University Press 1996

First published 1996
Reprinted 1997
First paperback edition 1998

Printed in the United Kingdom at the University Press, Cambridge

A catalogue record for this book is available from the British Library

Library of Congress cataloguing in publication data applied for

ISBN 0 521 48138 4 hardback
ISBN 0 521 65389 4 paperback

Starting from the days of slavery and following through to the first two decades of the twentieth century, this book traces the evolution of Carnival and secular black music in Trinidad and the links that existed with other Caribbean territories and beyond. Calypso emerged as the pre-eminent Carnival song from the end of the nineteenth century and its association with the festival is investigated, as are the first commercial recordings by Trinidad performers. These featured stringband instrumentals, 'calipsos' and stickfighting 'kalendas' (a carnival style popular from the last quarter of the nineteeth century). Great use is made of contemporary newspaper reports, colonial documents, travelogues, oral history and folklore, providing an authoritative treatment of a fascinating story in popular cultural history.

Carnival, Canboulay and Calypso

For all devotees of Carnival and its music.
In gratitude for my mother's support
and in memory of my father

Contents

Illustrations

Acknowledgements

The scope of this work entailed gathering information in Trinidad and Tobago, France, the United States, and Britain.

In Trinidad and Tobago, I am greatly indebted to Jean Pearse. Her encouragement from the onset spurred my efforts. She graciously allowed me access to Andrew Pearse's papers, and the material he collected in Trinidad in the early 1950s is a foundation for this study. I am especially grateful for her hospitality and wisdom. I owe a similar debt to Peta Bain and Diane Dumas, through whose generosity I was able to visit Trinidad and Tobago during the Carnival season in 1991. Their friendship, hospitality, and efforts are singularly appreciated.

The staff of the West India Reference Library, in Port-of-Spain, gave me access to newspapers not available in Britain, and Edwina Peters (National Archives of Trinidad and Tobago), allowed me to inspect similar periodicals. Garth Murrell photographed relevant columns from these precious nineteenth-century documents. His speed and efficiency in delivering the prints before my departure were particularly helpful.

At the University of the West Indies, St Augustine, Bridget Brereton (Senior Lecturer in History) smoothed my passage in using the Library's West India Collection and my purpose was advanced by Kim Gransaull. I also spoke with Gordon Rohlehr (Professor of West Indian Literature), whose work on calypso parallels my own. Bridget Brereton helped subsequently with additional sources.

The late Neville Marcano (Growling Tiger) kindly shared his reminiscences and I have had useful conversations with Hollis Liverpool (Mighty Chalkdust) on his visits to Britain.

I am grateful to Alain Boulanger in Paris, who sent recordings and information on biguines from the French Antilles that allowed accurate comparison with French Creole music in Trinidad.

Many friends in the United States have assisted. I owe a great deal to the unstinting support of Dick Spottswood. Joseph C. Hickerson (Archive of Folk Culture, Library of Congress), located obscure items; and Archie Green tracked down references that appeared to be figments in the imaginations of bibliographers. Donald R. Hill sent a great deal of material, and I have benefited from correspondence with Lise Winer, and Lorna McDaniel (who helped with important references). Léonie St Juste-Jean and Lise Winer kindly translated the French Creole songs.

This work is based on my PhD thesis at the University of Warwick, where I received the support of the Higher Degrees Committee with a Graduate Award for three years. Professor Alistair Hennessy supervised the research and several departments facilitated completion; in particular the patient tenacity of Inter-Library Loans and specialist assistance of William Pine-Coffin in the Library. Anne Lakey and Barbara Owens were responsible for the original typescript.

All the libraries in Britain, where most of this research was conducted, provided a friendly and efficient service. I utilised the resources of the British Library at the National Sound Archive, the Newspaper Library, and the Reference Division (where Ilse Sternberg was very supportive). My requests were dealt with efficiently at the library of the Foreign and Commonwealth Office and in the Public Record Office. Terry Barringer and her staff were of great assistance, at the former library of the Royal Commonwealth Society, together with David Blake and his colleagues at the Institute of Commonwealth Studies, University of London. Malcolm Taylor, of the Vaughan Williams Memorial Library, English Folk Dance and Song Society, aided my endeavours as did the library of the Folklore Society.

Howard Rye and Richard Noblett reciprocated knowledge and followed up leads and Marina Salandy-Brown helped with encouragement. Paul and Valerie Oliver have done likewise. Many of the ideas in this analysis were first articulated during long discussions with Bruce Bastin in the early 1970s, when we were researching black North-American folk music. Keith Summers, whose magazines *Musical Traditions* and *Keskidee* mirror my xiv *Acknowledgements*

interests, provided a much needed forum. The final text could not have been edited without the loan of equipment by Keith and Janet Fanshawe. 'Patrick' Fitzpatrick helped with proof reading. Many family friends supported this endeavour, especially my godfather Charles L. Pickering, but my greatest debt is to my mother; as a pensioner, she shared her income in order that the work be completed.

I apologise to any person or organisation inadvertently omitted from these acknowledgements.

All views expressed are my own.

Extracts from Crown Copyright Records in the Public Record Office appear by permission.

Excerpts from the interviews with Patrick Jones are with the permission of the Center for Folklife Programs and Cultural Studies of the Smithsonian Institution.

Permission is gratefully acknowledged for the use of the following illustrations:

6	Crown Agents and Institute of Commonwealth Studies
8 (a)	Crown Agents and Institute of Commonwealth Studies
(b)	Crown Agents and Institute of Commonwealth Studies
9	Crown Agents and Institute of Commonwealth Studies
10	Institute of Commonwealth Studies
13 (b)	Alain Boulanger
16 (b)	Richard Noblett
17	West India Committee and Institute of Commonwealth Studies
18 (c)	Richard K. Spottswood
21 (a)	Richard K. Spottswood
(b)	Richard K. Spottswood
(c)	Richard K. Spottswood

Abbreviations

bis	twice
c.	chapter (British legislation)
c.	circa
C.	Command paper (Britain)
Cd.	Command paper [different series] (Britain)
CO	Colonial Office
DC	*da capo* (repeat)
EN	*Evening News* (Trinidad)
FP&TN	*Fair Play and Trinidad News* (Trinidad)
F. Supp.	Federal Supplement (United States)
M	*Mirror* (Trinidad)
MM	*Melody Maker* (Britain)
NE	*New Era* (Trinidad)
POSG	*Port of Spain Gazette* (Trinidad)
PRO	Public Record Office (Britain)
SG	*Sunday Guardian* (Trinidad)
SOTW	*Star of the West* (Trinidad)
TC	*Trinidad Chronicle* (Trinidad)
ter	thrice
TG	*Trinidad Guardian* (Trinidad)
TP	*Trinidad Paladium* (Trinidad)
TR	*Trinidad Review* (Trinidad)
TRG	*Trinidad Royal Gazette* (Trinidad/Britain)

1

Background to West Indian music

Popular fascination with music from the Americas has been of great significance in the twentieth century. The United States is usually recognised as the source of this trend, with African-American styles the most prominent. Less documented, but equally influential, is equivalent black music from the Caribbean and Latin America. This rose to prominence from early in the century with the tango (from Argentina), and includes rumba (from Cuba), biguine (from Martinique), and samba (from Brazil). Each style reflects contributions from differing European languages – Spanish (tango and rumba), French (biguine) and Portuguese (samba). In the English-speaking world, calypso (from Trinidad) gained popular recognition from the 1930s.

Calypso, samba, biguine and (sometimes) rumba are each associated with Carnival, the ever popular Shrovetide festival throughout Latin America. All have African-American origins that date from slavery. The evolution of black music in Trinidad has cosmopolitan importance. Some of these developments can be traced in the United States, mainland South America and other islands in the Caribbean.

Prelude – Trinidad Carnival, Canboulay
and black music in the 1870s

Vernacular music formed the core of the popular masquerade, especially Canboulay the midnight opening activity of the festival. Some 50 years later Lewis O. Inniss described 'the bands' in this decade:

As a preliminary to enjoying a good Carnival it was necessary for its votaries – especially those who intended to jeur Pierrot (play as clowns) to visit Gasparillo in order to select a suitable stick. For it was supposed that Gasparillo was the only *habitat* of the Baton Gasparee which was recognised by all as being the weapon *par excellence* for the part. This stick had to be prepared by singeing over a fire to remove the bark and then rubbed with coconut oil in order to be Bien Bandé i.e. properly prepared for use.

At twelve o'clock on the evening of Shrove Sunday the blowing of horns, or empty bottles as a substitute, was the notice for the assembling of the bands, Belmont, Corbeaux Town, New Town, Dry River, Dernier point, etc., etc. These headed by the champions who could hallé baton skillfully with a grande tambour and a collection of shack-shacks to give the music, torches made of resinous wood to give light, marched down the streets yelling ribald songs.

The city was in total darkness at night in those days. When they came to some convenient spot the drummer put down the drum and sitting astride it proceeded to batte tambour, the women who carried the shack-shacks making a vigorous accompaniment whist the crowd danced Corlindas, the women singing Bel-Airs and hallé baton (stick-fighting) waged among the men.

It is not difficult to foresee that bands of men marching through the streets armed with sticks would lead to altercation. The Canboulay Riot – the most serious confrontation in the history of Trinidad Carnival – took place in 1881. This melee led to an investigation by the Colonial Office in London and the future of Carnival was examined carefully:

Some feel that the Carnival if left alone will die out. With this view I do not concur. Experience does not show that fewer people from year to year take part in it. On the contrary, one of the most objectionable features of it, namely the bands, are a creation of quite recent times, and they are largely fed by immigrants from other islands, the number of whom is constantly increasing. With reference to this point, it is worthy to notice that the census thus taken for 1881 shows that during the last ten years the number of natives of other West Indian Islands residing in Port of Spain has been increased by upward of 5,000 or upwards of 100 per cent. Others urge that the Carnival should be stopped altogether, on the ground that in itself it is a senseless and irrational amusement, and affords a pretext for the indulgence of unbridled licentiousness on the part of the worst of the population. But I do not either agree with this view. However objectionable some of the features of the Carnival are, I believe it is looked forward to as the only holiday of the year by a large number of the working population of the town, who derive amusements from it and I think to stop it altogether would be a measure which would justly be regarded as harsh and might lead to serious dissatisfaction on the part of the working classes.[1]

This was the considered view of R. G. Hamilton, in his report to the Colonial Secretary (the Earl of Kimberly). Many of the underlying reasons for such actions, however, are not explained in these two complementary accounts. Indeed, they pose the question where and how did these traditions evolve? In addition, Carnival did not 'die out': the festival remains a principal event in the island's annual calendar, with music its fundamental component.

To answer these questions, and explore ways in which black culture developed in the Caribbean, it is necessary to know something of the region's complex history from its European discovery by Columbus in 1492.

European colonisers, post-colonial conquests, and the slave trade

Slave culture in the West Indies reflects the relationship of peoples from three continents – Europe, America and Africa. This was forged by European exploration, conquest and trade, beginning in the late fifteenth century.

Different geographical conditions in each Caribbean island (or mainland America), and interactions with differing European traditions, were modified by fortunes of war and other political circumstances. These produced complicated cultural patterns that became entangled with the traditions of the area's original inhabitants.[2] Native Americans were decimated by diseases introduced by Europeans. This, and hostility to territorial overthrow, led their conquerors to seek African labour for large-scale plantations, growing staples for expanding European economies. Black people were coerced to replace the indigenous population. Like the Native Americans, with whom they sometimes intermarried, African slaves did not represent one 'culture' but were drawn from many areas of that continent, adding to the evolving complexity.

Throughout the seventeenth and eighteenth centuries, the importation of Africans was the most consistent factor in a region that epitomised the instability of European nations jostling for trading supremacy. Many West Indian islands changed hands, some on several occasions. Both Jamaica and Trinidad were originally Spanish – their British acquisition was almost one-hundred-and-fifty years apart; the first in 1655, the second in 1797.[3]

Individual territories were subject to differing material developments. Trade (and therefore cultural contact) was maintained with Europe, the American mainland, Africa, between islands, and elsewhere, but enterprise fluctuated with political circumstances. Trinidad is a particular example, with ties to several European countries, Africa, the Orient, Spanish-speaking Latin America and most of the islands in the Eastern Caribbean, as well as the United States and Canada.

Cultural 'repression' and African 'resistance' of slaves

Opinions differ whether slaves maintained a degree of cultural integrity in the face of oppression. One theory argues they were overwhelmed by the ideas of their 'European masters'. Notwithstanding, while African tradition was actively discouraged, this was not absolute. Cultural values were sustained and developed in resistance to enslavement, especially in activities beyond the compass of the repressors. This 'African' fidelity was dynamic and varied according to space, time and circumstances of enslavement, manumission, escape, or eventual emancipation.

During slavery, complicated class structures developed. In very simplified terms African-Americans can be divided into two groups: slaves newly arrived from Africa, and creole slaves (born in the Americas). Often, they preserved the identity of their African 'nation'. There were also free(ed) Africans, and people of mixed (African/European/Native-American) ancestry. Free Europeans were generally the controlling plantocracy. They maintained a class hierarchy based on skin-colour gradations.[4] In the British Caribbean, this structure operated virtually exclusively until the slave trade was abolished in 1807.[5] Ensuing changes allowed the evolution of almost wholly black creole populations and cultures in respective territories.

Emancipation – consolidation of new African-American cultures

Slaves were granted freedom on 1 August 1834 in the British West Indies, but a scheme known as 'Apprenticeship' was introduced to retain the plantation labour force. This failed in 1838 when 'Apprentices' became free citizens on 1 August in that year.[6] In one sense, this parallels the liberty gained by slaves who escaped and established free (Maroon) communities away from plantation control – a radical change in their circumstances.

The result of this change varied from territory to territory. In general, a new culture evolved that transformed, developed and replaced earlier patterns with a positive response to freedom. Descriptions of black culture by the white elite reflect these circumstances.

Some cultural traits continued, such as the call and response singing of work songs, including shanties (or chanties) – this remained, because black people were employed, or employed themselves, collectively, in the slavery- and post-slavery periods.[7] A similar apparent stability can be demonstrated for the use of certain musical instruments known or believed to have been brought from Africa.[8]

Indentured labour – a substitute for slavery

Planters looked for means to maintain a reliable and cheap labour force. Several methods were adopted. Free Africans were encouraged to migrate across the Atlantic or were rescued by the British Navy (while in transit to countries where slavery still existed); Chinese were engaged as indentured labour; and, most successfully (for the planters), so were many people from the sub-continent of India. From the mid-nineteenth to the early-twentieth century, a steady stream of East Indians was brought to Trinidad, Guyana and, to a lesser extent, Jamaica. Indentureship tied workers to plantations, providing the continuity for which estate owners had been looking. Although considered only in passing, East Indians became part of the cultural *milieu*; they responded to dynamic circumstances that influenced their heritage in much the same way as people of African origin.

The significance of the drum

From slavery, most white observers associated drums, drumming and related dancing with Africa: this was both direct (performances by newly arrived Africans) and indirect (drum dances performed by creoles). Europeans in the Caribbean feared the drum and always controlled it as a 'nuisance' or, prior to Emancipation, because of its potency in signalling revolt.[9] The complex pattern of drum rhythms was outside European compass and posed an additional threat founded in incomprehension. Proselytising Christian missionaries saw drum dances as sacrilegious and tried to stamp them out. The drum symbolised not only 'uncivilised' Africa, but also violent disorder and the work of the devil.

For European missionaries, drumming posed a particular dilemma. In their homelands it was the fiddle rather than the drum that was sometimes cast in the role of the 'devil's instrument', especially when providing accompaniment for 'wild' dancing. The association of unbaptised black people with 'non-Christian' belief was enough to transpose this symbolism to drum dances. Unaccustomed dance movements, sound, and the continuous rhythmic playing of the drummers, added to missionary opposition.

These interpretations are far from the truth, even in the eyes of diarists and travel writers. Dances were not exclusive, nor the accompaniment of drums. Activities might include other styles involving different musical instruments. Drumming was also dependent on circumstances of place, time, and precedent.[10] In one respect, however, the potency of the drum was sustained as a signal for African integrity: by its use for sacred ceremony. Despite changes, exacted by separate evolution and cross-fertilisation, links to both sacred and secular events were maintained. On this level, the drum remains a symbol of Africa in black music from the Caribbean.[11]

The role of the fiddle

The fiddle was used in two principal categories of performance: dances and processions.

Among factors that encouraged black slave musicians to adopt the fiddle were creative adaptability, the instrument's relative availability, and a nostalgic inclination by the plantocracy for music from their homelands.

This led to absorption of European melodies and dances, especially at festive occasions when ritual licence allowed black and white people to mix on terms of 'equality'. 'African' dances were also performed by black participants.[12]

While there is a strong tradition of playing string instruments in the West African savannah, which may account for easy adoption of the fiddle by black slaves, in manufacture and design the instrument was European. Alongside association with dances from that continent, the instrument gained an allegorical status representing 'civilisation' (or, 'decorum') in the New World. This does not deny the role of the fiddle for other music-making, but emphasises a singular factor among black musicians and white observers of their playing.[13]

In parallel with the drum being a most appropriate musical symbol for Africa, it can be said that the fiddle became the symbol for the European contribution to black music in the West Indies. These are simplifications, but provide reference points for considering complex cultural evolution in the region, especially in the nineteenth century.

In the British Caribbean, music ranging from the 'mother country's' social 'elite' to the 'folk' had considerable influence. Military repertoire is represented by African-American membership in bands of the armed forces and police, after black musicians were allowed in their ranks.

Sacred and secular rituals and social institutions

One way in which links with the African past can be explored, is by sacred and secular rituals and associated music and dance.

The European nations that conquered the Caribbean were nominally Christian and imposed an annual cycle of religious festivals on the area. These had evolved from the seasonal rotation of the northern hemisphere, adopted and adapted by the Church during conversion to Christianity. In turn, some cross a divide between sacred and secular that was developed to accommodate the delicate relationship between Church and State. A further complication was the split between the Roman Catholic and Protestant churches.

The most persistent musical evolutions in the Caribbean are associated with sacred or secular events that sometimes combine – as with Carnival. Usually, they show evidence of cross-fertilisation stemming from the adaptation to new circumstances by people in the world diaspora to the Americas.

In Jamaica, where the predominant Christian influence has been Protestant, the primary black sacred and secular celebration is known as 'Jonkonnu'. It has been held at Christmas for over two centuries and, since 1838, on 1 August, in commemoration of the ending of Apprenticeship. Among other 'Protestant' islands, St Kitts-Nevis have their 'Christmas Sports' (including mumming), Bermuda its 'Gombey' parades, while the Bahamas also use 'Jonkonnu' as the name for their Christmas festivities.

Caribbean-French sugar planters and their slaves, from Martinique and other French territories, settled in Trinidad in the 1780s. They sustained the influence of Roman Catholicism, consolidating the island's most important sacred/secular festival – Carnival. To a lesser extent, Christmas is also celebrated. The history of both events can be traced from the time the British took the island. Shrovetide Carnivals are held also in Carriacou, Dominica, Grenada, St Lucia, St Vincent and Tobago[14]

Dances, processions and seasonal occasions

Festivals provide a focal point for different musical styles that have evolved in each Caribbean territory. They also integrate with common elements such as language and migration of people (from island to island, or elsewhere) in the course of international circumstances.

Hierarchical groups (usually elected), that perform at festive gatherings, have existed since slavery. Music is fundamental to these celebrations and includes dressing, singing, dancing, and marching competitively to music. In the historical record, these associations were widely distributed throughout the Caribbean, Latin America and United States. Black 'Kings and Governors', for example, provided an extra feature of election days in eighteenth-century New England. Generally revolving around the Christian calendar, celebrations incorporated European and African masquerade traditions (also founded in the agricultural season).[15]

Festivals in the English-speaking Caribbean were of great significance in the development of the region's musical traditions. Reports of topical themes in African-American songs range from slavery to the present. Calypso is a famous example of this genre. This evolved in Trinidad from the heritage of slave dancing societies, Carnival bands and other influences.[16] The history of Trinidad Carnival provides a means of tracing and understanding these proliferations. In turn, the annual cycle of the festival allows greater appreciation of the island's cultural (and political) position in the Caribbean and its contribution to popular culture in the English-speaking world.

Carnival and black music in Trinidad

Trinidad was discovered by Columbus in 1498 (he named the island for triple peaks representing the Holy Trinity). The island was ruled by Spain for virtually 300 years and remained one of her most 'underdeveloped' American possessions. Only in the 1770s, with the 'Bourbon reforms' of Charles III – designed to rejuvenate flagging colonial efficiency – did the Spanish crown pay attention to this thinly populated, almost uncultivated territory. A *Cédula* issued by Charles in 1776 highlighted the neglect. With no Catholic Europeans available for emigration, this invited West Indian French planters to transfer slaves for work on new estates. They were encouraged by land grants

Influenced by France, and set on maintaining Spanish control and the Roman Catholic faith, Charles III extended this provision in 1783 by issuing a further *Cédula de Población*. Any Catholic was allowed to settle in Trinidad providing he agreed to certain conditions, including a loyalty oath to the crown.

At this point, the population was very small. It comprised white Spanish- and French-speaking colonists, 'coloured' people, black slaves, and remnants of the Native American community, whose forebears had originally inhabited Iere (their name for the island).

Over the next fourteen years a great number of French planters grasped the opportunities to settle in Trinidad, escaping the maraudings of the Napoleonic wars. In consequence, when Britain conquered the island in 1797, there was a significant French-speaking and mainly creole constituency. The French elite had established themselves as a landed aristocracy, using their black slaves to create flourishing plantations growing tobacco, sugar, cotton and coffee.

A large and speedy increase in settlement followed 'capitulation', with migrants coming from the Spanish Main, North America, Africa and British West Indian islands. There was also some French emigration.

Despite this, the French community remained in control of the island's economic core.[17]

With virtually all of the early slave population having 'been born in the French islands', black culture also reflected this African-French-Caribbean bias, including the establishment of 'patois' (Caribbean French Creole) as a lingua franca. The arrival of new slaves did not change this pattern. The unusual French character of late-eighteenth- and nineteenth-century Trinidad was remarked upon by L. M. Fraser in his important memorandum to the Colonial Office on the 'History of the origin of the Carnival' (1881).[18]

From the arrival of French planters, the history of Carnival can be divided into four phases. These cover slavery, the period immediately following Emancipation, the last quarter of the nineteenth century, and the period from 1897 to the aftermath of the First World War.[19] This complex development illuminates the interrelated evolution of black music in the island.

2

'Pain nous ka mangé': music, carnival and events, 1783–1869

Shrovetide festivities were almost certainly introduced into Trinidad by early Spanish settlers. There is no concrete evidence, however, for the existence of an annual celebration before the influx of French Creole planters and their slaves in 1783.

Pierre-Gustave-Louis Borde paints a picture of the social whirl of the plantocracy in this period:

> The pleasures of meals at the dining table and picnics were added to those of music and dancing. There followed nothing but concerts and balls. There were lunches and dinners, hunting parties and expeditions on the river, as well as carnival which lasted from Christmas time until Ash Wednesday. It was nothing but a long period of feasts and pleasures.

He notes also that free 'blacks and people of colour' formed a parallel society that adopted the same 'customs and manners' as the white elite.

While this may reflect a romanticised view, Borde's description conforms with divertissements enjoyed by the white and quadroon (coloured) French Creole population in New Orleans, Louisiana. Carnival was a similar feature and balls were held most frequently between Twelfth Night and Shrove Tuesday.

In New Orleans, black people participated in Carnival from the early 1800s. Black fiddle players performed at public Carnival balls in 1802 and on Carnival Tuesday in 1803, two groups (by inference slaves) danced the *bamboula* and contre-danse 'side by side'.[1]

Such direct slave activity, especially dancing *en masse*, seems not to have taken place in Trinidad, at least after the capture of the island by the British (in 1797). They viewed free black inhabitants and 'people of colour' as a threat to authority over the slaves and increasingly discriminated against them. This was one of several controls the British endeavoured to introduce. In their Protestant territories, Christmas-New Year revelry did not extend to Shrovetide, and there was an unsuccessful attempt to demote the celebration of Carnival in Trinidad.[2] Early in the cosmopolitan island's existence as a British colony a pattern of contradictory pressures soon became apparent. By virtue of differing traditions – strands of European, African and creole-American cultures, to which were added attitudes from the Orient – the complexity of the population ensured a multitude of social ideals, some working in opposition to one another.

As in other Caribbean islands, black slaves were quick to exploit any weakness in the social order, including the celebration of Christmas. According to one report, uninhibited behaviour was a feature of white society at this season.[3] It is not surprising, therefore, that one of the principal so-called revolts, in Trinidad's short period as a slave colony, took place just before Christmas, in 1805.

The Shand Estate Revolt – Christmas 1805

Writing in 1838, the Trinidad historian E. L. Joseph summarised this disturbance, pointing out 'the principal evidence in the case' came from 'a mad woman!' The Governor and planters, however, were convinced of the authenticity of a plot to murder 'all the whites and free coloured inhabitants':

> A revolt was to have commenced on Shand's estate. The conspirators, it is said, meditated the destruction of all the white men, and the dishonour of all the white women of the island. It seemed to have originated with some French and African negroes. I have inspected the papers of the courts-martial held on these people, and fully believe that their *judges* were convinced of their guilt. The result was, four slaves were executed, many were disgustingly mutilated, and a few were ordered to be flogged and banished.

Referring to a pamphlet by G. Dickson, Joseph thought it most likely that the participants 'only meant to have one of their African dances', noting how readily this would 'be understood by those acquainted with the manner of our West India slaves of the period'.

The importance of this event is not simply that the uprising was to have taken place on Christmas Day, but the way in which black slaves had organised themselves.

Slave 'Societies, for the purpose of *dancing* and *innocent amusement*' were common throughout the island. They were known generally as *Convois* but had recently adopted the name *Regiments*. Each having a distinguishing name and location, they were concentrated 'especially in Maraval, Diego Martin and Carenage (Districts which were chiefly inhabited by French settlers)'.

According to the 'Minutes of His Majesty's Council' held in Trinidad on 20 December 1805, four of the *Regiments*, based mainly in Carenage, were principals in the 'plot'. These were: the *Cocorite* (probably Cockerels) from Port of Spain and its environs; the *Macacque* (Monkey) from Carenage; the *St George* with branches in Carenage and Port of Spain; and the *Sans-peur* (Dreadnoughts), again with branches in Carenage and Port of Spain. In addition, a list of those punished, or to be punished, published in the *Barbados Mercury and Bridgetown Gazette* (1 February 1806) shows that the *Regiment Danois* (Danish, known also as *Marine*), was also implicated. Other societies mentioned in this report were the *Guadaloupe* (*sic*), *La Fantasie* (Fancy) and *Martinique*. Some of these names probably reflect islands of origin for the slaves. The 'Danish Regiment', for instance, is likely to have been founded by black slaves transported from St Thomas, or St Croix.

The *Regiments* were hierarchical. In addition to regular participants, the *Barbados Mercury* identified some seventeen different officials, including 'royal' leadership by Kings, Queens and a Dauphin (or Prince), 'royal' households, and political, legal and military personnel – for example Ambassadors, a Prime Minister, Grand Judges, an Admiral, Colonels, Generals, Majors and Alguazils (police).

Membership of these dancing societies was spread between groups whose creole origin had been elsewhere in the Caribbean – for example, Martinique, Guadeloupe, or Grenada. Participants also included slaves who had arrived in Trinidad direct from Africa, and free blacks. Many members were given titles (and, presumably, functions) and there were ceremonial and disciplinary formalities.

Flags and uniforms (probably cast-offs from the European military) were part of the paraphernalia. The groups used them as symbols of parody and power. With the same purpose, they also adopted and adapted aspects of Christian ritual and allied them to religious and magical perceptions that originated in Africa.

It was a song in this vein, said to have been 'in common use amongst the labourers for some months previous to the detection of the plot', that was the principal evidence against the dancing societies. Sung in French Creole, it had the recent and successful slave rebellion in San Domingo (Haiti) and the Christian sacrament as its theme. One couplet and its refrain are reported by Fraser. This is probably the earliest song that can be dated specifically in the history of Trinidad music:

Pain nous ka mangé	The bread we eat
C'est viande beké	Is the white man's flesh
Di vin nous ka boué	The wine we drink
C'est sang beké	Is the white man's blood
Hé, St Domingo,	Hé St Domingo,
songé St Domingo	remember St Domingo

For the 'Supreme Tribunal' the connection of these 'allusions' with a plot for insurrection was overwhelming, as was a ceremony held four times a year that was said to be 'a profane and blasphemous parody of the Christian Sacrament'.

While this signifies religious and recreational purpose for these groups, it is not absolute proof of rebellious intent. The song and ceremony might be seen as an imitative homage to Christian ritual. This seems unlikely, however, in the light of magical powers ascribed to one of those executed, King Sampson, of the *Regiment Macacque*. Reportedly, he appeared an old and foolish African of Ibo descent but had a hidden reputation as a powerful obeahman.[4]

The main purpose of these organisations was probably 'feasts and rejoicings', such as those described by Borde:

> On Saturday evenings and on Sundays after Mass, they gave vent to their passions for dancing and music. For long hours and without rest they performed the dances called the 'calinda,' and the 'jhouba,' which had come down from their ancestors, and also the dance 'bel air' which was their own invention. All these were carried out to the sound of their voices and the African drum.[5]

These activities fit the general pattern for the Caribbean, and French-speaking West Indies in particular.

It is almost certainly via the latter tradition that a direct rapport between black songsters and their white masters was fostered in Trinidad. This is apparent in oral history stories and songs relating to improvisatory singers employed by, among others, the influential French Creole planter St Hilaire Begorrat. Arriving in Trinidad from Martinique in 1784, his attitude symptomised a singular love-hate relationship between slave and master. He sustained particular black chantwells, or lead singers, for their skills in spontaneous composition, but was instrumental in meting out macabre punishments to slaves who were believed to have transgressed. Begorrat was heavily involved in devising the mutilations inflicted on those found guilty in 1805. His cultural knowledge meant he was very familiar with the way in which black people organised dancing societies and the motives that underlay their music. For him fear was the principal means of maintaining control over slaves.[6]

Spanish law remained in operation in Trinidad until the 1830s, but Police Regulations, published two or three months after the British took the island, strictly controlled dancing in the free coloured and slave communities. In essence, a permit was required for coloureds to hold dances, entertainments or wakes after eight o'clock at night; slaves were allowed to dance, where licenced, only until eight o'clock.

Further regulation followed in 1801, with the 'Prohibition of Negro Dances in Town', and from 1807, it appears that 'people of colour' were permitted 'to hold Balls and Assemblies subject to a donation to paupers of 16 Dollars'.[7]

An even more stringent control over the free coloureds was known as the 'Fandango licence'. Dating, perhaps, from later in the era, this required 'any free coloured proprietor wishing to give a dancing party in the night' to 'first obtain permission to do so from the Commandant of the Quarter'. In addition, they were 'forbidden under penalty of a fine of $25 to admit any slave to the party'.[8]

Christmas and Carnival – 1810s–1820s

While it is difficult to overemphasise the harsh regime of slavery and persecution of free coloureds as scapegoats for British policy towards black people, this does not mean there were no controls on white inhabitants and their forms of entertainment.

Probably from the establishment of the Militia, by proclamation on 29 November 1800, it was general practice to declare Martial Law at Christmas. One of the reasons for this was to control abandon among white inhabitants. In addition to ebullience, a further serious problem became honour between aggrieved parties and consequent death, or serious injury, by duelling.

Before the appointment of Sir Ralph Woodford as Governor (he took up the post on 14 June 1813), duelling was commonplace, even among house slaves. Woodford determined to scourge Trinidad of this 'pernicious custom' and 'used his own almost unlimited power and the severe enactments of the Spanish laws against duellists'. The initial effect was to concentrate encounters at Christmas, when Civil Courts were closed. Service in the Militia was compulsory in the white community and with courts martial this limited individual confrontations. In order to control them further, Woodford used the Court of Royal Audience (that remained open to him) to punish offenders.[9]

Reports of the Christmas–New Year season in 1820–21 show the juxtaposition of compulsory military service and luxurious ceremony. Proclaimed on 23 December 1820, Martial Law was to have terminated on 2 January 1821, but remained until the following Monday (8 January) due to 'assembly of the General Court Martial ... and the duties which crowded upon it'. With great pomp and circumstance, swearing in of the 'Illustrious Board of the Cabildo' of Port of Spain took place, followed by a Levee at Government House. Companies of the West India Regiment and Militia were reviewed by the Governor, who provided refreshments for onlookers. He also hosted 'an elegant Ball and entertainment' on '*Twelfth Night*'.[10]

By 1824, Woodford's disciplinary measures had altered considerably the way in which Christmas was celebrated. Contrasting past laxity with the present, the *Trinidad Gazette* commented: 'The times since then have changed. The noise, the mirth, the revelry, and the inebriety are now found chiefly amongst the slaves and lower classes.'[11]

Contemporary descriptions, published by Mrs Carmichael in 1833, indicate the way in which slaves took part in seasonal vivacity. The accounts confirm a pattern of role reversals common in the English-speaking Caribbean. During her first Christmas at Laurel-Hill, she was invited to a ball given by slaves from St Vincent, who had recently moved with her and her husband to Trinidad. On the afternoon of Christmas Day, food, wine and the plantation house kitchen were given over to the slaves. In the evening, Mrs Carmichael visited the dance, where participants paid great attention to dress and decorum; there was no drinking or fighting. Music was provided by four female singers, accompanied by a drum and three women playing 'shac-shacs'. The dance was in favour of slaves acquired in the new island.

At a later Christmas she and her husband were awoken at daybreak by a party of their slaves complimenting the season. They quickly arose, dressed and reciprocated, after which several slaves made speeches expressing good wishes. 'Songs and dances followed', she reported; 'the songs of their own composition, and full of good wishes for a good crop and good sugar'.

Another feature was 'the giving out of the Christmas allowances', described by her as a 'very merry scene'. The slaves floured 'each other's black faces and curly hair' calling out 'look at he white face! and he white wig!' in fun, but emphasising skin-colour and class role reversals that are reported in post-Emancipation Carnivals.

There were also Christmas and New Year waits:

> About eleven in the morning, a party of negroes from Paradise, the adjoining estate, came to wish us a good Christmas. They had two fiddlers, whose hats and fiddles were decorated with many-coloured ribbons. They said they wished to come and play good Christmas to the 'young misses'. They were very nicely dressed, in clean white shirts, trowsers [sic] and jackets. We told them to come back and see us on New Year's Day; as we wished now to be quiet, and read the service for Christmas-day. They went away very good-humouredly, and returned on New Year's Day; and pleased and entertained us with their songs and merriment.

On the evening of Christmas Day, estate slaves partook of a special supper. This was followed by another ball, for which the participants had made special preparation, again paying particular attention to dress. Mrs Carmichael attended:

> The drum and the song were soon distinct; and we shortly reached C.'s house, where, before her door, a large space was left clear for the dancers, surrounded on three sides by seats of all kinds. The musicians were at one end. They were engaged in a dance of eight persons when

> we reached the spot; it was similar to a French quadrille, and they were dancing to the air of 'Garcon Volage'.

> Every grown person paid C. half a dollar for coming to this dance; and for this they had refreshments and supper ... Many dances of all kinds were performed: among the most interesting, a *pas de deux*, by the two oldest negroes present – the driver and his wife. During this dance there was the profoundest attention and the deepest silence. The supper took place at a late hour and they danced till sunrise.

The concentrated exertions of the two drummers are described and Mrs Carmichael noted how much it was 'considered a first-rate accomplishment to beat the drum well', as with the playing of the fiddle in Europe.[12]

References to French Creole dances sustain the view that the mainstream of black tradition in Trinidad was African-French. Another supposed plan for a slave rebellion, discovered in the autumn of 1823, adds weight to this assertion. It confirms black dancing societies, like those identified in 1805, continued to flourish in the same vicinity.

Plans for what was believed to be a slave insurrection in the plantations between Carenage and Diego Martin were discovered on 25 October 1823. The revolt was to coincide with the Feast of All Saints (1 November) when slaves had a holiday. An official inquiry quickly discovered that sacrifice of a cock and sprinkling its blood over ceremonial drums were part of an Ibo (or Igbo) ritual of purification. This practice was usual prior to a dance of religious significance. Eight slaves who had been arrested were acquitted of 'intention to revolt'. Judge L. F. C. Johnston found, on 21 November, that 'various societies or meetings of slaves for dancing ... are referred to [as] ... "Regiments" ... synonymously with or for the word "party" or "society" ... to be used on the occasion of Dances on Holy days.' The slaves had been overheard talking about a 'regiment' and a revolutionary purpose had wrongly been assumed.[13]

A song heard by Mrs Carmichael 'soon after coming to Laurel-Hill, and subsequently to the meditated insurrection in Trinidad' may have some connection with these events:

> I heard some of the young negroes singing, as I thought, rather a singular song. I asked J. to sing it for me; he hesitated and said, 'Misses, it no good song.' Why do you sing it then? ''Cause, misses, it a funny song, and me no mean bad by it.' At last I prevailed on J. not only to sing the song (which turned out to be an insurrectionary song), but to explain it. The words are these –

Fire in da mountain,
Nobody for out him,
Take me daddy's bo tick (dandy stick)
And make a monkey out him.
        Chorus:
Poor John! Nobody for out him, &c.

Go to de king's goal,
You'll find a doubloon dey;
Go to de king's goal,
You'll find a doubloon dey.
        Chorus:
Poor John! Nobody for out him, &c.

The explanation of this song is, that when the bad negroes wanted to
do evil, they made for a sign a fire on the hill-sides, to burn down the
canes. There is nobody up there, to put out the fire; but as a sort of
satire, the song goes on to say, 'take me daddy's bo tick', (daddy is a
mere term of civility), take some one's dandy stick, and tell the
monkeys to help to put out the fire among the canes for John; (meaning
John Bull). The chorus means, that poor John has nobody to put out
the fire in the canes for him. Then when the canes are burning, go to
the goal [sic], and seize the money. The tune to which this is sung, is
said to be negro music; it is on a minor key, and singularly resembles
an incorrect edition of an old Scotch tune, the name of which I do not
recollect.[14]

This is the second song available that can be dated with any certainty in
the history of black Trinidad music and, unlike the first, is in the English
language. The interpretation by Mrs Carmichael seems, in part, question-
able; for instance 'make a monkey out him', may be idiomatic for foolish (as
at present), and it is likely that 'goal' is a misspelling of gaol. It is significant
that 'satire' is identified as a lyrical theme early in the history of the music.
Reference to the tune being in the minor key is a consistent observation
regarding black music in the Americas, as is the possible influence of
Scottish music.

Cannes brulées (*Canboulay*) – a component of Carnival

In the first verse of the song, accidental or premeditated burning of sugar
canes (in French *cannes brulées*) serves to introduce another component in

the evolution of Trinidad festivals. At the time of a plantation fire, *bandes* from different estates, each with its whip-carrying slave driver, were assembled, by the blaring of horns, to deal with the emergency. The *nègres jardins* (or field slaves), who comprised the *bandes*, carried torches (for night-time illumination) and drums (for rhythmic accompaniment to their work songs). 'In such cases', recalled 'X' in the *Port of Spain Gazette* in 1881, 'the gangs of the neighbouring Estates proceeded alternately, accompanied with torches at night, to the Estate which had suffered, to assist in grinding the burnt canes before they became sour. The work went on night and day until all the canes were manufactured into sugar.'

In addition, burning canes from the edges of a rodent-infested field was used 'to trap and kill an entire rat population'. An emergency harvest would have been required in these circumstances and this may account for an association of the term Canboulay (a French Creole form of the word) with the cane rat, reported in Trinidad in 1912. A less intensive method of working (without firing canes) would have been adopted at a conventional sugar harvest.[15] Sometimes the cane stubs were burnt after cutting, both to control pests and fertilise the soil prior to replanting.

Cannes brulées seems to have acquired several meanings, each becoming associated with Carnival in certain Caribbean islands. The term probably originated in feasts celebrating the completion of concentrated-manual-cropwork, such as Cropover. Almost certainly, Canboulay became attached to Carnival celebrations via this relationship with the plantation work cycle. It is curious, however, that in Trinidad this occurred before Emancipation.

In 1881, L. M. Fraser provided a good summary of the way in which Carnival was celebrated:

> In former days and down to the period of the emancipation of the slaves the Carnival was kept up with much spirit by the upper classes. There are many persons still living who remember the Masked Balls given at St Ann's by the Governor, Sir Ralph Woodford and also that the leading Members of Society used in the days of the Carnival to drive through the streets of Port of Spain masked, and in the evenings go from house to house which were all thrown open for the occasion.
>
> It is necessary to observe that in those days the population of the Colony was divided into the following Categories, whites, Free persons of Colour, Indians and Slaves.
>
> The free persons of Colour were subjected to very stringent Regulations and although not forbidden to mask, were yet compelled to keep to themselves and never presume to join in the amusements of the

privileged class. The Indians kept entirely aloof, and the slaves, except as onlookers . . . or by special favour when required to take part had no share in the Carnival which was confined exclusively to the upper class of the community.[16]

With these entrenched positions of race and class, and the accepted licence of Carnival, it is less surprising that the plantocracy enacted a parody of *cannes brulées*. In 1881, 'X' described how: 'The favourite costume of our mothers and grandmothers was the graceful and costly one of the "Mulatresse" of the time, whilst the gentlemen adopted that of the "Negre de Jardin" or in creole *Négue jadin*, that is to say, the costume of the field labourers.' He recalled that: 'These pretended Négues jadin were wont to unite in *bandes* representing the gangs of different Estates, and with torches and drums to represent what did actually take place in the cane districts when a fire occurred on the plantations.'

Further particulars are in a letter published a few days earlier in the *Trinidad Chronicle*. They were obtained from an old man who remembered 'Canboulay was played (in the streets?) during slavery by many members of the middle and in some cases the upper classes'. He observed 'it was intended to "take off" slave life on a plantation, and hence' included 'the driver with a whip pretending to drive the people before him to extinguish a night-fire in the cane-piece' and 'the slaves tramping in time and singing a rude refrain, to a small negro-drum and carrying torches to light their way along the road'.

The writer emphasised the old man's reminiscence that masqueraders 'came from the principal houses of the Town in an orderly way, bent on amusing themselves in a harmless manner and at the same time amusing others'. He stressed that 'the whole thing was done as a lark to laugh over afterwards. It was a laughable burlesque, and the performers respectable people.'

Alongside these enactments, 'X' reported that the white elite similarly chose to perform black drum dances, such as the *'bamboula,' 'belair,' 'calinda'* and *'ghouba'*.[17]

Masqued balls and other Carnival entertainments

Symbolic inversion by the plantocracy was only one feature of the Carnival season. In parallel with New Orleans, where duelling was also common, there were numerous masqued balls and other entertainments. The latter probably would have included the puppetry of Jack Bowel, a slave whose escape in January 1826 was advertised early in February. Theatrical performances, under the Governor's licence and patronage, also became popular. Pre-Shrovetide dramas were staged, such as 'The Tragedy of The Orphan' followed by 'the French FARCE of "George Daudin"' advertised for performance at the Amateur Theatre, St James Street, on 21 February 1827. In the event, 'MASKING and all other Public ENTERTAINMENTS' were cancelled on news reaching Trinidad of the death of Frederick, Duke of York, in Britain on 5 January. The Carnival was not abandoned altogether. Sir Ralph Woodford allowed the festival to take place at Easter. A notice published by the Police Office in the *Port of Spain Gazette* on 4 April reads:

> THE Public having been deprived of their usual Entertainment at the Carnival, in consequence of the late General Mourning, MASKING will be permitted on Easter Monday and Easter Tuesday, under the usual Regulations.

It is signed by the Chief of Police, James Meany.

The source for these powers was probably Spanish Law. The statutes operating in Trinidad had been translated into English by Judge Lewis F. C. Johnston in 1825; he dedicated his work to Sir Ralph Woodford. Johnston's translation specifies:

> *Masks.*
> Plebeians are prohibited with masks under pain of one hundred stripes; and nobles under pain of banishment or transportation for six months; and it being in the night time, the punishment is doubled.

The effect of these controls does not appear to have muted the celebration of Carnival by the elite. The 1827 Carnival at Easter (one of the few for which contemporary reports contain a modicum of detail) provides a useful sample of their activities.

Major W—., a British army officer wrote to his compatriot F. W. N. Bayley, on 4 May:

> I wish, Bayley, you had been here in the time of the carnival; you have no idea of the gaiety of the place during that season. Ovid's Metamorphoses were nothing compared to the changes that took place in the persons of the Catholics of Trinidad. High and low, rich and poor, learned and unlearned, all found masking suits for the carnival.

Despite describing the town (17 April) as 'alive with ... gaiety and

(a)

MARRON DEPUIS LE 14 DU COURANT,

LE Nègre nommé *Jack Bowel.* Il est connu
pour faire danser les Marionnettes. On
le croit dans le Quartier de St. Joseph où il se
fait passer pour libre. Le propriétaire prévient
ceux qui peuvent l'employer qu'ils s'exposent à
être poursuivis conformément à la loi.

31 Janvier, 1826

(b)

POLICE OFFICE, PORT of SPAIN,
15th February, 1827.
NOTICE.

THE Public is hereby notified, that
during the MOURNING for His
Royal Highness the DUKE OF YORK,
MASKING and all other Public EN-
TERTAINMENTS are prohibited.

JAMES MEANY,
Chief of Police.

(c)

MASQUERADE DRESSES
AND COSTUMES.

MR. LASALLE begs to inform the Amateurs of the Carnival, that he has a
splendid assortment of
DRESSES & COSTUMES,
at his Chambers in Charlotte-street, on moderate
terms.
☞ MASKS may also be had at the same
place.
28th Feb. 1829.

1 Jack Bowel absconded prior to Carnival and was also pursued by advertisement in
English. British Governance is emphasised by cancellation of Shrovetide masquing in
1827. Participants would have patronised Mr Lasalle.

amusement' the *Trinidad Guardian* thought that the 'energy' and 'spirit' of
Shrovetide were lacking. They noted, nevertheless, that 'Colonel and Mrs
MALLET, were at home to their friends', and their residence provided a
sparkling focal point for the social elite. Another was the saloon, which 'was
crowded to excess and in which was seen all the Beauty and Grace for
which our Island is so eminently conspicuous'. There were numerous
masques 'and the parties active in the performance of their several parts'.
One group of ladies identified by the British major 'converted themselves
into a party of brigands' and 'assailed' him in his 'quarters'.[18]

A retrospective on Carnival published in the *Trinidad Sentinel* in 1860
provides a few more details, including the *nègre jardin* personifications:

> We remember the time when the princes and lords of the land did not
> disdain to parade in the open streets in the sooty disguise of the *negre
> jardin* and when the respectable upstart joined without reservation the
> convivial bands of man-o-war's men, and clownish *Pierrots*, which
> once made so great a figure in the days of yore – when indeed the
> princely balls given at the Governor's residence did not disdain to
> admit its aristocratic guests in all the varied and ludicrous disguises
> which the imagination could conceive or the good times procure.

It is evident that Sir Ralph Woodford had achieved a successful social mix among the majority of white inhabitants. Major W—. lauded his praises, as did Mrs Carmichael, and Colonel Capadose. His regime was viewed subsequently with great nostalgia by French Creole residents.[19] By the late 1820s, therefore, the celebration of Carnival had brought together all these elements in the island's community. It was to continue in this way, following Woodford's death in 1828, changing only gradually in the prelude to slave freedom (from 1833 to 1838) and maintaining something of its homogenous quality into the 1840s.

Carnival – 1831–1834

The principal Carnival event reported in the *Port of Spain Gazette* in 1831 was a 'Masquerade Ball' at Mrs Bruce's Hotel. Announced originally for Shrove Tuesday (15 February), it was brought forward a day 'By particular request of the Ladies'. The function provides extra evidence for disguises and festivities favoured by the elite.

In what appears to have been a rather lack-lustre season, the newspaper's reporter had expected apathy, but was agreeably surprised by the ball's success. The recent arrival of the 'Admiral and his squadron', allowing for a presence of naval officers, had galvanised the community and all 'the beauty and fashion of Port of Spain' attended. As well as 'elegantly dressed ladies', some in disguise as 'lovely Swiss damsels', the male contingent came in a variety of masques including 'French marquisses [*sic*], English noblemen, grooms, postillions, priests and friars'. The reporter attended in guise of the inquisitive Paul Pry. He was pleased to announce 'hilarity and good humour outlived the night' and praised Mrs Bruce for the 'sedulity' of her arrangements.

The diary of Frederick Urich (a merchant's clerk) shows that black people had begun to participate in Carnival. On Shrove Sunday he 'went to see the negroes dance'. On the Monday, he 'followed various masked bands', commenting that 'the dances are usually African dances, and the enthusiasm of the negroes and negresses amuse us very much, for these dances are stupendous'. The ball at Mrs Bruce's Hotel was viewed from the street. Masqued bands continued to parade on Shrove Tuesday.

In 1832 he saw fewer masques. There was another ball at Mrs Bruce's on Shrove Monday. On the Tuesday (6 March) he again 'went to see the masks'. In this he noted that 'nearly all were coloured people'. Urich also provides early evidence for a Carnival tradition common in the French-speaking West Indies. A group of 'acquaintances and our negroes [slaves] had organised a funeral procession to mark the end of the carnival'.[20]

The early 1830s was a period of great change. From outside the colony there was increasing pressure to reduce the powers of slave owners. This was to culminate in the British legislation of 1833 and 1838 that succeeded in ending slavery in her colonies. In 1831 a new form of government was introduced, an Executive Council and a nominated Legislative Council being established. From 1832, the latter began to produce laws in the English language.

It is evident that slaves began to question openly both their working conditions and social position. This is reflected in Carnival. Black creoles who, by inference, may have been slaves, featured in a report of premature masquing in the *Port of Spain Gazette* on 22 January 1833:

> On Sunday afternoon an attempt was made by Mr Peake (Assistant to the Chief of Police) to check the shameful violation of the Sabbath by the lower order of the population, who are accustomed about this time of the year to mask themselves and create disturbances on a Sunday. He arrested two persons who were in masks, and lodged them in the Cage. On his return from performing this necessary duty, his house was assaulted by a large concourse of rabble who broke all the windows, and attacking Mr Peake, pelted, beat, and otherwise ill-treated this officer.

There is a resume of the way in which Carnival was celebrated:

> In reference to the above affair, it may be as well to remark, that the custom of commencing the Carnival several weeks before Ash Wednesday, is contrary in Spanish custom as well as law. In Spain, and in all Spanish Colonies and *ci-devant* Spanish Possessions, the Carnival is kept up but three days; the custom of extending Bacchanal diversions for the space of a month or two, is Italian, and was introduced by foreigners. This has of late become a great nuisance in this Island, as the most criminal and indecent events occur during the extended Carnival, which the local Magistrates do well in endeavouring to suppress.

The authorities reacted swiftly to this confrontation and issued a notice from the Police Office, on 21 January, stating:

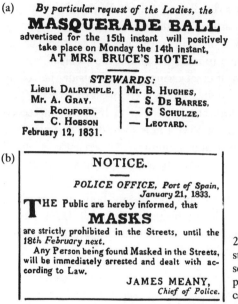

(a)   *By particular request of the Ladies, the*
       MASQUERADE BALL
       advertised for the 15th instant will positively
       take place on Monday the 14th instant,
       AT MRS. BRUCE'S HOTEL.

       STEWARDS:
       Lieut. DALRYMPLE, | Mr. B. HUGHES,
       Mr. A. GRAY, | — S. DE BARRES,
       — ROCHFORD, | — G SCHULZE,
       — C. HOBSON | — LEOTARD.
       February 12, 1831.

(b)   NOTICE.

       POLICE OFFICE, Port of Spain,
                   January 21, 1833.
       THE Public are hereby informed, that
                   MASKS
       are strictly prohibited in the Streets, until the
       18*th February* next.
           Any Person being found Masked in the Streets,
       will be immediately arrested and dealt with ac-
       cording to Law.
                   JAMES MEANY,
                       Chief of Police.

2 The names of Mrs Bruce's stewards represent a diversity of settlers. Black slaves began to take part openly in the festival and in 1833 caused a premature disturbance.

THE Public are hereby informed, that
MASKS
are strictly prohibited in the Streets until the 18*th February next.* Any person being found Masked in the Streets, will be immediately arrested and dealt with according to Law.

Signator was James Meany, Chief of Police.[21]

Association of violence with Carnival (and the pre-Carnival season) has been long-standing. The response to incarceration of the two premature masquers is in keeping with this tradition. In addition, use of a 'cage' to confine these prisoners adds weight to the supposition they were slaves. Such devices were employed to emphasise chattel status and maintain separation from white inhabitants; the latter were usually confined to the gaol.

In many respects, the 1833 Carnival was the last the hierarchy was able to sustain almost exclusively to itself. This was due to the passing of the Act that abolished slavery and introduced Apprenticeship (28 August). The latter was to commence on 1 August the year following.

With confirmation of freedom on the horizon, and a plantocracy depressed by the imminent loss of their slaves, black participation in

Carnival came of age in February 1834. Although the festival was reported in the *Port of Spain Gazette* there was 'a complete change of tone'. An 'unctuous self-congratulation', that characterised previous descriptions, altered to an 'apprehensive expectation of disgust tempered by condescension in case of disappointment'. Making a contrast with the past, the report begins:

> Nothing can more decidedly mark the great change which has taken place within this Colony, than the want of spirit, and we might add, deficiency of elegant bustle, which was to be seen during the Carnival week in olden times. We have traversed the town at all hours during the two days allowed for the exercise of fun and frolic, and with the exception of witnessing a large crowd of idle negroes and little people, accompanying a party intending to represent the Artillery, we met no other in character deserving a moment's notice.

The writer describes the members of this masquerade band:

> The Artillery party with their mock Commandant was not badly got up; their Chief, however, was but an indifferent representative of the portly original. The Lieutenant Colonel was also a most sorry figure, and the Adjutant a very bad copy. But we cannot withhold praise of the two jolly Subs, who were done to life – the spectacles of one were admirable, whilst the bold strut of the other was inimitable. We were sorry, however, to observe that the mock detachment were so defective in their wheelings and marchings, much more ought to have been expected from their two weeks drill by Major Expediency.

At this he took mild, but qualified, offence:

> The mockery of the best Militia Band that has ever been embodied in the West was in very bad taste – and if intended to ridicule, must have missed its aim; but we are rather inclined to believe that this was not the case, and that the whole was got up by the Maskers in the same spirit with which it was received by the Public – viz., in good humour and as a mere piece of fun.

On a somewhat supercilious note, he ended with a comment that the Carnival had passed 'without the slightest outrage'.[22]

Imitation of the Militia by black masqueraders appears to have struck a raw nerve. This was probably intended. Although their parades and other activities had been the subject of a farce by E. L. Joseph, white Trinidadians took great pride in their Militia. Joseph himself commented on its

quality in his *History of Trinidad* and this praise was echoed by other con-
temporaries. The force, which had been honed to a high standard of readiness by Sir Ralph Woodford, maintained this tradition after his death.[23]
The services of the Militia were utilised on and immediately after Emancipation Day, when former slaves protested that they were not at liberty but
Apprenticed for from four to six years.

Emancipation Day – 1834

A concise summary of Emancipation Day in Trinidad is provided by E. L.
Joseph:

> The negroes of Trinidad, on this occasion, behaved less riotously than
> those of some of the neighbouring colonies. The greatest difficulty was
> in making them comprehend the difference between slavery and what
> is called praedial and non-praedial apprenticeship; they shewed much
> resistance, but this in most cases, was of a passive nature. The use of
> the cat-o'-nine-tails convinced some of the most refractory that they
> were in the wrong, and the rest returned to their duty, patiently to
> await the four or six years probation. Contrary to the desire of many,
> martial law was not proclaimed; no life was lost, save that of one negro,
> who was shot at Band de l'Est: his murderer escaped to the opposite
> coast of Columbia.

While this describes rudiments of the occasion, several other factors are
of relevance. These revolve around protestations by the 'apprentices', on
learning their new status had left them less than free.

According to the *Port of Spain Gazette*, even before 1 August slaves had
not been prepared to accept the Apprenticeship provisions. 'It was decided
by them', the newspaper reported, 'that the King had freed them right out
and that the apprenticeship was a job got up between their masters and the
Governor. Their masters were "dam tief" the Governor an "Old Rogue"
and the King not such a Fool as to buy them half free when he was rich
enough to pay for them altogether.'

Apparent in this is a traditional belief in the impartiality of Kingship – of
the King as an arbiter of justice – as well as a perceptive understanding that
Apprenticeship was not full Emancipation. Some in the plantocracy were
alarmed at the attitude of the slaves, and four companies of the Militia were
placed in readiness, should there be disturbances in Port of Spain.

The *Gazette* took the view that there was a distinct threat of violence, when former slaves gathered to enquire their status on 1 August. In contrast, the recollection of Henry Capadose, a military officer also present, inclines to a peaceful interpretation of the crowd's intentions. They 'appeared to be a deputation from a few French Estates' and comprised 'for the most part very old men, old women, and children' with a younger man as spokesman 'probably selected because he spoke the French language well'.

On being told terms of their Apprenticeship by the Governor, they 'vociferated "*pas de six ans, point de six ans*"'. Advancement of the same message by different representatives of the administration, culminated in the ex-slaves exclaiming: '*Pas de six ans, nous ne voulons pas de six ans, nous sommes libres, le Roi nous a donné la liberté.*'

Despite exhortations to withdraw, and heavy rain, the crowd stood their ground, none 'had even a stick in their hands'; a point made also by the *Gazette* when describing this and similar protestations during the next two or three days. The crowds were cleared by the police at night and Hardy, the Lieutenant Colonel in charge of the military, astutely declined the wishes of planters for Martial Law.

On the night of 1 August, Capadose recalled driving through Port of Spain with Hardy in his gig. They passed the Militia 'as if prepared for a fierce encounter'. 'As the gig rolled on', however, 'a number of girls danced about it in the streets, singing French *arriettes* of, probably, their own composition on the goodness of King William in granting them freedom'. At this, Hardy commented in humour that it '*looked mightily like insurrection*'.[24]

In addition to the subtle tactic of unarmed protest, to which Hardy responded likewise, it is also apparent that the beau stick (or 'bo tick' in Mrs Carmichael's insurrectionary song) was sometimes carried by black people. As early as 1810 an Order by the Cabildo (12 September) had been passed in this respect:

> Negroes are forbidden to carry bludgeons or other weapons, on pain of
> a month's imprisonment and being worked in the chain gang.

Such evidence implies that some form of stickfighting was a recognised activity among black slaves.[25]

The African-French character of slave culture in Trinidad is demonstrated by protestations in French, dancing in the streets and singing of short songs – *ariettes* is the usual spelling. Emphasis on the British monarch as the ultimate authority for their freedom suggests a belief in the role of Kingship that may well have originated in Africa.

Carnival and Emancipation Day – 1835–1838

The Carnival of 1834 had been limited to two days by Police Order. Presumably because of the good behaviour of the masquers, and controls exercised over former slaves through Apprenticeship, the period was extended during the next four years. Orders in the *Trinidad Royal Gazette* show that masqueraders were allowed six days for their festivities in 1835, four days in 1836, four days in 1837, and four days in 1838.[26]

In 1835, '*An Ordinance for establishing an effective system of Police within the town of Port of Spain*' was passed, which specified powers allowing masquing. These provisions were extended to the environs of the town in another Ordinance passed in 1837. The same laws also restricted the locations and time of day various musical instruments could be played: namely 'any drum, gong tambour, bangee, or chac-chac'. The exact meaning of 'bangee' is not certain, but there are newspaper references to the 'banjee drum'.[27]

It is unlikely that there were special celebrations for Emancipation Day between 1835 and 1837. In the same period, the Carnival appears to have continued much as in earlier years. In 1838, however, perhaps reflecting dissatisfaction with Apprenticeship, the black presence in Carnival made its first significant mark of protest with the white establishment.

As with a number of later confrontations, a principal issue was the relationship of Carnival to Christian worship on Shrove Sunday. For white colonists of strict Protestant persuasion, this was of particular consequence. The conflict, when it was politically expedient, was between paganism and Christianity – symbolising Africa and Europe respectively. To this effect, 'A Scotchman' harangued the authorities in a letter to the *Port of Spain Gazette*. Fortuitously, this prompted the earliest Carnival report with detail of participation by black masqueraders.

Defending the plantocracy against the 'lower order', warning of the consequences of the ending of Apprenticeship on 1 August 1840, and heightening criticism by half declining to describe 'the outrageous desecration of the Sabbath which took place "*by Authority*" last Sunday,' the report is both disdainful and desperate in its tone:

> We will not dwell on all the disgusting and indecent scenes that were
> enacted in our Streets – we will not say how many we saw in a state so
> nearly approaching to nudity, as to outrage decency and shock modesty
> – we will not particularly describe the African custom of carrying a

(b)

N O T I C E.

POLICE OFFICE, PORT OF SPAIN,
25th January, 1839.

(a)

POLICE OFFICE, *23d February* 1838.

HIS Excellency The Governor has been pleased to grant Leave to any person to appear in Mask in the Streets, from Saturday the 24th to Tuesday the 27th instant.

JAMES MEANY,
Police Magistrate.

ALL Persons are hereby strictly prohibited to appear MASKED in the Public Streets of this Town, except upon the Two undermentioned days, namely,

Monday the 11th ⎫
and   ⎬ of February :
Tuesday the 12th ⎭

And all Persons found disobeying this Notice shall be arrested and punished according to Law.

JOHN JOSEPH CADIZ,
Police Magistrate.

3 'Noisy' celebration by black creoles on Shrove Sunday in 1838 led to a clampdown the next year.

stuffed figure of a woman on a pole, which was followed by hundreds of negroes yelling out a savage Guinea song (we regret to say nine tenths of these people were Creoles) – we will not describe the ferocious fight between the 'Damas' and 'Wartloos' which resulted from this mummering – but we will say at once that the custom of keeping Carnival, by allowing the lower order of society to run about the Streets in wretched masquerade, belongs to other days and ought to be abolished in our own.

The bias that started in 1834 must again be stressed. The sensational, and thereby threatening actions of black masqueraders on days when role reversals were permitted, became the scapegoat for the plantocracy (and subscribers to the newspaper). The celebrations of this group (whatever the complexion of their skin) were ignored, or treated separately. This was to become the pattern for the majority of nineteenth-century newspaper reports. The structure of the event (and, therefore, the society in which it took place) was far more complicated than most newspapers were prepared to accept (especially the dogmatic line adopted by editors of the *Gazette*).

Despite histrionic language, certain aspects of this structure can be deduced from the description:

* African custom is pinpointed – the carrying of a stuffed figure of a woman on a pole. Such totems were not identified in later accounts of Carnival
* fighting (or other competition) between masquerade bands is featured
* the names of these bands probably distinguish African-French- and

African-English-speaking creole groups. The *Damas* are likely to have been the former, and the *Wartloos* the latter

* the greatest proportion of the masqueraders were black creoles, who had no direct contact with Africa
* near nudity in costume
* parades and individual masquers running 'about the streets'
* yelling (or singing) of a 'savage Guinea song' in chorus (again, the African coast of Guinea was not identified in later accounts of singing in Carnival)

Even European 'buffoonery' and 'mummering' are equated with brutalisation of 'the faculty of the lower order of our population'. They are portrayed as the antithesis of the pretended 'civilisation' of the hierarchy. It was this white elite, however, or rather the proportion of Spanish- and French-speaking Roman Catholics, who had established Shrovetide in the island. In resistance to the Protestant English and Scottish colonists, and sometimes separate British administration, they defended the festival when threatened by others in the hierarchy. On occasion, this linguistic and religious split allowed for alliances between differing factions, including those in the black population.[28]

As the nineteenth century progressed, Carnival can be taken as a measure of the increasing polyglot nature of Trinidad society. This approach is not without difficulties. The two principal bands of black creoles who fought one another in 1838 provide a good example of problems of interpretation.

Later in 1838 'a group of Dama people from Port of Spain presented a thanksgiving petition to the Governor ... on the ending of apprenticeship'. They can be classed as an African nation – 'an eastern Nigritic tribe' from the Cameroons. Although possible, it seems unlikely that the band of black creoles called Damas in the Carnival simply represented this group. It is much more probable they were a more general aggregation of black people aligned with French sentiments. Thus the Wartloos were almost certainly named after the victorious British at the battle of Waterloo – as can be shown for equivalent carnivalesque organisations in Jamaica, and St Lucia. Neither explanation is certain. Despite the French (and some English) influence on black creoles, associations that identified their African origin persisted. There was a similar petition to the Governor by the Mokos (from Benin), and the Yoruba Friendly Society was also founded in 1838. The latter was allied to the Roman Catholic Church.[29]

The ending of Apprenticeship on 1 August 1838 was brought about by 'An Act to amend the Act for the Abolition of Slavery in the *British Colonies*'. This received Royal Assent on 11 April 1838 and, in the British West Indies, popularly associated the abolition of slavery with Queen Victoria, who had sanctioned the Act in the second year of her reign.

Plantocracy opposition to the revised date was swept aside by circumstances outside their control. When the time came, the *Port of Spain Gazette* was happy to report there was no 'excitement of any kind'. In Port of Spain, 'the different Churches were tolerably well attended by the Laborers [*sic*], the Roman Catholic particularly so, as the greater number of them belong[ed] to that Religion'. A pattern of limited celebration appears to have continued in subsequent years or, if festivities took place, only the most formal attracted attention in newspapers.[30]

Despite the scanty evidence, more popular celebrations seem likely. In 1881, it was reported that Canboulay was enacted annually by black people on Emancipation Day 'as a kind of commemoration of the change in their condition'. The event 'was kept up much for the same reason as the John Canoe dance in Jamaica'. Later, 'the day was changed, and for many years the Carnival days have been inaugurated by the "Cannes Brulées".' In the same year, 'X' recalled that *'cannes brulées'* (performed by newly freed black people) had become the starting point for Carnival when the authorities limited the festival to two days.[31]

In common with 'John Canoe' in Jamaica, it is possible that black people in Trinidad enacted Canboulay on Emancipation Day and during Carnival. Indeed, it may be that elements of the ceremony were already present in the Carnival of 1838. For example, 'near nudity', the yelling of songs, and ferocious fighting between bands, were components of the event as it was performed in the third quarter of the century. It must be remembered, however, that these particular features were hardly mentioned in accounts of the Carnival during the next decade.

Carnival and Christmas in the 1840s

After Carnival disturbances and the ending of Apprenticeship in 1838, the festival was confined to two days the next year.[32]

A letter from 'A Subscriber', published in the *Trinidad Standard* on 7 February 1842, indicates that this had been the case 'for the last two or

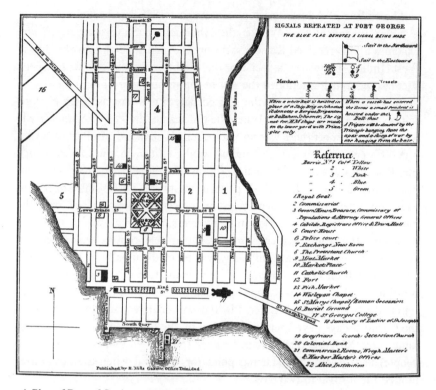

4 Plan of Port of Spain, *c.* 1839. The French steeets (or 'shores') spanned from Henry
Street to the River St Anns.

three years' and the practice 'appeared on the decline' because of official
restriction. The writer complained, however, of 'wanton desecration of the
Sabbath Day' by masquers which he put down to lack of 'such judicious
measures' and, more particularly, the holding of a masqued ball that
evening (Carnival Monday) by the Governor, Sir Henry MacLeod.

The paper defended 'the revelling of maskers in the streets on Sunday'
on the grounds that 'to the majority of the population (the Catholics)
recreation is as much permitted on that day as on any other'. They also
noted that they could not 'flatter our correspondent that the lower orders
will be tempted by these revelries from the path of virtue' and continued
'we should rather wager that it tended to keep them from vices of a
darker character, not that we intend to impute anything very bad to
them'.

This spells out the Protestant versus Catholic split over the holding of Carnival and almost certainly implies that black participation was not perceived as a threat. Later reports of the celebration in the 1840s are usually tolerant of the role played by black people.

The *Standard* was highly critical of their 'Subscriber's' views on the ball, believing that his 'squeamishness' would 'only be laughed at by at least the 500 or 600 people' expected to attend. *'Vive la Bagatelle'* said the *Standard*, and the report of the ball in the *Port of Spain Gazette* (8 February) maintained this happy vivacity. It noted 'the costumes were various and of all nations pearly – Greeks, Turks, Germans, Spaniards, French', and that the event compared favourably with similar balls held by Sir Ralph Woodford. The paper was even moved to report 'that never within our memory has the conduct of all classes of the people been so correct – so free from any sort of offensive demeanour or licence, as during the present Carnival'

The exact year in which Carnival was fixed at two days has not been determined but it was so limited in 1844; a notice to this effect was published on the front page of the *Port of Spain Gazette* (6 February).[33]

Upper-class masqued dances remained a feature of Carnival in this period. They probably continued to be held annually at this season throughout the century, although not always reported in the press. In 1844 the *Port of Spain Gazette* carried an account of a ball in St Ann's, a district of elite residences in Port of Spain and there was a similar bulletin in the *Trinidad Standard* the following year. From the same edition of this newspaper (5 February) there is a description of Carnival that serves as a reference for considering the street festival during the 1840s:

> The streets are thronged by parties and individuals in every variety of national and fanciful costume, and in every possible contortion and expression of 'the human face divine'. Some are gay and noble – some are as ignoble as rags and uncouth habiliments can make them. Some are marching to the sound of well-played music – the violin, the guitar, the castinet, the drum, and the tambourine strike the ear in every direction. Some delight themselves in the emission and production of sounds of the wildest, most barbarous, and most unearthly description imaginable, and their instruments are as extraordinary as the sounds they make. Now we observe the Swiss peasant, in holiday trim, accompanied by his fair Dulcima – now companies of Spanish, Italians and Brazilians glide along in varied steps and graceful dance ... But what see we now? – goblins and ghosts, fiends, beasts and frightful birds –

wild men – wild Indians and wilder Africans. Pandemonium and the savage wilds of our mundane orb are pouring forth their terrific occupants. It would seem as though the folly and madness and fitful vagaries of the year had been accumulated in science and solitude to burst forth their exuberant measures and concentrated force in the fantastic revels of the Carnival.[34]

One of two accounts of Christmas available from the 1840s was published in the *Trinidad Spectator* on 27 December 1845. This complained of 'Christmas Nuisances', and the exhibition of 'a scene anything but becoming a civilised country'. In common with the protest of 'An Unitarian' about 'the Sabbath' in Arouca, published one month before in the *Gazette*, the *Spectator* notes that 'the wild banjee drum abounded'. It was 'accompanied with sounds the most unmusical and grating'. Fireworks were also set off and, to mark the beginning of Christmas Day, 'the bells of Trinity Church commenced a furious peal' at midnight.[35]

'Uncivilised' is associated with the 'banjee drum' (and, thereby, 'savage' Africa). Together with Protestant antagonisms towards Catholics, this probably underlies these criticisms. There appears also to have been a change of mood in the colony, a tension that was to reach a climax at Shrovetide.

On 17 February 1846 'A Proclamation' and 'Notice' affecting the Carnival were issued by the Colonial Secretary. The 'Proclamation' related to the dry weather, and required Port of Spain citizens to keep 'a hogshead of water' at their abode because of frequent fires – it emerged an arsonist was at large. The 'Notice', which restricted masquing, appears to have been another measure against the fire raiser, but was seized upon by those opposed to the festival. 'We trust this will prove a final, instead of a temporary stop to the orgies which are indulged in by the dissolute of the Town, at this season of the year, under the pretence of Masking' was the stance of the *Port of Spain Gazette*. The 'Notice' read:

> WHEREAS the practice of MASKING in the open streets has frequently led of late years to the disturbance of the Public Peace, NOTICE IS HEREBY GIVEN, That MASKING in the open streets will not hereafter be permitted; and that all persons found so Masked in the open streets, in the Town of Port of Spain, or any other Town or Village, will be apprehended by the Police as idle and disorderly Persons, and dealt with accordingly.

TRINIDAD.

By His Excellency Colonel Sir HENRY
MACLEOD, K. H., K. S. W., Governor and Commander-in-Chief
in and over the said Island and
its Dependencies, Vice-Admiral
thereof, &c.

A PROCLAMATION.

WHEREAS the present dryness of the weather, the probability of its continuance,
and the frequent Fires that have occurred in the
Town of Port of Spain, render it necessary and
expedient to establish the Regulations that have
been from time to time made in this Colony, for
the prevention of Fire in the Town.

I do, therefore, hereby call upon all Her Majesty's Loyal Subjects immediately after the pro-
mulgation of this Proclamation, to cause to be
placed and constantly kept contiguous to the entrance of his or her abode, a hogshead of water.

And I do hereby further call upon every such
Loyal Subject to cause twice in each week, until
further orders, and oftener if need be, such hogshead to be emptied and refilled with water.

And the Surveyor General, the Inspector of
Police, and all Justices of the Peace are hereby
requested to see that this Proclamation is carried
into effect.

Given under my Hand at Government-House,
in the Town of Port of Spain, this 17th day of
February, in the year of Our Lord One Thousand
Eight Hundred and Forty six.

By His Excellency's Command,

ARTHUR WHITE,

Colonial Secretary.

NOTICE.

Government-House, 17th February, 1846.

WHEREAS the practice of MASKING in
the open Streets has frequently led of
late years to the disturbance of the Public Peace,

NOTICE IS HEREBY GIVEN, That MASKING
in the open Streets will not hereafter be permitted ; and that all persons found so Masked in the
open Streets, in the Town of Port of Spain, or
any other Town or Village, will be apprehended
by the Police as idle and disorderly Persons, and
dealt with accordingly.

By Command,

ARTHUR WHITE,

Colonial Secretary.

5 A spate of fires threatened Port
of Spain during Shrovetide in
1846 and the Government took
special precautions.

Two days later (19 February), the *Trinidad Standard* explained the Governor was 'anxious to prevent what might be resorted to by the incendiary as a cloak for . . . his evil purpose'. It hoped, in the circumstances, that prohibition of masques would be 'perfectly understood and appreciated'. The *Gazette* (20 February) shifted its position, following a representation to the Governor to rescind the ban. His rumoured favourable response was denied but, it was pointed out, masquing was prohibited '*whilst in the streets*'. There was no objection to 'parties dressing in such apparel as they may see fit, and on arriving at any of their friends' houses putting on the masks they may carry with them, and there enjoying themselves as much as they choose'. The pro-Carnival lobby appear to have won a small but significant victory in this change. This seems to have encouraged a degree of tolerance towards other masquers, judging by a report of the first day of the festival (*Standard*, 23 February). A comment hints that the celebration had begun to incorporate something resembling Canboulay: 'This morning, that is from midnight until day-break, the hour at which last year and former years the wildest uproar imaginable prevailed from one end of the town to the other, was remarkably quiet.'

Special Constables patrolled the town, and a detachment of the 23rd Regiment were bivouacked at the Town Hall to dissuade the fire-raiser(s) and ensure enforcement of regulations. There was some latitude, however, as the *Standard* explained:

> It was rather late in the morning before the votaries of the Carnival ventured to show themselves. But they gradually crept forth in their fancy dresses, and have continued their antics with growing confidence, as they find the proclamation has reference only to the use of the mask. They appear, however, to feel themselves shorn of their chief delight in not being able to conceal their faces, and some of them have endeavoured to compensate this deprivation by other substitutes as spectacles, beards, and even paint and chalk.

Despite occasional heavy handedness by the police, the Carnival appears to have been celebrated without disturbance. At its conclusion the *Trinidad Spectator* (25 February) praised the populace for conducting 'themselves with great propriety', as had the *Standard* two days earlier. The *Spectator*, however, was against the wearing of masques on any occasion. Its stance stands as a measure of the anti-Carnival lobby in this period, and indicates a principal element in their objections was fear.

> Formerly, at this season, we were left to our own guidance, which in all conscience was wayward enough: indeed, a large number of the

inhabitants used to act more like the liberated inmates of a madhouse than sane beings. The order prohibiting the wearing of masks was a rational and wise measure. Moral honesty and the safety of society require that all should exhibit their *native face*, however fantastically they may bedeck or disfigure the remaining portions of their corporiety. No Government should allow man woman or child to appear in public with *a false face*. There is already in every human being too much falsity under the skin, and in the original features. The tolerance of *masking* is a disgrace to an enlightened government, and happy we are that our Governor has, at last, wiped off this disgrace; at least as far as Port of Spain is concerned. It may be true that circumstances prompted him to prohibit the practice; but, be that as it may, we are grateful for the prohibition, and sincerely trust that *masking* will never again be tolerated by the rulers of Trinidad.[36]

The advice of the *Spectator* was not heeded and the Carnival continued annually, the 1847 event being witnessed by Charles William Day. His description is the fullest available for this decade:

I was residing in Trinidad during the Carnival, which commenced on Sunday, the 7th of March, at midnight. I had seen the Carnival at Florence, at Syra in Greece, and in Rome; and was now about to witness a negro masquerade, which, from its squalid splendour, was not unamusing, cheapness being the grand requisite. The maskers parade the streets in gangs of from ten to twenty, occasionally joining forces in procession. The primitives were negroes, as nearly naked as might be, bedaubed with a black varnish. One of this gang had a long chain and padlock attached to his leg, which chain the others pulled. What this typified, I was unable to learn; but, as the chained one was occasionally thrown down on the ground, and treated with a mock bastinadoing it probably represented slavery. Each mask was armed with a good stout quarter-staff, so that they could overcome one-half more police than themselves, should occasion present itself. Parties of negro ladies danced through the streets, each *clique* distinguished by boddices [*sic*] of the same colour. Every negro, male and female, wore a white flesh-coloured mask, their woolly hair carefully concealed by handkerchiefs; this, contrasted with the black bosom and arms, was droll in the extreme. Those ladies who aimed at the superior civilization of shoes and stockings, invariably clothed their pedal extremities in pink silk stockings and blue, white, or yellow kid shoes, sandled up their sturdy legs. For the men, the predominating character was Pulinchinello; every second negro, at least, aiming at playing the continental Jack-pudding. Pirates too were very common, dressed in Guernsey frocks, full scarlet trowsers, and red woollen cap, with wooden pistols for arms. From the utter want of spirit, and sneaking deportment of these bold corsairs, I presumed them to have come from the Pacific. Turks also there were, and one Highlander, a most ludicrous caricature of the Gael, being arrayed in a scarlet coat, huge grenadier cap, a kilt of light blue chintz, striped with white, a most indescribable philibeg, black legs of course, and white socks bound with dirty pink ribbon. There were also two grand processions, having triumphal 'wans,' one of which was to commemorate the recent marriage of a high law-officer; the other, judging from the royal arms in front (worth a guinea of anybody's money, if only for the painting – the lion looking like a recently drowned puppy), and a canopy of red glazed calico, trimmed with silver tinsel, shading a royal pair, who in conscious majesty, sat within, represented the Sovereign pair of England. This brilliant *cortége* was marshalled forward by a huge negro, in a celestial dress, made after the conventional fashion of the angel Gabriel; and who stalked along, spear in hand, as if intent on doing dire deeds. The best embodiments were the Indians of South America, daubed with red ochre; personified by the Spanish peons from the Main, themselves half Indian, as testified by their exquisitely small feet and hands. Many of these had real Indian quivers and bows, as well as baskets; and doubtless, were very fair representatives of the characters they assumed. In this costume, children looked very pretty. One person-ation of Death, having what was understood to be a skeleton painted on a coal-black shape, stalked about with part of a horse's vertebra attached to him, and a horse's thigh bone in his hand; but his most telling movements only elicited shouts of laughter. I noticed that whenever a *black* mask appeared, it was sure to be a *white* man. Little girls dressed *à la jupe*, in the *vrai* creole negro costume, looked very interesting. All parties with the assistance of bands of execrable music, made a tremendous uproar; and most of us were glad when the priestly saturnalia was over.[37]

Day was also in Trinidad for Christmas. His account, more graphic than the *Spectator*'s in 1845, shows this feast had already become something of a mini-Carnival. It incorporated elements of 'lower class' celebration, to which attention would be drawn in many subsequent descriptions of Shrovetide:

> On Christmas Eve, it seemed as if, under the guise of religion, all Pandemonium had been let loose. At intervals during the night, bands of execrable music paraded the streets, and bad fireworks filled the atmosphere. Drunkenness bursting forth in yells and bacchanalian

orgies, was universal amongst the blacks; and fiddles, fifes and har-
monicons resounded on every side, making night hideous. Sleep was
quite out of the question, in the midst of such a disgusting and fiendish
saturnalia. One band which came forth at two o'clock on the morning
of Saturday merits particular notice. It seemed to be composed of an
enormous *tambour*, a thousand times louder than the drum of a *fanto-
ccini*, and banged with a maniacal violence; a fiddle or two, a triangle,
and an infinity of cow-horns! The musicians were attended by a multitude of drunken people of both sexes, the women being of the lowest
class; and all dancing, screaming and clapping their hands, like so
many demons. All this was the effect of the 'midnight mass', ending, as
all such masses do, in every species of depravity. Of course the priests
encourage this, as it serves to keep up their influence over their flock.[38]

In addition to general disparagement, Day's report implies his opposition to
the Roman Catholic church.

A continuing deprecation of Carnival, and Catholicism, is evident in the
Trinidad Spectator's brief account of the festival on 8 March 1848. Referring
to a 'relic of barbarism – nursery of vice, – and fostered imp of a super-
stitious faith', the newspaper believed the event to be on the wane. This was
not the case, however, as can be seen by a report published in the *Port of
Spain Gazette* on 20 February 1849 (Shrove Tuesday):

> Since midnight on Sunday, this Festival has broken the slumbers of
> our peaceable citizens with its usual noisy revelry and uproarious
> hilarity. Bands of music (*soi disant*), including those 'elegant' instru-
> ments the tin kettle and salt box, the banjee and schack-schack [*sic*],
> have paraded the town in all parts, and at all hours of the day and
> night. Still, although 'the fun grew fast and furious', but slight infrac-
> tions of the peace have taken place, and exhausted by the incessant
> dancing and antics, the greater portion of the noisy groups have
> already retired to their houses.[39]

Celebrated for its description of 'bands of music' this bulletin provides a
point for assessing Carnivals from the previous decade. They can be
divided into two principal categories of exotica – civilised and primitive.
It must be remembered that accounts available include black *and* white
participants. A recall of Carnivals in the 1840s, published in *Fair Play and
Trinidad News* on 6 March 1879, provides an overview for comparison.[40]

Perhaps one of the most significant statements in this recollection is that
'people of all classes enjoyed themselves, and commerce was extensive –
benefited by the lavish expenditure of those easy monetary times'. It
appears that a principal reason for the degree of tolerance between mas-

queraders in the 1840s rested on financial stability and a willingness to share both wealth and the ceremony between different sectors of the community. Inevitably, *Fair Play* concentrates on the 'civilised' aspects of the festival; it notes also, that 'anything of an objectionable character was exceptional and confined to the purlieus of the town'. The masqued balls are confirmed, as are 'rich and characteristic costumes' (including 'kings and queens' in chateaux 'drawn by numerous horses'). There were 'bands of musicians' (who accompanied the 'kings and queens'); 'cavalcades of gentlemen finely dressed up in character'; specialised 'living caricatures'; and 'a thousand and one personated characters' (including 'jesters' and 'tumblers'). The satire was both 'cutting and wholesome' and provided 'a magnificent and masked *abandon*'.

Allowing for nostalgic romanticism the overview is remarkably accurate. Thus, in the 'civilised' category the *Trinidad Standard* (1845) reports 'gay and noble' masqueraders that fit this pattern (including Brazilians, Italians and Spanish, as well as the Swiss Peasant and his fair Dulcima). The 'bands of musicians' (1879) are equivalent to the 'sound of well-played music'. These equate with 'the violin, the guitar, the castinet, the drum and the tambourine'. Charles William Day (1847) was not impressed by any of the musicians that he heard but recalls two grand processions representing 'triumphal "wans"' (or wains), one of which featured a canopy and was in homage to Queen Victoria and her consort Prince Albert (married in 1840). Day also mentions what appear to be 'sets' of black women dressed in 'boddices [*sic*] of the same colour' (similar to Jamaican 'John Canoe' bands of several years previous) and 'little girls dressed *à la jupe*, in the *vraï* creole negro costume'

Fair Play's only reference to the primitive exotica of 1840s Carnival is to 'all the conceits and peculiarities of human, and even sometimes animal life', although it drew attention to the 'Indians with bows and arrows'. The latter are mentioned by the *Standard* in 1845 (wild Indians) and Day describes 'the Indians of South America' as having been 'the best embodiments' in the Carnival of 1847.

In line with *Fair Play*, the *Standard* mentions 'fiends, beasts and frightful birds', wild Africans, other wild men, goblins and ghosts. The ghosts can be equated with 'Death', seen by Day in 1847. Together with the personification of Pirates and Turks, each masque represents an incursive force threatening social life. Caricatures include Day's Highlander, and numerous Pulinchinellos (described as a 'continental Jack-pudding' – or, 'fool' in British masquing terminology).

There were also masquers 'ignoble as rags and uncouth habiliments can make them' (*Standard*, 1845), who may have been similar to the 'primitives' observed by Day. From his description, this band could have been participating in Canboulay, for they included a man in chains, perhaps symbolising a prisoner or, more likely, slavery.

Day mentions that each band of black masqueraders carried sticks (in defensive-offensive symbolism) but this appears not to have been perceived as a threat by other bands. Indeed, racial role reversals, with black participants wearing white masques and white mummers wearing black masques, were the order of the day in 1847.

The 'sounds of the wildest most barbarous and most unearthly description' (1845) or 'bands of execrable music' making 'a tremendous uproar' (1847) were probably synonymous with the 'bands of music (*soi disant*)' that included 'those "elegant" instruments the tin kettle and salt box, the banjee drum, and schack-schack' (1849).

It is likely that the musical instruments Day heard, on Christmas Day in 1847, were also featured in black Carnival processions in this period – 'an enormous *tambour* ... a fiddle or two, a triangle, and an infinity of cow horns'. It seems possible that the *tambour* he describes was the banjee drum, but this is conjecture. These instruments, together with the 'dancing, screaming, and clapping of hands like so many demons' perhaps provides a link with the Carnival description of 1838 and the 'yelling' of 'a savage Guinea song'. Also in common with 1838 and the 1840s was the near nudity of costume, street parades by competing bands and individuals, and reference to Africa.

In addition to 'wild Africans', other migrant groups are identified in Carnival parades. The Spanish were the original European settlers, but the Spanish-speaking African-Amerindians from Venezuela were recent arrivals. The Scots formed part of the wave of British settlers, while the 'little girls dressed *à la jupe*, in the *vrai* creole negro costume' probably reflect the origin of many French-speaking ex-slaves in Martinique and Guadeloupe.[41]

Migrants and music – 1840s–1850s

The 1840s and 1850s saw a flow of migrants to Trinidad, amongst them French and German settlers from Europe, and indentured labour from Africa, China and India. Black creoles also arrived from English-speaking islands such as Antigua and St Kitts, and French-speaking islands such as Guadeloupe and Martinique. 'The yard where the Martiniquians dance' is mentioned in a court case in 1846 and is identified with the 'Society of the Rose' (or St Rose of Lima). All these emigrants contributed to Trinidad's cultural development, including the Carnival.

On 1 October 1849 there was a riot about prison conditions. Present were 'all the rabble of Port of Spain', among whom were 'a large number of loose women including the vilest of their class, girls, boys and little imported Africans, etc.' Many of the 'mob' were armed with 'sticks and stones'. The *Port of Spain Gazette* found scapegoats among outsiders, or the marginalised. With their French republican inheritance, Martiniquians were particularly suspect. In an attack on their presence after the riot the *Gazette* described each as:

> strutting through the streets of Port of Spain as if they belonged to him, exciting our quiet population with stories of shooting and relating the '*sacres colons*' of the Islands he came from, and *endoctrinaire*-ing our loyal Creoles with the outrageous notions imbibed by himself, at second hand, of equality and republicanism, and rights to be enforced by cries of '*aux armes*', '*au feu*', and other sounds, strangers to Trinidad ears, which were pretty plentiful in the French side of the Town on Monday afternoon last.

If black French Creole migrants had imbued the population with republican sentiments, there was little sign of revolution. The cries '*aux armes*' and '*au feu*', however, were echoed by stickfighting bands in the 1870s, and sticks had been carried in the riot.[42] More pertinent is the flow of kith and kin from Martinique that reinforced the French Creole character of black music and Carnival. This is true in particular of the '*Bel Air*', first identified in the *Port of Spain Gazette* in 1838 as 'half licentious, half unmeaning, songs' of slaves.

Martinique is named as the source of a *belair* reported in the *Trinidad Sentinel* in 1841:

> There was a pretty little *belair* recently imported here, he understood, from Martinique ... A *belair* was a sort of song – a Creole tune with a few verses attached, generally in the French patois. This *belair* has become very popular with the lower orders.... It was called, he believed, 'Coq-d 'Inde ponde'.... [He asks the Chief Justice to sing it, being assured that he knew it].

The *belair* (or *bele*) is a generic name for a drum dance and song form in the French-speaking Caribbean. The words to these songs circulated orally. In some instances stanzas spread from island to island. Others remained exclusive to a particular location, relating to subjects not of general interest. Two lines from a satirical '*bel-air*' from 1852–3, were printed by José M. Bodu in 1890. They refer to a failed attempt by Numa Dessources to found a settlement of Trinidadians in Venezuela:

Creoles charriez bois (ter)	Creoles carry wood (ter)
Pour nous bruler Papa Dessources.[43]	For us to burn Pape Dessources.

The *belair* was not the only old Creole drum dance with singing. The black Trinidad scholar J. J. Thomas compiled much of his famous *Theory and Practice of Creole Grammar* (1869) from the words to songs of three different types: '*bellairs, calendas, joubas*'. Each may have existed independent of this musical instrumentation.

A retrospective description of old-time drum dancing published in *Fair Play and Trinidad News* in 1883 provides a summary of such occasions:

> These entertainments were held in neatly built edifices, thatched and enclosed with coconut branches and ornamented with festoons of fruits and flowers. There was an elevated platform at one end where the King with his gorgeously apparelled Queen sat surrounded by her almost equally highly dressed attendants. The drum players, sometimes many in number, who sat in front of them, were well dressed and wore white kid gloves. Whilst the Chorus and Dancers, all gaily dressed females, with bright colored head dresses and sparkling with jewelry, sang in cadence or danced.

With its emphasis on the presence of a 'King' and 'Queen' overviewing the dance this was probably a *belair*. Similar dances were witnessed by Charles William Day in the late 1840s. He described 'a negro *ladies*' ball'. This was held in 'a spacious shed, rudely thatched with palm branches; from the joists of which hung a clumsy wooden chandelier, and at intervals, stuck upon high poles, serving as candelabras, were large tallow candles, casting a fitful glare over the place'.

Although Day saw no 'King' and 'Queen' (his condescending attitude towards black people met with necessary stonewalling), virtually all other elements tally with the recall in *Fair Play*. There were five male drummers accompanied by twenty females singing the chorus. About twelve women, all highly dressed and adorned with jewellery, performed the dance – each

6 Richard Bridgens identified dancing as the principal recreation for black people, sometimes with special dressing, and pinpointed accompaniment by keg drum, 'shak-shak' and vocal chorus (*c.* 1830s–40s).

had paid a subscription in order to participate. They were 'chiefly servants and laundresses', with costumes apparently in the Martinique fashion favoured for this type of performance. At other dances, he noted each woman played 'a "shock-shock"'. This was 'a little calabash filled with peas, by which a rattling is produced in cadence with the *tambours'*.

Day also saw another type of dance, held in a private yard, the function of which is unclear, although his description hints at ritual, rather than recreation. There were two drums ('tum-tums'), a chorus of 'young negro females' and dancing by 'old women'. Tallow candles, held by boys, provided the light.[44]

While Day was opposed to black culture on principle, he was also fascinated, and compelled to detail his dislikes. Paradoxically, therefore, his descriptions provide numerous insights for establishing African-American integrity. Day's opposition was founded in British 'upper-class' snobbery, including a Victorian perception of 'savage' Africa. This allowed him to note 'an infinity of African customs can be traced in the West Indies' and single out 'drumming on the abominably monotonous tum-tum' plus 'singing in chorus, accompanied by the simultaneous clapping of the hands'. He described how black inhabitants circumvented restrictions on playing drums:

> The noisy tum-tum being prohibited after eight o'clock at night, to evade the regulations they begin at eleven o'clock and keep drumming all Saturday night until broad daylight on Sunday morning, and that without the slightest interruption from the police who, being chiefly negroes, are readily bribed by a glass of rum to wink at any illegal proceedings.

Black musicians, who had mastered European instruments and formal dance music, were also castigated for not being prepared to play for the white elite. Essentially, Day had met his match, but on no account was prepared to accept black West Indian equality, let alone superiority. He had little time, also, for the local white population. Fortunately, but with his usual condescension, he indicates the variety of European musical instruments played by black people in Port of Spain, during the late 1840s:

> Another nuisance is the barbarous music of that dark season [night]. The guitar, flute or violin, played by the coloured people and negroes, salute the ear in excruciating strains; whilst in the principal street of Port of Spain (Frederick Street), almost every house resounds with

musical efforts. One coloured young lady in my neighbourhood used to fill half the street with her stentorian lungs. Nearly opposite, two young 'gents' indulged in fierce blasts on the *cornet-à-piston*, or some equally diabolical instrument. Two doors beyond resided a crazy flute, filling up the measure of my torments.[45]

Further torment, for those who had no tolerance, were wakes. These varied in line with religious affiliations of the mourners. They were an integral part of black culture in the English-speaking Caribbean.

In January 1847, the *Trinidad Spectator* criticised the general conduct of wakes as 'crying violations of the social compact'. It asked: 'Is there propriety in holding a revel beside the dead body of a friend or neighbour? Is piety promoted by singing hymns, &c. during the *"live long night"* around or near the mortal remains of a fellow creature?' and answered: 'Such a practice is at once dishonouring to God and injurious to man. Yet it is common in this community, even among those who pretend to not a little piety and enlightenment. Wakes as conducted are a nuisance – a breach of the peace – and ought not to be tolerated.'

As well as 'singing hymns', complaint lay with the 'unbecoming and inane mirth and revelry' that had accompanied a recent death, disturbing local residents. On these occasions, 'dancing and howling' were usual.

Similar patterns were noted in a letter to the *Port of Spain Gazette*, published on 3 October 1848. Without permission, the wake took place in the yard of the writer's lodgings. Signing himself C. W. D. (presumably Charles William Day), he contributed (as usual) a tirade full of detail:

> The relations of the deceased are Methodists of the lower class – his lady cousin being my washerwoman.
>
> At 7 o'clock in the evening the riot began by psalm singing over the corpse, and at 9 o'clock at night the yard was literally crammed with women and girls of very doubtful character, a band of drunken sailors and all the lawless ruffians of Port of Spain – yelling in chorus, dancing in circles, and clapping their hands until the uproar was fearful – the saturnalian orgies being further enlivened by every variety of swearing and profane language. To such a height at last were these hellish revels carried that, at the desire of the landlady, the police were sent for, but were utterly unable to quell the disturbance and the psalm singing was thoroughly overpowered by a fearful din that ensued – in fact the original purpose of the meeting was but a pretext for the assembling of the most lawless characters of both sexes that infest Port of Spain to

the annoyance of the whole neighbourhood, from which sleep was effectually banished, and an absolute breach of the Queen's peace. This riot did not terminate until four o'clock the next morning. The police were defied, the landlady grossly insulted, and myself threatened to be beaten with sticks by the fiendish ruffians who predominated – instigated by the natural son of a former proprietor.

Alongside assimilation of psalm singing into the Trinidad musical corpus, this particular wake also represents the upside-down tradition of Carnival. An editorial in the same issue of the *Gazette* pointed out that wakes were a custom of long-standing, and recommended specific legal constraints. None, however, were introduced until the early twentieth century.[46]

The principal reason for failure of a prosecution brought against the 'Congo Society' in 1853 was lack of restraint against wakes. The clause selected from the 1849 Ordinance '*to consolidate and amend the Laws relative to the Police*' concerned imposition of a 'Penalty on persons keeping disorderly houses, &c.' Proceedings were heard in the Police Court, Port of Spain, five days before being reported in the *Port of Spain Gazette* (12 November 1853). The opening paragraphs of this account place the case in context:

> Joseph Allen appeared to answer an information laid against him by Mr F. C. Bowen under the '26 Clause of the Police Ordinance'.
>
> It appeared from the evidence, that the defendant, Allen, is a trustee of certain persons, Africans of the Congo nation, who have associated themselves together as 'the Congo Society', and who have purchased certain premises in Charlotte Street, known at the Congo yard, where three or four nights every week they hold public dances, to the music of the banjee drum and shack-shack until the hour of 10 p.m. – and often much later – that when any of the society die, whether in the town or environs, the dead body is brought to this yard to be 'waked' as it is termed; on which occasion the whole neighbourhood are obliged to pass a sleepless night. An occasion of this kind formed the subject of the present complaint. According to the deposition of the witnesses – on Wednesday night last a 'wake' was held in the yard in question; it commenced at 8 p.m., and only finished at 6 a.m. the next morning; during the whole of which time, a crowd of upwards of fifty persons, male and female, were bellowing out at the utmost pitch of their voices – the noise becoming greater as the hours got later – *not* hymns, or canticles, or any other kind of devotional exercises, but French Chansons de Societé – having forfeits attached to the omission to join

in at certain periods, with certain words – any forfeit imposed for such neglect being announced with yells of laughter, and shouts and vociferations audible several streets off, and entirely destroying the sleep of all in the immediate neighbourhood.

The report contains additional cultural information. Principally, stones were beaten together at intervals in accompaniment to songs (a custom attributed to Africa) and 'coffee and syrup and water were served round to the assembled company'. Accordingly, the complainants endeavoured to prove the Society's private yard was a public hostelry where disreputables were entertained. This was rejected by the judge.

Although the Congo Society wake had no Christian component, there are several elements in common between this and earlier descriptions. In addition to direct African association, there were signs of French Creole influence – in particular, *Chansons de Societé* sung 'in the French language'. As was pointed out in the *Gazette*, the defending lawyer had made play of the African nature of these 'hymns of mourning'![47]

It is important to place this institution alongside the Yoruba Friendly Society and other organisations representing African 'nations'. Such associations met for secular and religious activities. For the Congo Society, these would have taken place in its Charlotte Street yard. In addition, societies representing African nations participated in Carnival. This is likely also for related migrant affiliations, such as the Martiniquian Society of St Rose.

Attempted suppression of the 'people's festival' – Carnival in the 1850s

Consolidation of the Police laws in 1849 restated restrictions on dancing and playing music at specific times and appearing masqued in the streets of towns. A clause not in previous Police Ordinances concerned the singing of profane or obscene songs or ballads. These were now perceived as a threat.

It is evident also that songs of social comment had begun to make their mark in public. This is witnessed by a letter published in the *Port of Spain Gazette* following Shrovetide in 1851. The writer identifies a Church scandal that had become the subject of a Carnival personification and songs:

when an individual whose immoral conduct has led to his personification and exposure to the scorn and derision of the multitude during the last two days of 'Pagan revelry' ventures, whilst the names of his victims are being sullied in the streets, and made the subject of the ribald songs and jests of the people, to take his seat as a member of the Roman Catholic Vestry, and assume a conspicuous part in matters in which the interests of religion are concerned, it is high time that he should be made to understand the disgust his conduct excites.

The correspondent continues with his moral stance and notes the effect of the satire with advice to the perpetrator:

It is currently reported that two of this individual's victims, a young couple, have left the island, unable to face the unenviable notoriety which he has cast upon their fair fame; let him, their evil spirit, so far follow their example, as to retire from public observation.

In conclusion, he threatens that if his letter produces no result the cleric will 'hear again from A FRIEND OF SOCIAL ORDER'.[48]

This is a very early example of the popular power of Trinidad Carnival burlesques. It is doubly important in that it shows satirical songs were also part of the masquerade tradition; performing a function similar to that of the calypso in the twentieth century.

With a few exceptions, such as the *belairs* mentioned previously, evidence for the subject matter of songs from this era is very difficult to discover. The full shape of Carnival is similarly elusive, although sporadic accounts in newspapers provide a more complete picture. Two letters from 'A *Friend* to MIRTH but an *Enemy* to FOLLY' published in the *Port of Spain Gazette* in 1856, are the next available documents. The first was printed on 30 January, before Carnival, and the second on 6 February after the event.

Complaining in his initial letter of the issue by police of the annual proclamation allowing masquing (limited to two days as usual), 'A *Friend* to MIRTH' is at 'a loss to know why this *barbarous* custom has not long been put a stop to'. He declares that 'none but the lowest of the low, and vilest of the vile now think of appearing in masks in the public streets at this season' and calls for the abolition of Carnival, although this is not mentioned by name. He is assured that Roman Catholic and Protestant clergy are opposed to the festival as well as all 'well thinking people in the community'. He asks, therefore, for a second proclamation in line with his views. In this, the '*Enemy* to FOLLY' was disappointed.

Following the revelry, the same writer is incensed by a pro-Carnival bulletin published by the *Trinidad Reporter* and, castigates 'all hands connected with it, from the *Editor down to the Printer's Devil'*. At the core of his criticisms is the behaviour of '"*the Majority*"(!) during the night of Sunday and morning of Monday last'. This appears to be a reference to Canboulay, for the '*Friend* to MIRTH' scorns the masqueraders, describing them as 'such out-and-out devils as filled the streets of Port of Spain from half-past 10 o'clock Sunday to 3 a.m. on Monday last'. He believed that they (and staff of the *Trinidad Reporter*) 'would disgrace a community of *savages*'.

If it was Canboulay, the '*savages*' that 'filled the streets' were recalled by 'an old lady' in 1881, who had seen 'a Canboulay some thirty years' before and 'described it in a way which suggested the idea of it being a representation of the slave driver and his slaves'. In this 'she spoke of the "Negres Jardins" with their baskets, and of a man with a long whip, who pretended to drive them on to work and flog them when they refused'.[49] Accompanied by drumming, singing and cries, this accentuated reminder of slavery was too close to past reality for the comfort of a guilty (and fearful) plantocracy – who had mimicked Canboulay when Carnival was their prerogative. Yet, there was no single reason for objections to Carnival (including Canboulay). For example, Canboulay might be seen as a vindication of the fight against slavery, not simply by ex-slaves but also by white abolitionists. It is also evident that the festival had its supporters in the white elite (abolitionists or not) whose influence was augmented by an increasingly articulate black (and 'coloured') population.

The *Port of Spain Gazette* continued its anti-Carnival stance in 1857 and also indicated some of the external influences on entertainment in the island: 'We continue to be well furnished with amusements. A Conjuror, and a Company of Acrobats have been doing their best to afford us recreation; and a less harmless pastime, that annual noisy nuisance of masking, seems to be preparing to make a prominent exhibition this year.'

In the same issue (7 February), the arrival of a new Governor, Robert William Keate, was reported. In the next two years his attitude towards Carnival was to have a profound effect.[50]

There was a belief that 'in 1857 the Carnival was dying out'. This was a sentiment often expressed, but never resolved. A revival of cross-sectional interest appears to have been triggered by the negative attitude of Governor Keate in 1858. Those who were against masquing had the ear of the Governor – it seems he was advised by the then Chief Justice – although there were always others in the elite who were opposed to any interference.

Following the Governor's holding of 'a Fancy Ball in honour' of the

Queen (complained the *Trinidad Sentinel* on 25 February), the anti-masqueraders had their way and a proclamation 'forbidding all persons to wear masks' at Shrovetide, was issued one month before.

That this was unlikely to have the desired effect is evinced by a letter from 'DUTY', published in the *Port of Spain Gazette* on 3 February, soon after announcement of the prohibition. He complained of excessive pre-Shrovetide revelry, comprising *'noise'*, *'tumult'* and *'barbarian mirth'* that was 'certainly beyond anything [he] had experienced hitherto'. The correspondent asked fiercely: 'If the "Police Law" can prohibit "Masking", or rather I should say wearing a "Mask", one can be masking without the "paper face", can not the same law prohibit unnerving noise such as *howling*, *yelling* and other *savage signs* of mirth, now to be heard every night from 6 p.m. to 12 p.m?' The police were criticised for doing little to quell disturbances, but shopkeepers commended for not selling masques pending the Carnival.

A letter published in the *Gazette* after the festival provides further evidence that Canboulay opened Carnival in this period:

> commencing the orgies on Sunday night we have the fearful howling of a parcel of semi-savages, emerging from God knows where from, exhibiting hellish scenes and the most demonical representations of the days of slavery as they were forty years ago; then using the mask the two following days as a mere cloak for every species of barbarism and crime.

These included 'innumerable petty robberies in broad day and to insult and assault everyone whom cowardly malice could not reach under other circumstances'.

Like previous letters, from which quotations have been taken, the sobriquet of the signator (in this instance 'PAX') is in the carnivalesque tradition, as are characteristics of the festival about which he complains. The latter appear to refer to activities that later became known as 'Ol' Mas' (Old Masque/Old Mask). Behind the cloak of anonymity these letter writers generally expressed stereotypical elitist attitudes towards race and class, a subject that was to come into the open in exchanges between the *Sentinel* and the *Gazette* in the aftermath of Keate's measures.

Philopolis, writing in the *Sentinel* (4 March), explained the pro-Carnival position regarding the violence that accompanied Keate's attempt to control masquing:

> Some days before Carnival, we saw posted up in the corner of our
> streets a bill forbidding all persons to wear masks, and intended to
> prevent those masquerades, that, since the days of Columbus, have
> been the entertainment of our people in this island. The people
> resented, murmured a little, and obeyed the cruel enjoinment: *the
> masks were dropped*. But, by way of compensation, they betook them-
> selves to fancy dresses, and in droll accoutrements led many pro-
> cessions through the streets. The Police was immediately set on move-
> ment, and some of the gay fellows were *arrested, prosecuted and fined*.
>
> Now, we would ask, were these orders and harsh measures just or
> prudent? Were they not provoking and mischievous? They may be
> judged of by their results and the sad events that followed, will answer
> for us. The people, excited by these last provocations, would not
> submit; they assembled in different bands, set the Police at defiance,
> paraded with or without masks, hissed or hooted the Policemen,
> attacked them in their stronghold, beat and knocked them down,
> wounded some of them, and presented such boisterous scenes as we
> had never witnessed before.

Heavy-handedness by the police on Shrove Tuesday, especially in the
so-called 'French Streets', in which many who were 'dressed up, but not
masked' were 'dragged' to the police station, appears to have incited this
confrontation.

According to the *Gazette*, the police 'wavered in the performance of their
disagreeable duty' and in consequence 'the whole force was called in and the
whole town left free to the rabble to do as it chose'. Sensing their victory, a
large band of black people paraded before the police station and gave 'a
derisive shout of triumphant defiance', but soon after 'every vestige of the
immense crowd of boisterous maskers and mummers' dispersed on arrival
of armed troops (redcoats), at the behest of the Government.

In addition to issues of race and class, that followed this stalemate
between masqueraders and 'authority', there was the question of 'custom'.
Competition between French- and English-speaking Trinidadians was predominant. Clashes between police and populace in the 'French Streets' (to
the east of Henry Street, on the eastern side of Port of Spain) reflect this
extra consideration in Keate's attempt to stop masquing.

The *Sentinel* (owned by a group of black people, and with French Creole
sentiments) identified this issue squarely in its editorial on 25 February:

> It is sought, say the advocates of this iniquitous and silly proceeding,
> to make this Colony English in its manners, habits and customs. The

absurdity of this assertion appears upon its face, and requires no keenness of perception to discover it. As well might our ruler desire to make this community English in habits of thought, nay in language, or better still in religion. Is he likely to succeed in such an attempt – yes, just as likely to succeed as in changing our habits and customs.[51]

Without direct reference to French-English rivalry, the point is emphasised in a later description, noting the ban produced:

> another and far more serious consequence which had not been foreseen. Many persons who had noticed with much satisfaction the gradual decline of the Carnival, thought it a very high-handed act to endeavour to put down by armed force that which, however absurd and objectionable, could scarcely be called illegal and which had the sanction of immemorial custom.
>
> The result was that new life and vigour was given to the almost defunct Carnival and in 1859 preparations were made to carrying it out on a more extended scale than had been the case for years.

Keate appears to have wavered slightly in his attitude in 1859. This was presumably in the light of overt opposition and his experience the year previous. A post-Carnival report (*Port of Spain Gazette*, 19 March) gives this impression. It notes that 'at first it was stated that no interference with the mummers would be made – that they were to be allowed the full licence they claimed; then the orders given to the Police were far from exact – not to say intentionally equivocal – then the assistance of the Military was obtained in an irregular and inefficient fashion'. The *Trinidad Sentinel* (10 March) indicates, however, that special preparations were made to constrain the Carnival – soldiers were posted at key positions, and the police force was strengthened. There was also police interference with the masquers from early on Monday morning 'until a band of about one thousand persons forced them to retreat'.

The police appear to have had little contact with the masquers for the rest of the day but on Shrove Tuesday became very active in making arrests. The *Sentinel* highlights a case where a man who had painted his face with red ochre was compelled to wash off the colouring. In addition, 'a large canoe on wheels [was] taken away from a certain band, and a canopy viciously destroyed'. The constabulary endeavoured to enter the 'French Streets', but were driven back as in the year before. At this 'another detachment of Soldiers was sent for' who 'soon after marched into Town'.

Veterans of the Crimean War, some with decorations for bravery, these troops had dissipated the masqueraders in 1858 by virtue of their arms. In 1859, however, they were dispatched without weapons. This led to their ignominious downfall for, in the words of the *Sentinel* 'like fiends [they] commenced an attack on the people of Corbeau Town, who, to their praise be it said, drove the heroes of Sebastopol like chaff before the wind'. The location for this confrontation was the 'Western end of Lower Prince Street' (in the 'English' part of Port of Spain), and 'stones and bottles' were the missiles of the defenders.

After this, the populace 'had their pleasure out without further molestation' and the satisfaction of having obtained a symbolic victory over the Executive that had been achieved only in part the year before. A similar attempt to put down masquing in San Fernando also ended with the police 'shamefully beaten and put to flight'. This brought strong criticism in the press, especially from the *Port of Spain Gazette*, and the *Sentinel* confessed that it had 'no confidence in, nor respect for, the Governor'.

In 1858, it is likely that organised opposition to the actions of the authorities had been concentrated among French and French-Creole speakers. Overt resistance to the military by an English-speaking district of Port of Spain in 1859 suggests linguistic barriers had been put to one side among representatives of all sectors. Issues of race and class had merged with the sentiment of the French-speaking elite, opposed to the attack on 'custom', and disdain of the English-speaking elite for an ineffectual administration. Symptomatic of this is a comparison in the *Sentinel* between Carnival and festivals of the exclusive group of indentured East Indians. These migrants were 'allowed anniversarily to have their fêtes without molestation', despite the fact 'they generally fight, and on the last occasion even a murder was perpetrated'. 'Yet', it said, 'no Police, no Military Force, is put in requisition to prevent them from enjoying themselves'. The latter is presumably a reference to the 'Muharram' or 'Hosien' which has a parallel history to Carnival in this period and in which black inhabitants also began to participate.[52]

The rise of the *jamettes* – Carnival in the 1860s

For those opposed to Carnival, 1858 rather than 1859 was seen as a turning point in an increasing decline into degeneracy. The festival, however, 'went on much as before' until the late 1860s. The events of 1858–9 had their repercussions in 1860. In January 'there were rumours that Keate was planning to ban Carnival completely'. The consequences were so unpredictable that the *Trinidad Free Press* argued 'to let Carnival die a natural death would be a safer procedure'. A circular was sent to merchants to obtain their views and, in the light of pecuniary interests, they supported continuation. As early as 1860, therefore, commerce had come to be a mainstay of the event. Keate acquiesced and allowed Carnival to take place.

Without the politics of confrontation with the authorities, there was a change in attitude by the *Trinidad Sentinel* (23 February). While it maintained 'that the people have a *prescriptive right* to mask', it also wished to see the festival 'modernised' by the influence of 'civilisation'. This was a theme worthy of their erstwhile opponents, the *Port of Spain Gazette*. The *Sentinel*'s attitude appears to have been influenced by what it saw as 'savagism'. It was 'sorry to have to state that several skirmishes ensued – not with the Police, for there was no interference on that score – but among the maskers themselves. One man (report says) lost his life; another was severely wounded by a weapon and others came off with broken heads, &c.'[53]

This suggests that battles between rival bands (parallel to the confrontation between Corbeau Town and the soldiers in 1859) had already become a feature of the Carnival. They may have included stickfighting.

In 1861, the *Port of Spain Gazette* believed that lifting of restrictions on masques deterred those who had previously protested against the attitude of the Executive. It reported that 'the [Carnival] display fell again entirely into the hands of the idle and vagrant' and was unimpressed. Most masquing seems to have taken place in a particular section of Charlotte Street (one of the 'French Streets') which it described as 'continental'. Presumably, it was here that there were: 'the usual ostentatious promenades of those ladies whose existence is usually ignored or accepted as a necessary evil ... the usual fantastic mummers who represent the continental *Pierrots*' and a smaller number than before 'of unclad creatures who sometimes take advantage of the general laxity to outrage public decency'. In other streets 'a distant Babel of discordant noises' was heard and occasionally a small band passed by. Unlike 1860, there appears to have been 'no conflict or serious quarrelling'.[54]

An increasing distaste for the type of masqueraders who took part in the Carnivals of the 1860s is apparent from these accounts. In this vein, 1862 was the last year the Archbishop of Port of Spain gave sanction to masquers by visiting 'some of the houses where the inmates were dressed up and drove through the town to see the less refined amusements in the evening'.[55] It is necessary to be cautious about these reports, however, as the judgements reflect aspects of contemporary elitism and racism.

For the *Port of Spain Gazette*, in 1863 'the annual two day's saturnalia' was becoming 'less and less engaged in every year'. Its account, however, suggests a more elaborate festival: 'the few masqueraders of the Carnival got their frolics somewhat damped, and their finery damaged by showers'. Leaving aside the rain, it was prepared to mention only 'one single piece of mummery' (and then not describe the masque). This highlights the usual obsession with 'the grade of a licensed exhibition of wild excesses by the least reputable classes of society to the annoyance of all the others'. In turn, 'noise and ... nuisance continues unabated while it lasts; but the pageantry and the fun are clipped of all their former attraction'. Again, attention was drawn to the 'annual parade of ladies less accustomed to the privacy of domestic life, than to what in London parlance would be termed life on the streets'. Their companions were 'idle dissolute youths'. It noted 'the former dress as showily as they can; the latter make a hideous uproar, both with the same intention of attracting public notice'. The newspaper had heard of no conflict between the masquers and the authorities.[56]

The *Gazette* carried no Carnival bulletin the following year, excepting 'the Masquerade of 1864' was 'marked by a midnight fire of the most serious description ... by which the most valuable portion of the town was threatened with destruction'. This was a case of arson. A fire was started in a store in Frederick Street (then known colloquially as Rue de Anglais, or Almond Walk) and spread to several similar properties before it was brought under control.

In 1865, a letter from 'Anti-Masquerader' described early morning Carnival music and what may have been Canboulay (*Trinidad Chronicle*, 3 March). The writer complained of 'the barbarous din which disgraced the town during the last few nights' between 12 p.m. and 5 a.m., and noted that after midnight control of specified musical instruments was outside provision of the Police Ordinance (operational only between 10 p.m. and 11.59 p.m.). The 'beating or playing of instruments' he protested, was usually accompanied by 'filthy and obscene songs'. The latter were to become a continuing source of indignant censure for the next forty or fifty years.[57]

For 1866, the *Port of Spain Gazette* provides more varied information on

Carnival than three years before. Despite good weather, however, it still believed the festival was a 'very stale, flat and unprofitable affair' with 'street-masquers ... less numerous and less effective ... than on any previous occasion'. This sentiment was echoed in the *Star of the West*, which also thought 'the performances were a little less noisy than usual'. The *Gazette* shows there were activities in both the French and English sections of Port of Spain:

> In one or two of the streets at the East end ... there was a good deal of the drumming and dancing for which the denizens of that quarter are locally celebrated; but as far as we have been able to learn, there were no grand 'dignitys' as in former times. At the West end of the town on the Tuesday, there was a very fair burlesque of the recent trial of Thomas McGrath, before the Supreme Criminal Court here, in which the law was somewhat stripped of its majesty by the extravagant imitations given of one or two of the legal and lay personages who were engaged on that trial.'

Commenting on this burlesque (which represented a recent murder case), the *Star of the West* believed 'the Governor, Chief Justice, Attorney General and Mr McGrath were personated with considerable care', but said disparagingly 'the representations were scarcely deserving of note'. It was happy to report the holding of 'fancy dress parties in several private houses'.[58]

Just over two weeks prior to Shrovetide in 1868, the same newspaper wrote 'there is at present much of evil and abuse in the popular observance of the Carnival'. Like other broadsheets, however, they had become resigned to holding the event and believed 'reformation is better than destruction, and that to elevate and refine the amusements of the people is better than to forbid them altogether'. An example of the behaviour about which they complained is an affray on the morning of Carnival Monday, 24 February – described as *cannes brulées* in an ensuing court case.

There were seven bands of women 'parading the streets in fantastic dresses': Black Ball, Dahlia, Don't-Care-A-Damn, Magenta, Maribun (usually Maribone), Mousseline and True Blue. Dahlia, at least, had male auxiliaries and, it may be some, if not all, of these bands had male counterparts with whom they were directly associated.

The Mousselines carried baskets filled with bread and cheese, and flambeaux to provide light for dancing. The whole band appears to have been on bail (their Queen, Clementina Mills – alias Mamselle Janette – had been tried for affray but acquitted). The women, nevertheless, armed themselves with concealed batons (*boutous*). They were dancing in Duke Street, between the intersections of St James' Street and Henry Street, suggesting alliance with the French-speaking section of Port of Spain. This is given credence in that their attackers came from the direction of Corbeau Town (the English-speaking area). They were assaulted by the Dahlias, possibly assisted by the Black Balls and/or True Blues at about 1.45 a.m. The attackers, probably encouraged by 'grog', had put out their flambeaux, and were armed openly with sticks and baskets full of stones and broken bottles. Men appear to have been in the forefront of the onslaught, but the band was led by their Queen, Elizabeth Simmons. 'The Prince Consort of the Mousseline Queen was knocked on the head, and the forces ran away but, as remarked by the counsel, they lived to fight another day'. The *Chronicle* (in its summary of the court case) described how 'the princesses of the Mousselines gave their evidence against the Dahlias with a great deal of gusto'. L. M. Fraser, the historian, was Acting Inspector Commandant of Police. He told the court how the wounded man was assisted by members of his party, as they carried their flambeaux running down St James' Street to escape the missiles of their assailants.

Alongside the violence, this event is important in demonstrating the way groups of black women participated in Carnival (and Canboulay). It is possible that band membership was synonymous with the 'ladies of the street' who paraded in this period, but this seems too simplistic. The associations appear to have been dancing organisations, probably based on territory. Participation usually reflected linguistic and religious groupings as well as other social circumstances. A confrontation in June 1864 provides a little more background via another case, involving two bands. The Mousselines challenged the Don't-Care-A-Damns in George Street (in the French section), but while the disturbance lasted all day, fighting was very limited. Some of the same women took part, including Clementina Mills. The Mousselines were seen 'dancing in the yard opposite Richaud's'. The witness also described the purpose of these societies as for 'dancing and fighting'. The Chief Justice paid particular attention to this observation. Summing up, he commented:

> He . . . did not know what that could mean, but he dared to say it was within the knowledge of the jury that some of these societies – originally founded no doubt for innocent purposes – had become mere factions and that during the present Session they had had two of them

before the Court in a very disgraceful case between two women belonging to the 'Holy Trinity' and the 'Immaculate Conception'.

Women of violence, brutalised initially by slavery, played an important role in black society in Trinidad throughout the nineteenth century. Many belonged to dancing societies whose activities reflected the turmoil of changing circumstances. Some organisations appear to have been devoted to aggression, such as a recently disbanded 'society at St Joseph for the purpose of fighting all comers', mentioned in a court case in 1846. It seems, however, that until the 1870's this semi-latent violence did not manifest itself in a continual pattern of physical confrontation between bands at Carnival.[59]

Behaviour of black people in Carnival had again become an issue. In 1865, 'Anti-Masquerader' referred to 'the new Police Ordinance', but this did not reach the statute book until three years later. Ordinance No 6 of 1868 *'for rendering certain Offences punishable on Summary Conviction'*, included a revision of the times when it was permitted 'to play or dance . . . to any drum, gong, tambour, bangee, chac-chac or other instrument of music', encompassing the period between midnight and 6.00 a.m. In addition, it was decided to place Carnival under 'Police Regulations'. A system of this type was used in European countries. The *Port of Spain Gazette* adjudged (in 1899) that the method was adopted 'in recognition of the fact that [Carnival] was essentially an un-English amusement and one, if allowed to continue, had to be dealt with in the same manner as in the countries from which it originated'. This, of course, denies any African component, let alone other non-European influences. There were further considerations. Control of Canboulay and other aspects of the festival was designed not to affect the East Indian celebration of Hosien. The maxim 'divide and rule' was being sustained, albeit subtly, between the black creole and East Indian communities.[60]

The Carnival of 1869 was 'quiet as usual', reported the *Star of the West* (11 February). Masquing was generally confined to 'the lower classes'. In this, 'there was a burlesque Cricket-match in the Almond Walk far from complimentary to the "Trinidad Eleven"' and 'a member of Council was represented with a cart whip slashing his lieges right and left'. Finally, the Attorney General was depicted 'with a long document in his hand which appeared, from the few sentences that were read, to be an "impeachment" of a high authority'.

CIRCUS.

A CARD

BY PERMISSION OF HIS EXCELLENCY
THE GOVERNOR,
AND THE
ILLUSTRIOUS BOARD OF CABILDO.

MR. W. R. DERR, the *American Samp-son*, most respectfully informs the Ladies and Gentlemen of Port of Spain, and its Vicinity, that his **BENEFIT** is fixed for Monday Evening, March the 5th, on which occasion there will be brought forward the greatest variety of Performances ever witnessed in this place.
   1st March, 1838.

   For particulars see Small Bills.

BOXES— 10s.
CHILDREN under 10 years half price.
PIT— 5s.

7 Circuses toured the West Indies throughout the nineteenth century and were an influence on Carnival bands.

A possible influence on these burlesques was travelling showmen and other theatrical personalities who toured the Caribbean, from Europe, North America and, perhaps, South America. There are advertisements (located at random) for travelling Circuses from the United States in the *Port of Spain Gazette* in March 1838, and January 1846.

Another type of burlesque (performed initially by whites in blackface) was minstrelsy. Originating in the United States, this appears to have made an appearance in Trinidad with concerts by local amateur Christy Minstrels in the mid 1860s.

Formal entertainments by black creole musicians continued, featuring European music played on European instruments. Such musicians were versatile in different types of performance. For example, in 1858 'a Band of Creole Amateur Musicians' attended a banquet celebrating Emancipation Day and 'enlivened the meeting with their strains'. At the funeral of Archbishop English (September 1862), 'the Dead March in "Saul", specially arranged for the occasion by Mr Renaud, was played by the Creole Band under the direction of the talented native musician, Ernest Monteil'. The same band 'under the direction of Mr C. S. Renaud' provided music at the inauguration of a new fountain in Brunswick Square (now Woodford Square) in 1866.[61]

These factors augment the background to Carnival and black music in the same way as remarks by outsiders such as Day. A similar observer was the cleric, historian and writer Charles Kingsley. In late-1869–early-1870 he paid a visit to his friend Arthur Gordon, the Governor of the island, and published an account of his experiences in 1871 – *At Last: A Christmas in the West Indies*.[62] Kingsley did not write about the Carnival; he attended 'The Races' – 'to wander en mufti among the crowd outside and behold the humours of men'. His description provides pertinent cultural characteristics.

Horse races had been staged on the 'Grand Savannah' in Port of Spain as early as 1828, according to Capadose. Kingsley's experience probably took place in January 1870. By this time, Trinidad had begun to accommodate a stream of English-speaking black migrants from Barbados, in search of employment. Together with local French-speaking black creoles, they formed enthusiastic groups at the turf. Accordingly, he wrote how 'the Negro, or the coloured man, was in his glory' and noted that:

> He bawled about island horses and Barbadian horses – for the Barbadians mustered strong and fight was expected, which, however, never came off; he sang songs, possibly some of them extempore, like that which amused one's childhood concerning a once notable event in a certain island –

> > 'I went to da Place
> > To see da horse-race,
> > I see Mr Barton
> > A-wipin' ob his face.

> > Run, Allwright,
> > Run for your life;
> > See Mr Barton
> > A-comin' wid a knife.

Oh, Mr Barton,
I sarry for your loss;
If you no believe me,
I tie my head across.'

As this is in English, it was sung presumably by Bajan partisans. Rivalry with the French-creole speaking element is shown by possible conflict with the Barbadians. At the same time, Trinidad's popular links with metropolitan France were being maintained in the shape of 'one of those great French merry-go-rounds, turned by machinery, with pictures of languishing ladies round the central column. All the way from the Champs Elysees the huge piece of fools tackle had lumbered and cracked hither across the sea to Martinique, and was now making the round of the islands, and a very profitable round to judge from the number of its customers.'

That evening, Kingsley who was staying in St Ann's, to the north of the Savannah, heard in the distance both 'the weary din of the tom-toms which came from all sides of the Savannah save [his] own ... and ... the screams of an European band which was playing a "combination tune," near the Grand Stand, half a mile off.'

He observed that 'to the music of tom-tom and chac-chac, the coloured folk would dance perpetually till ten o'clock, after which time the rites of Mylitta are silenced by the policeman, for the sake of quiet folk in bed'. Despite the *Summary Convictions Ordinance*, he complained in similar fashion to Day and 'Anti-Masquerader': drummers were 'but too apt, however, to break out again with fresh din about one in the morning, under the excuse – "Dis am not last night Policeman. Dis am 'nother day".' Such dances were 'not easily seen', but he managed to catch a glimpse of one from a distance, sitting with his host on the steep slope of the Belmont hill. 'A hundred yards below we espied a dance in a Negro garden; a few couples, mostly of women, pousetting to each other with violent and ungainly stampings, to the music of tom-tom and chac-chac.'

Some ten or more years earlier E. B. Underhill had attended 'the little gatherings of the Africans and their children at Dry River' (in similar vicinity). This group were post-Emancipation migrants from Africa who came to Trinidad as indentured labour. They had settled in Port of Spain, building 'mud and thatched houses' and 'a large shed devoted to night dances, and to the noisy music of the banjo or drum'. The location might be one of the Belmont Valley Road settlements of Africans, recalled from *circa* 1890, which included plots occupied by Radas, Mandingos, Ibos and Congos.

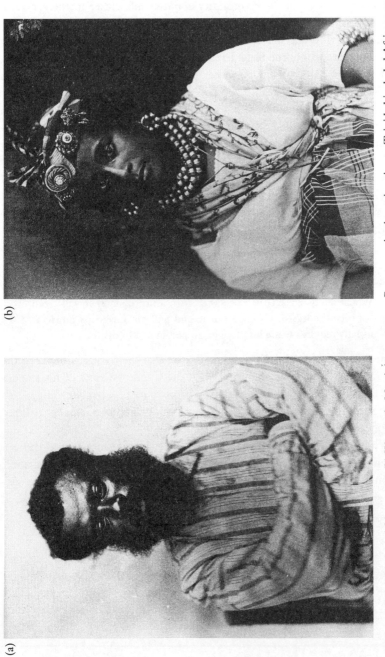

8 Views of Trinidad (a) African man; (b) Woman in Martinique costume. Post-emancipation migration to Trinidad included Africans and Martiniqians – women from the latter island dressed in traditional costume. Both groups participated in Carnival.

There was also a Yoruba community about a mile closer to the centre of Port of Spain and, just east of the Dry River – a more likely situation.[63]

Reports by Underhill and Kingsley re-emphasise African-Caribbean undercurrents within the black French-creole- and English-creole-speaking communities in Trinidad. Another consideration was the relationship between peoples of African-American and East Indian origin. At the race meeting, Kingsley mentions that East Indians were equal participants in the activities, including joyriding by women on the French merry-go-round. There was also black creole – East Indian rivalry. A pertinent example is stickfighting.

It appears that from the time East Indians began to arrive in Trinidad (1845), African-Caribbean stickfighting traditions (including absorption of European and Amerindian techniques) met with those of the Indian sub-continent. Day notes this rivalry in the late 1840s, reporting:

> A fight between the two races is a most ludicrous spectacle; for the physical inferiority of the Hindoo, is amply compensated by his super-ior strategy, and a well-organised combination amongst themselves. Whilst one is engaged stick to stick with a negro, another will creep between the legs of his countryman and pull his antagonist down. It usually requires white interference to put an end to the fray.

Some twenty years later Kingsley indicated that 'heavy fights between the two races arise now and then, in which the Coolie, in spite of his slender limbs has generally the advantage over the burly Negro, by dint of his greater courage, and the terrible quickness with which he wields his beloved weapon, the long hardwood quarter staff'.[64]

While, during the 1870s, East Indian participation in Carnival did not become an issue, stickfighting between rival bands of black masquers became its dominant feature. This characteristic was attributed to the *dia-metres* or *jamettes* – the underworld – who gradually took over Carnival, in the eyes of the white elite.

3

'Not A Cent To Buy Rice': poverty, revelry and riots, 1870–1896

The rise of the stickbands – Carnival 1870–1876

An account of Carnival in the *Port of Spain Gazette* for 9 March 1870 sets the scene for what was to become the focus for festival reports throughout the 1870s. This identifies elements that made up Canboulay, and hints at 'obscenities'.

> The masqueraders began their saturnalia on the night of Sunday the 28th ultimo, and kept up an unremitting uproar, yelling, drumming, and blowing of horns till the sun was well up on the following morning. There was no possibility of sleep during this 'hideous' night; but beyond that inconvenience to the more respectable portion of the inhabitants everything passed off without calling for police interference.

The newspaper called for the time 'when the influence of the Clergy alone' would be 'sufficient to put an end to the obscene and disgusting buffonery [*sic*] to which the *fundus* of the population devote themselves during the two days and nights that precede Ash Wednesday'.[1]

One of the songs performed during this Carnival probably concerned the tarring and feathering of the Chief Medical Officer, Dr Bakewell (an Englishman) 'on the steps of Government House by three unknown Negroes' in January. Bakewell had clashed with Dr Espinet 'a well-known and respected coloured Creole', regarding 'the treatment of leprosy' and offended both black and white inhabitants. Atilla the Hun (*sic*) recalled the song as *Bakeway* and the action as having been carried out by two black people, but these lyrics almost certainly commemorate the same event:

Bakeway, *qui rive*	Bakeway, what happen
Qui moon qui fair ca	Who is this person who did this?
Is two blackman tar poppa	Is two blackman tar papa
Moen ca garde con yon negre	I look like a Negro
Moen moen blanc mes enfants	Me, I am white, my children
Is two black man tar poppa	Is two black man tar papa
Is two black man tar poppa.	Is two black man tar papa.

Other songs that can be dated to 1870 concern the murder of Abbé Jouin in Diego Martin (May) and subsequent trial of Nicholas Brunton, a local coloured-creole landholder (September). Two, in French Creole, are reported to have been sung respectively by the chantwells Hannibal and Zandoli; a third (in English) was performed by Cedric le Blanc. Similarly, le Blanc is rumoured to have composed *Not A Cent To Buy Rice*, critical of contemporary migration by Barbadians.[2]

From their subject matter, all these songs fall into the categories of topicality and/or social commentary later associated with the calypso. Masquerades in Carnival sometimes served a similar purpose. This can be deduced from descriptions of the 1871 Carnival. Four reports are available and their interlocking commentaries provide the first overall contemporary account of the festival in the nineteenth century.

The regular proclamation declaring confinement of masquing to Shrove Monday and Tuesday (20–1 February) appeared in the *Trinidad Chronicle* on 14 February 1871. Particular attention was drawn to the fact that assault, blowing horns, playing other noisy instruments, and carrying torches were punishable with imprisonment and hard labour. This was in response to a report 'that some of [the] lowest class of people whose great annual fête this is and with whom amusement without uproar is no amusement at all, threaten to carry out their customs in despite of the Police'. The *Chronicle* recommended no half measures in exerting discipline on 'the lawlessness of the mob', should this prove necessary.

Just before Carnival (18 February) the *Echo of Trinidad* printed a letter from Mathias Raymond complaining of a flagrant breach of this proclamation. A band of 'aristocratic sprouts in St Ann's Road' were masqued and dressed as cavaliers to attend a local night-time fancy ball. Two black policemen were on hand and began to disperse onlookers. At this Raymond pointed out that some of 'the masked men [were] disguised in female attire' and should therefore be apprehended. Caught between the white masquers and Raymond's comments the police turned on him, although he was not arrested. The following day, his complaints to police officials met with stonewalling. In a comment the *Echo* doubted the writer's veracity. The letter, however, indicates one of the elements it was to distinguish in its own account of the masquerade on 25 February. This provides the best summary of the social attitudes of race and class apparent in Carnival at this time:

> It is the great annual festival of most of the various nationalities of this polyglot community, and each has observed [it] in its own way. There were the costume-dances of the European and Europeanized section, where additional charms were lent to natural beauty by artistic adorn-ment; there were the burlesques and mummeries of serious things by another section; and there was the barbarous *Cane-bouler* of the lower orders, by which Sunday-night was made so hideous.

The form of the celebration is also established:

Monday
Beginning at midnight the '*Cane-bouler*' lasted until the small hours. There were 'brutish cries and shouts' together with 'horrid forms running to and fro about the town with flaming torches in their hands, like so many demons escaped from a hot place not usually mentioned in polite society'.
At dawn, these 'unmeaning and noisy demonstrations ... [were] resumed in another shape'. The *Echo* noted that 'dressed in filthy garments, with their features concealed by dirty masks, men and women walked the streets, singly or in couples, in solemn and measured tread, as if performing some religious duty'.
Later in the day, there was an improvement in the costumes.
'Towards the evening', the paper related that 'in many instances' the masquerades became 'elegant and picturesque'. These appear to have been a 'better class of people' who 'seemed to have begun to take part in the frolic' and participated as 'disguised parties ... on horseback, or in carriages'.

For the same day the *Chronicle* reported 'numerous bands paraded round the streets' and 'the behaviour of the maskers was on the whole good'.

Presumably in reference to the '*Cane-bouler*,' however, it noted the occurrence of 'a fight or two ... between some of the rival factions or "bands"' that rejoiced 'in such illustrious names as "True Blues", "Danois", "Maribones", "Black Ball", "Golden City", "Alice", "D'jamettres" and so on'. In one confrontation '"True Blue", after expending all of its ammunition in stones and broken ware, ingloriously fled the field, pursued and mauled by the gasparil and guava stings of the "Maribones"'. The *Echo* paints a slightly different picture, mentioning 'there were one or two fights here and there between rival parties of maskers', who were 'mostly women' and 'barring slight bruises' these were 'without any very unfortunate results'.

Some bands identified by the *Chronicle* were similar to those that had existed in 1868. The 'True Blues' were an English-speaking group (later named Free-grammar – presumably on this account). They came from 'Coburgtown'. The 'Maribones' (or Maribons – wasps) were a French-speaking affiliation from Belmont. Gasparil and guava were woods used for fighting sticks.

Despite the police notice, there appears to have been no interference with Canboulay in Port of Spain. In San Fernando, however, an unconfirmed rout of the police proved false; masquers were apprehended before dawn on Shrove Monday. This caused local acrimony, especially as a rumour circulated that the action resulted from a bet between the Commandant in Port of Spain (Fraser), and the Inspector in San Fernando (Fitz-Simmons).

Tuesday
> 'The scenes were repeated with some variations'. According to the *Echo*, these included 'parties of tumblers' performing 'in various parts of the town for half-pence' together with 'a body of clerks from the dry goods' stores ... dressed as prisoners of the hard-labour gang'.
> The *Chronicle* recounted there were fewer bands on Tuesday. Other coverage, however, does not specify the exact occasion for masquing.

In the Carnival as a whole, the *Chronicle* noted there had been 'fully as many ridiculous parodies as in recent years' while the *Star of the West* believed that a lack of previous brilliance was due to 'the dearth of proper masks' consequent 'to the war in France'. It identified 'grotesque groups and ludicrous representations', picking out 'some of the political ones' which 'were not a little significant and amusing' – probably, 'the burlesques and mummeries of serious things by another section' (*Echo*). The thrust of these masqued satires can be seen to parallel lyrical themes that became associated with calypso. The 'section' who performed them were presumably articulate black and/or white mummers who used the anonymity of masquing to both flatter and criticise the hierarchy.

The burlesques can be grouped into two principal categories – political and legal. The press was also subject to caricature (newspaper editors), as were clerics, a medico and a representative of the Town Hall. There is mention of a traditional masque reported to have come to Trinidad from the Spanish Main – the 'little donkey or jenny' (in Spanish *burraquita*). Thus, the *Star of the West* described 'a very lame *bourrique*' who 'personalised "Lothair"' and on 'whose tail' was displayed a card with the words "Art Society's Plate"'. The exact satire is lost but the sarcasm is evident in the comment: 'the poor animal was evidently indisposed, seemed weak in the epigastrium, and was indeed obliged to wear slippers, and have a Madras handkerchief round its head. People said it was a shame to bring it out at all in that state.'

Less oblique in its message was the depiction of the previous Governor (Arthur Gordon) and his circle. He was represented as the '"lord of *mis-rule*"' wearing 'a Russian imperial crown and carrying a wizard's wand', and 'supported on either side by Professor Kingsley (with a copy of *Good Words*) and Inspector Fouché' (of the police – presumably a burlesque of Fraser, the subject of particular ridicule). They were followed by caricatures of three key members of the legal profession, including the Solicitor General.

Personifications of 'Clergymen of different churches walked arm in arm in a fraternal manner, and appeared to be soliciting money from the crowd, for various objects in which they were interested'. In addition, 'other groups represented several failures of justice last year, and cases of political unfairness'.

Despite this detail the press maintained its regular condescension and criticism – possibly a reason for singling out the editors of the *Star of the West*, *Chronicle*, and *Gazette* for burlesque. The latter two were Englishmen. Perhaps on this account the *Chronicle* wrote that the festival 'has been as tawdry and absurd as usual' and the *Port of Spain Gazette* decried the 'performances' as 'poorer and more foolish than ever'. It described 'the large proportion of the actors of these miserable harliquinades' as 'vagrants and vagabonds'.[3]

These 1871 newspapers show the Carnival was a complicated ritual, reflecting different symbolic purposes for each strata of Trinidad society. Notwithstanding, vagrancy and vagabondage were to be singled out as the festival's major components throughout the next decade.

While there appears to have been little understanding of this growing poverty, a principal cause was economic depression in the Eastern Caribbean. This encouraged migration from smaller islands (including Barbados) and increased pressure on accommodation, jobs and all other aspects of survival among the poor in Trinidad. Unfortunates were seen as an incomprehensible underworld, and feared and loathed accordingly. Thus the *diametre* came to be made up of stickmen, singers, drummers, dancers, prostitutes (another meaning of *jamette*), *bad johns* (swashbucklers), *matadors* (madames), *dunois* (*jamette* rowdys), *makos* (panders), obeahmen (practitioners of magic) and corner boys. All were associated with a culture that revolved around the barrack-tenement yards of Port of Spain and similar locations elsewhere in the island. Migrant groups competed with one another, and more established settlers, for territory. At the same time, the *diametre* flaunted themselves (especially during the masquerade) to sustain their identity and draw attention to their plight in a society in which they were decried.

Similar defensive-offensive symbolism is exemplified by a band called the Beka Boys who 'caused public indignation by their habit of tossing foul-smelling handkerchiefs into the faces of respectable women and using obscene language in the streets'. This was reported in the *Echo* on 15 October 1873, and five days later a correspondent in *New Era* was addressing another aspect of 'City Morals' (or rather the behaviour of the bands). He declared 'one of the most fruitful and common sources of Trinidad demoralization, may be traced to that *Pandemonium* known as the "Bel Air" dances, where vice parades its hideous standard in all its grimness; drunkenness and its concomitant attendants being the order of the day'.

Other commentaries show this was a continuing problem for the elite. Just before the Carnival of 1874 the *Port of Spain Gazette* wrote of the 'increase of *"vagabondage"*' and detailed how:

> By day and night the streets are thronged with herds of disreputable males and females, whose time seems to 'hang heavy on their hands', and who are always ripe for any mischief. They are organised in bands

and societies for the maintenance and propagation of vagrancy, immorality, and vice and some of the most noted members are those who have paid their footing by an unlimited number of visits to the Royal Gaol.

As early as the Carnival of 1871 there was a stickband named 'D' jamettres' that, by its very existence, symbolised the era. It is also evident that such groups maintained themselves by holding drum dances and other functions which, although considered to be 'depraved', were essentially collective endeavours to provide sustenance in conditions of extreme deprivation. In this they represent an antithesis of the idealised 'decorum' or 'civilisation' claimed by the elite. Bands, thereby, resorted to fighting one another when they believed it necessary to establish or maintain their territories throughout the island.

A description of the Carnival in the *Chronicle*, in 1874, exemplifies these two contrasting ideals, simply by concentrating on the behaviour of the *jamettes*:

> This wild revel, which grows coarser by degrees and scandalously low and too often bruted, has taken possession of the streets as usual for those two days. Broken heads and torn finery are more frequent than ever. As for the number of girls masked and in men's clothing, we cannot say how many hundred are flaunting their want of shame. As many men, also generally of the lowest order, are in like manner strutting about in female dress, dashing out their gowns as they go.

In addition, the *Port of Spain Gazette* identified 'beating of drums', 'blaring of horns', and 'yellings' that heralded Canboulay, as well as throwing of 'stones, broken bottles and other missiles' in confrontations between bands. The latter, they adjudged, had trebled in number from previous occasions. The principal areas of conflict were 'the streets to the east of the town' (the French Streets, or French Shores).

If the accounts of Carnival in 1871 newspapers can be said to establish the shape of the festival in this period, these two 1874 reports distinguish key elements that signify the *jamette* component:

* an increasingly wild, noisy and violent Canboulay;
* 'lewdness' in costume, gesture and song lyrics;
* transvestism in masquing by both females and males;
* confrontations between bands;

* stickfighting contests between individuals in which the combat involved the dismantling (or tearing) of the stylised finery of an opponent's costume, and blows at the head.

In April 1874 the *Echo* summarised the purpose of the bands but did not address the underlying social reasons for their existence. For them, the 'only objective' of these groups 'was to hold riotous dances and at Carnival to "do battle against each other with stones, long sticks, glass bottles and missiles to the danger and terror of peaceful people"'.

The account of the 1875 Carnival in *Fair Play* maintains the same approach, reporting 'fewer than ever of maskers either of a gorgeous or grotesque character, the usual episodes of fighting and disorder, and much more than ever of filthy and indecent dancing and obscene conduct of every description'. There was a 'riot' in Port of Spain on Shrove Tuesday but none of the participants were apprehended. As the *Port of Spain Gazette* explained, the police relied on observing the miscreants as thousands swarmed 'through the streets inflamed with drink and excitement, and ripe for a row'. Having identified those who could be prosecuted with certainty, these were arrested once Lent commenced.

Police reticence was due in part to the failure of Keate's measures in 1858–9, and a lack of confidence in the statutes available. Another factor may have been the covert encouragement of fighting bands by individual members of the hierarchy. As in Keate's time, this almost certainly involved rivalry between French- and English-speaking members of the elite. Sponsorship was along linguistic lines, although fights between bands did not always conform to this pattern.

In January 1876, prior to Carnival, the *Echo* described how bands paraded 'their disorderly designs with effrontery unimaginable to strangers' and wore 'distinctive dress' carrying 'remarkable cudgels as the badge of their order'. The festival, however, had 'less of rioting than there was reason to anticipate', according to the *Chronicle* (29 February), which reported increased police activity. In addition, there was 'a good deal of harmless humour and caricaturing of oddities or conspicuous individuals' and 'less of coarse rampant vulgarity, such as men all but naked, their bodies daubed with tarr [*sic*]'. Notwithstanding, in the 'Eastern streets' there was 'abundant ruffianism' with 'parties mauling individuals of an opposite band met with in the street or yard – with sticks, stones, broken bottles – anything that came handiest'. The special core of Carnival activity continued in the 'Eastern streets' (or French Shores) of Port of Spain, an area singled out in press reports since the late 1850s.

In summation, the *Chronicle* expressed nostalgia for past Carnivals in bewilderment at the style of masquing and violence: 'It is many years since the respectability of the town has taken any part in these amusements. Some wasteful, ill-assorted and badly-fitting extravagances were to be seen; but of the taste of other days, rich or simple, nothing came under our notice.'

In Port of Spain, the police were 'mildly criticised' for their actions, 'especially in the use of batons'. Fitz-Simmons in San Fernando, however, averted a Canboulay fracas between rival bands by arresting the ringleaders and swearing in 'two dozen gentlemen of the town as specials'.[4]

The increase in bands who participated in what had become almost a form of ritual combat can be seen readily from the press reports of Carnival between 1870 and 1876.

Inevitably, the values represented by the bands clashed with those of the colonial hierarchy and their sense of Victorian propriety ('civilisation'). This led to imprisonment for many band members. There was a high increase in female and juvenile convictions for crime, alongside those of males from the 'lower classes'. These reflected the lack of compromise by the elite in assisting those they considered to be idle vagrants and vagabonds. A description by L. A. A. de Verteuil published in 1884 exemplifies both the camaraderie of band members and the arrogance of the elite:

> Generally, when such prisoners as are members of the societies or bands ... are discharged from the gaol, they are met at the gate by friends, male and female, and received with demonstrations of joy, but with not the faintest exhibition of shame; and they are accompanied home with triumph. When taken to gaol, they had been escorted by a retinue of followers. For the last two years, however, they have been conveyed to the prison in a closed van. Yet it is really painful to hear them – the female singers especially – singing at the top of their voices, as if in defiance of the law and of all decency. It cannot be surprising that the conduct, in prison, of creatures so callous to any feeling of shame is extremely bad, and that 'a fearful amount of depravity is practised between them when in an unwatched association'. Are they not, in the majority of cases members of *bands* notoriously formed for immoral purposes, and there practically taught to scorn all that society respects and appreciates, and to indulge in unbridled licentiousness?

9 Wilson & Co.'s store was on the corner of Frederick Street and Marine Square (formerly King Street) and was passed annually by Carnival parades (1876)

De Verteuil bases much of his evidence on reports by the Inspector of Prisons for 1874 and 1877. These were compiled by Fraser, who held this post in conjunction with his position as Inspector Commandant of Police. At some time in 1875, Fraser fell from his horse and struck his head. As a result he lost his nerve and a new police appointment was made in 1876, first to act in his behalf and then, in January 1877, to take over his duties. This was 'Captain' Arthur Wybrow Baker, who set himself the task of becoming the scourge of the stickbands in Carnival.[5]

The appointment of 'Brave Baker of the Bobbies' – Carnival 1877–1880

Like Fraser before him Baker was a man of military experience, although at the time of his departure from office in 1889 his exact credentials were found to have been somewhat dubious. He claimed to have been a Captain (and was known as such in Trinidad), but had only reached the rank of Lieutenant. He stated he had been in the 66th Regiment in India and 'had command of the Houssas on the West Coast of Africa'. The latter was presumably while he served under Lord Wolsey in the Ashanti Wars, or as Inspector General of the Gold Coast constabulary. There was doubt in 1889, however, as to whether he 'had any connection with Hausa police'.

Whatever his background, Baker was a disciplinarian who believed in authoritarianism. It was this aspect of his character that was to mark his attitude towards Carnival, and was welcomed initially as an active contrast to Fraser's less forthright approach. The *Trinidad Palladium* (3 February) commented how:

> Hitherto our valiant *Gendarmerie* have stood rather in dread of the clubs and bottles of the '*Diamètres*' and 'Bakers,' and have left them a fair field for their night riots and street frays; but under the new *régime* of a man who has not only expressed, but evidenced his *determination* to keep them up to the mark of duty, it is to be expected that they will 'screw their courage up to the sticking place'.

The *Palladium* also believed that there should be 'a guard of Police' to accompany 'the numerous bands of Maskers' to provide order, 'as is done with the Coolie processions'. The latter is the first reference in this era to what was to become a dilemma for the authorities. This was how to control the festivals of Trinidad East Indians and black creoles, while maintaining a policy of divide and rule between the two communities.[6]

On 9 February the *Trinidad Chronicle* printed two descriptions of the stickbands that are a primary reference for names, territories, and other aspects of their organisation:

> There appear to be about a dozen different bands, each generally representing the young vagabonds and semi-vagabonds of a street or *locale*. Thus the '*Free-grammar*' (formerly the True Blues) hail from Coburgtown; the *Bois d'Inde* (pronounced 'bois d'enne'), or Allspice tree, from Upper Prince Street; the *Bakers*, from the streets behind (i.e. east of) the Market; the *Danois* (Danes) from the Dry river suburb (between Faure's and Samuel's Bridges); the *peau de Canelle* (Cinnamon bark), from the streets behind (to [the] west of) the Gaol; the *Rose barrier* (Hedge-rose or rose hibiscus) from about the Toll-gate; the *Corail* (coral), from Newtown; the *'s Amandes* (almonds) boys and lads from about the wharves, allies of the 'Bakers', as the 'Danois' generally are of the next, the strongest band of all, the *Maribons* (wasps – pronounced 'maribones') from the Belmont road. The *Cerf-volants* (kites) come from Duncan Street; and there is said to be a St Ann's band, whose name we cannot learn. Two others, the *'s Hirondelles* (swallows) and the *Savanne*, a Newtown band, are said to have broken up.

Using the contemporary dividing line of Henry Street, which runs north from what was Marine Square, English bands can be distinguished to the west and French bands to the east (the 'French Shores' and east of the Dry River). To the south of Marine Square were the wharves. The Toll gate controlled the road to Arima.

ENGLISH	FRENCH
peau de Canelle	's Amandes
Corail	Bakers
Free-grammar	Bois d'Inde
Savanne	Cerf-volants
	Danois
	Maribons
	Rose barrier

No location is given for the ''s Hirondelles'.

The *Chronicle* goes on to comment on the membership of these bands:

it is said there is little cohesion or continuity in most of these, and that in some quarters of the town, both name and composition of the band are subject to frequent change. The name, as will have been observed, rarely has point or relevancy, and the band itself seems to be merely the loose, idler, younger members of the floating portion of the populace (it would not be always correct to call them the *working* class) in a district or neighbourhood.

These observations must be considered in the light of continuity in some of the band names (the meanings of which were not necessarily apparent to the newspaper). There is general agreement that Port of Spain had at least a nominal east-west divide defined originally by the areas inhabited by French or English speakers.

One band of long-standing, whose name was relevant to its fighting prowess, were the Maribones. The same, or another, reporter provides a fuller sketch of this group:

the 'Maribone' band will come out strong and, by permission obtained from the Police, will be armed with long sticks for quarterstaff play, and defence, if needed, from attack by 'the Bakers' or other bands. They say they will not go out at night, and have promised they will not provoke an attack, but if set-on are determined to give their rivals a mauling. They intend to come out in a uniform dress composed of a black hat (which they call a 'boum,' and which they are begging of the gentlemen of the town – any cast-off article that has seen better days will do, prime) a red shirt, and white or whitish trow[s]ers [*sic*] with a blue band down the seam or round the waist, the intention being to represent the national colors, the 'red, white and blue'. They will bind, *nègre jardin* fashion, a silk foulah round each leg below the knee. The women of this 'band' are also to appear, uniformly accoutred, namely, in short trowsers *a l'homme*, to the knee, wearing a short red jacket ending at the waist-band, over a chemise, round which on the stomach there is to be a narrow *tablier* or apron. Their top-gear is to be a sailor-hat covered with white, circled by a blue ribond [*sic*]. The 'band' will be led by a Captain or *Roi*, on horse-back, immediately behind whom are to come their children, uniform at least in hat the smallest in front, rising to the back, like steps. Each woman is to carry a wooden hatchet (painted to resemble iron). They will be accompanied by what they call music, *i.e.* a clarinet, 2 big drums, a fiddle, the *béké-nègre* of the Auctioneer (if not already brought off by others) with his small tattoo drum, a line of tom-toms (keg-drums, with goat skin top), and a triangle – that seems to be all they can collect this time. For safety, from a possible onslaught of road metal, sticks and broken bottles, the common ammunition of the 'Bakers,' the musicians (save the mark!) will keep in the centre of the procession, and 'fiddle' must look out for squalls and a fair port in case of a storm. The 'Maribones' (*Anglice*, Wasps) never came out in such fig.

In summary, in 1877 the Maribones intended to be a daytime band, comprising men, women and children, led by a 'Captain' or 'King' on horseback, accompanied by musicians. Although stating they would not provoke violence, precautions were to be taken in case of attack by other bands. The history of Trinidad Carnival in the 1870s shows that such peaceful intentions were not usually realised.[7]

'Captain' Baker's determination to control Canboulay (and the stick-bands) makes it necessary to establish as fully as possible the form of this event.

In the 1840s, once Carnival became a two-day celebration, black masquers adopted Canboulay as its opening feature. It depicted symbolically the extinguishment of a cane fire (and thereby, perhaps, the overthrow of slavery). In the 1850s it seems that the masquerade comprised black participants dressed as *nègres jardins* with baskets on their heads being driven by a man with a long whip. They cried out and sang to the accompaniment of drumming.

As well as parades by bands of men representing *nègres jardins*, and bands of women, masques depicting death, and demons (in which tar was used to cover the body) seem also to have been featured. All were unified by the use of flambeaux to simulate the effect of a cane fire and, perhaps, create an impression of 'hell'. In country districts, it appears, a conventional fire was ignited. Commencing midnight Shrove Sunday, bands were assembled by the sounding of horns and other audible signals. By the 1870s, Canboulay contained all of these components.

There was a difference (in costume) between stickbands that paraded at night, and those which marched through the streets during the day. Units were usually organised on the basis of territory. Prominent stickfighting exponents provided leadership, one being elected king of the band. In daytime parades the latter usually dressed as a pierrot. This masque appears to have been an amalgam of the 'Pulinchinello' – reported by Charles

William Day in 1847 – and 'country' king or *pays roi*. A queen might also be elected.

Each band had male and female members who usually comprised the marginalised section of the community. There were also supporters who might represent other aspects of the social strata, such as the *lom kamisol*, or jacketmen (gentlemen stickfighters). In some instances there was sponsorship from leading merchants and other worthies, especially in the French Creole elite.

Once assembled, the stickbands would march in procession through the streets, illuminating their way with the torches (flambeaux). Half intoxicated from drinking rum, they usually sang ribald or battle songs (that came to be known as *kalendas*) accompanied by drums, shac-shacs, and other instruments. The procession sometimes stopped for dances, which might be the *belair* or *old kalenda* ('corlinda'). One 1882 source also reports a dance called 'calypso'. Each of these dances were considered obscene by the elite. On meeting a rival band a fight would commence, the usual weapons being stones, loose macadam, and broken bottles. Sticks (carried by each band member) were used for individual combat – '*hallé baton*'. On occasion knives were wielded. There was vocal encouragement from non-combatant supporters.

Contests during the day differed. They commenced with challenges between pierrots that parallel competitions between Actor Boys in pre-Emancipation Jonkonnu in Jamaica. Gorgeously dressed in gown and cap (padded for protection), each pierrot cleared the way before him by cracking his long whip. He was accompanied by a 'page boy' (sometimes his paramour) carrying a stick. His stickband followed in formation. Proclaiming himself as he sought out a rival, a pierrot's confrontation began with bombastic speeches, then whip lashings (*combats a la ligueze*) and finally stickfighting. Stickmen supporters (*batonyé*) joined in at this point. In each instance the object of conflict was to dismantle an opponent's costume. The most elaborate costumes were worn on Shrove Tuesday.[8]

The difficulties in controlling this organised violence were well recognised, as was pointed out in a letter published by the *Trinidad Palladium* (10 February 1877). Press reports of the 1877 Carnival show, however, that Baker and his fellow police officers were assiduous in minimising confrontations – Baker on horseback being especially conspicuous. The masquerade itself was, according to the *Chronicle*, lacking in 'originality in idea, or taste in execution'. The newspaper also reported some 'tawdry finery torn' and 'broken heads' indicating that stickfighting was not completely stamped out. With bewilderment and a touch of sarcasm, the *Chronicle* was unable to understand why masquers found satisfaction in:

> the privilege of appearing in the streets in worse than common clothes and of being well stared-at, of playing what antics they choose, under mask, and of bawling dull refrains, discord and folly, by the hour, at the top of their voices during two days of unsexing themselves, and going in bands, or twos, or singly as they chose, almost taking possession of the roadway.

It must be remembered that while it was usual for stickbands to confine major encounters to Carnival, on occasion they also fought outside this season. For example, on 7 April, a letter writer complained to the *Trinidad Palladium* of a confrontation between the Bakers and peau de Canelle in George Street.[9]

The Carnival in 1878 was much like its predecessor. The police contained the stickfights, and 'Captain' Baker acted heroically. Single-handed, he arrested an assaulter, marched him towards the police station and, despite an attempted rescue by the crowd, managed to deliver the offender into custody.

Other details emerge, however, that indicate Carnival was not all stickfighting and similar defensive-offensive action by masqueraders. There was a band that humorously depicted the taking of Constantinople (the drummer was 'Mr Boyack's celebrated albino'). Another (comprising store clerks in costume), impersonated convicts acting as street sweepers. By inference there was also a black creole depiction of the 'Hosay procession' of Trinidad East Indians.[10]

Baker's methods were applied again in 1879, with similar effect and praise from the newspapers. The *Chronicle* also provides details of the masquerade that confirm a pattern of celebration closer to 1871 than had been apparent since that time. Noting 'there were much fewer character-groups or parties than usual', it singled out a Chinese pair (man and wife), girls schools, a squad of English redcoats headed by an officer, plus a 'Hosay procession', a 'Venezuelan army (rather *à la* Bombastes)', and 'a picturesque party of Venezuelan may-pole dancers'. The girls schools, like the Hosay procession, had also appeared in 1878. Other regular masques were gamblers, old dames ('*à la* Mother-Hubbard'), pierrots, 'pisanis' (men dressed as women and women as men), shoe blacks and South-American Indian warriors. It seems that *pisanis* were a particular feature of this Carnival, or at least 'the enormous proportion of masked men who unsexed themselves to enjoy the strange silly novelty of wrapping their big frames in a shapeless bundle of female apparel'.[11]

The confrontational approach adopted by the police met with its greatest success in 1880. To intervene where necessary, police were stationed judiciously on foot throughout Port of Spain. Baker controlled the streets on horseback, assisted by acting sub-Inspector Concannon and Sergeant Major Brierley. On commencement of '*Canboulé*', they interposed at each stickband conflict and forced the surrender of flambeaux, drums and sticks. Daytime skirmishes were dealt with in similar fashion. Stickbands were accompanied wherever they went in order to prevent affray. *Fair Play and Trinidad News* (12 February) mentions other masquerades: 'a Coolie Hosé band', 'a graceful dancing band of Venezuelans', 'a band imitating a wedding fête', and 'a ZULU band'. Stick fights took place in country villages such as Tacarigua.[12]

Baker's stand against Canboulay had met with press approval from its inception. Other undercurrents in Trinidad society, however, were far from satisfied. Canboulay was seen as an integral part of the Carnival. Essentially, the same emotions were aroused in the whole of the French Creole population as had surfaced at the time of Governor Keate's anti-masquing policy. In addition, merchants who gained extra trade from the Carnival viewed interference with mistrust.

More generally, the police were despised because of a high-handed attitude towards all levels of the population and general lack of discipline. There was also traditional antagonism between the police and black population that dated from slavery. Most black policemen were from Barbados and doubly disliked on this account.

A new Governor, Sir Sanford Freeling, arrived in Trinidad in November 1880 and stepped into this hornet's nest of authoritarian, linguistic, religious and pecuniary interests. An additional component of this potent mix was racism, manifested particularly in the forced isolation of the East Indian population.

The presence of a creole representation of 'a Hosay procession' in Carnival (noted in 1879 and 1880) shows that the policy of East Indian marginalisation was not wholly successful. In 1879, for example, the *Chronicle* reported the Carnival 'Hosay' featured 'dresses, shrine and paraphernalia' that was 'strictly or very nearly correct' as it had been 'chiefly made by coolies'. It will be remembered that as early as the 1850s black creoles are reported as having participated in 'Hosay'. There were similarities also between the 'Hosay procession' and Canboulay – both involved marching through the streets with lighted torches. The latter is reported in *New Era* on 7 March 1881. It noted that two months before, 'on the eve of the Coolie *Tajah*', the police had not objected to the carrying of lighted torches. This was not to be the case for Canboulay in 1881. Without special notice, marching in procession with uncovered torches became reason for police interference. The result was a riot.[13]

The *Canboulay* Riot – Carnival 1881

In many respects it was Baker's success in quashing Canboulay in 1880 that made a riot inevitable. According to the official report, in 1881 his exact intentions were kept secret. He appears to have avoided direct consultation with the Governor. His arrogant attitude, however, was self-evident to the pro-Carnival lobby. It made preparations to resist any attempt to interfere with the festival. As early as 14 February a notice was posted in Port of Spain and its environs:

> NEWS TO THE TRINIDADIANS
> Captain Baker demanded from our just and noble Governor, Sir Sanford Freeling, his authority to prevent the night of Canboulay, but our Excellency refused.

Baker seems not to have informed Freeling of this notice.

The exact circumstances of Baker's decision to take on the stickbands are unknown, although rumour suggested he made a wager he would put down Canboulay. Wager or not, the police were prepared for fighting on the night of 27 February and early morning of 28 February 1881.

The *Trinidad Chronicle* of 2 March provides the only contemporary account of the riot. Portions of this were later discredited in what appears to have been a 'consolidation of testimony' by the Governor. This was in the wake of vehement criticism by authoritarians. The description of hostilities was not questioned, however, and is corroborated by other evidence such as a recollection from a 96-year-old eye witness, Frances Richard, obtained in 1953.

Organised resistance (unexpected by Baker) is established by the united front presented by French- and English-speaking stickbands. In reporting this, the *Chronicle* gives details of some of the units:

ENGLISH		FRENCH	
Broomfield	*	Bakers	(Market Street)
Canelle	*	Danois	(Sorzanoville)
English	(Corbeau Town)	Maribones	(Upper Belmont)
Free-grammar	(short streets behind the Gaol)		

* No location given. In every instance the linguistic affinity has been surmised from earlier evidence.

The fight was concentrated in the 'French Shores' (at the upper end of Market Street). Here Baker and his men lay in wait to ambush the bands as they began their parades at midnight. Special effort was made by stickband supporters to lay down broken stones for ammunition against the police. There was also systematic breaking of the kerosene street lamps which had been installed at Christmas in 1878.

Without the element of surprise, which had aided him in 1880, the free fight between police and stickmen was a very bloody affair. It lasted three hours. Once again there were heroics from Baker – hence his nickname 'Brave Baker of the Bobbies'. His principal protection was his horse and his horsemanship. There were many injuries on both sides. The bands retired at about 3.00 a.m. and the police claimed a partial victory. They secured the streets with a force kept in reserve. The main unit returned to barracks at about 3.30 a.m.

Smarting at their lack of victory, the stickmen vowed to renew the fight in the daytime. Many of them were Martiniquians (or of other French-island origin). Their war song, according to Frances Richard, was:

Car ale le	Going there
Bio ba le	Give them a candle
Mete lumiere baio	Put a light for them
Car la lune leve mois passant trouvier.	When the moon rises, I will pass/go and find it

No attempt to suppress Canboulay was made elsewhere in Port of Spain, as *New Era* (5 March) pointed out. In the Newtown district, early morning celebrations took place without incident, and no street lamps were broken.

10 Scourge of Carnival stickbands, 'Captain' Baker's attempt to quash Canboulay in 1881 reputedly resulted from a bet.

There was a riot further south in the town of Couva. The police had difficulty in quelling a fight between Couva Savannah and Couva Exchange. Their action was preventative, however, rather than premeditated.

While the police in Port of Spain later claimed they had the situation under control, circumstantial evidence shows that although not defeated, they were heavily wounded. At 6 o'clock Baker withdrew the police from their stations in town to recuperate. He reported to Freeling at 6.30 a.m. and requested troops be stationed at the police barracks (they arrived between 8.30 a.m. and 10.00 a.m.). This secured the town in the event of further confrontation. Freeling was then left to pick up the pieces of this explosive situation. The first result was the continuation of daytime Carnival parades, as if nothing had happened. Thus, the *Chronicle* reports:

> the masqueraders had it all to themselves for several hours to do as they liked – and with the exception of a few fights between rival bandes or 'Negres Jardins' (who seem to have a strange liking for breaking each others' sconces) the masqueraders were, on the whole, more amusing than anything else. 'Pierrots' gorgeously and expensively dressed, their dresses being made of velvet and similar expensive material costing usually fifteen to twenty dollars (some over thirty!), with the usual *combats a la ligueze* (the whalebone whips costing $5 to 6 apiece), and the usual bombastic speeches were delivered by said Pierrots some of them being outrageously absurd – one player declaring his cousinship to the late Duke of Wellington – caricatures of old women, and representatives of 'Pinafore' by a party of young clerks who took the literal meaning of the word and acted on it by wearing pinafores, Chinamen, Coolies, all were well imitated and cleverly represented by players who took off their peculiar traits to a T. Bands of Pisanis not so vulgar as last year, stalwart school-girls, Spanish morris-dancers in beautiful costume representing Indian Caciques, shoeblacks – as importunate for a job as usual, and not over complimentary to those who refused their offers, Venezuelan soldiers, Spanish gentlemen as generals, cavaliers, &c., in cocked hats and velvet cloaks mounted on horseback – children, dressed in fancy costume, as Swiss Peasants &c., and one a miniature Spanish Grandee of the olden time – trunk hose, slashed doublet, small cap, tall red feathers, boots with rosettes – all deep red.

Many of these masquerades confirm the pattern established for this period.

Freeling, his authority usurped by the action of Baker, took careful stock of his options. His first move was to hold a meeting of the Executive Council. Shrewdly, he decided to isolate the hated police but also to swear in special constables in case of further violence.

He received a deputation from the Mayor and Borough Council at 3.00 p.m. Acting on their representations that further violence would threaten the town and in order to put Baker in his place, he agreed to address the masqueraders in the open. This he did in the Market Place at 5.00 p.m. The exact wording of his ameliorative speech was widely questioned subsequently and became notorious among authoritarians. He confined the police to their barracks and placed his trust in the black masquers and their allies in the white creole population.

Unknown to the populace, the police resigned *en masse* and had to be persuaded to reconsider their action. This was a further humiliation for Baker as he had little option but to maintain his police force. Freeling's action had the desired effect among masquers and no further violence ensued. Another subsequent contention, however, was whether he verbally allowed them to carry torches at night.

At some point there was a parade by a band of masqueraders dressed as police carrying a dummy, representing Baker, in funeral procession. Funeral music was provided by an imitation of the police band. The *Chronicle* places this on Monday afternoon, the official report on Monday evening (shortly before midnight), and Brierley (in his reminiscences) on Tuesday afternoon. The night-time parade is reported to have been lit by flambeaux in line with Canboulay. According to the official report the band 'sang in chorus songs reflecting on the police, of which the chief burden was, "the police can't do it"'. They deliberately marched past the police barracks, taunting the confined force, and subsequently conducted a mock funeral of Baker. The dummy was either jettisoned into the harbour (*Chronicle*) or burnt in proximity to the barracks (Brierley). It is possible that these accounts describe two separate incidents. Both are strongly reminiscent of the tradition in French-speaking Caribbean islands, where an effigy representing an unpopular person, or the spirit of Carnival, is consumed by fire on the first day of Lent.

One other event on the Monday evening (reported in the *Chronicle*, but subsequently denied in a despatch to the Secretary of State for the Colonies), was a visit by the stickbands to the Governor's residence. Whether this took place or not, the description is unique in establishing aspects of black creole music and their association with both stickfighting and Carnival:

> ON MONDAY NIGHT (after the assurances of the Governor in the Market-place – which had been widely and rapidly spread abroad with sundry variations and exaggeration) the interrupted Canboulay of Sunday night was resumed, and played without any disturbance worth speaking of. The Maribones and other amalgamated *bandes* repaired to Queen's House where orders had been previously given to the sentries at the gate for their admittance, and in fact that of all masquers who might present themselves. His Excellency and his Lady, Capt Ogilvy and other gentlemen and ladies who were present, came out on the balcony as soon as the bandes came up, and before them stick-exercises were gone through, the mens' drums beating as they never were before, extempore songs sung (in Creole, of course) in praise of his Excellency, composed on the spur of the moment by the *improvisatore* of the party. His Excellency, who with those around him seemed to enjoy the whole thing hugely (it being evidently a strange sight to himself and lady, and I believe to the gallant Captain) threw out money to the men, who vociferously cheered him on this evidence of his liberality and of their success in amusing him and party. His Excellency acknowledged their cheers by bowing to them, on which cheers and hurrahs made the usually quiet Governor's Garden ring. At the close of the stick-fight, the players were one and all, by order of His Excellency, treated to refreshments to which they did full justice, after which they retired, pluming themselves inordinately on having, as one expressed himself, '*Nous halla baton douvant Governour*'! an event I believe without precedent since Trinidad was Trinidad.

Freeling's denial relates to visits by masqueraders to Government House on the Tuesday when, he said, all were turned away. This leaves open the question as to activities on the Monday evening, a topic conveniently not pursued in the official report.

Recorded in the latter, however, was a letter written at 6.30 a.m. on Shrove Tuesday in which Baker advised the Governor's Private Secretary of the mock funeral procession with lighted torches the night before. No action was taken. Baker patrolled Port of Spain on horseback on five occasions during the day and found the town quiet. Troops were withdrawn to garrison at 6.00 p.m.[14]

With minor exceptions the press presented a united front against Baker's actions. They represent one aspect of what might be described as a three-way split in the ruling elite. On this occasion the newspapers took the Governor's part (British Colonial Office career diplomat's pragmatism). Baker was seen as a hot-headed authoritarian, and the French-speaking pro-Carnival lobby had no difficulty in siding with Freeling. It was a approach that was to receive support from R. G. Hamilton, the Colonial Office representative sent from London to investigate the riot. He spent a week in Trinidad (21 May to 27 May), interviewing as many interested parties as possible. His report was submitted to the Secretary of State for the Colonies on 13 June 1881. The text was printed by the Colonial Office in September, and officially received in Trinidad in late October. His conclusions were that Carnival should continue to start at midnight on Shrove Sunday. He believed, however, that the carrying of torches ought to be strictly controlled. He also called for greater regulation of Hosien (perceiving this as a future point of friction in Trinidad). There was a recommendation that during each Carnival season, the Admiralty station a man-of-war in the harbour at Port of Spain. The police were bolstered, but also heavily criticised.

These, and other recommendations, coupled with Freeling's personal appeal to the masqueraders, were important steps 'towards re-establishing a relationship based on mutual consent between the populace in its Carnival formation and the authorities'. Thus, in general the report was well received in the press, although there was some criticism of Hamilton's attitude towards the black population.[15]

The regulation of drum dances and stickbands – Carnival 1882–1884

Many of the recommendations in Hamilton's report were effected in 1882, including the man-of-war in the harbour at Port of Spain. Another result of the 1881 riot was that proclamations concerning Carnival were made public via the office of the Colonial Secretary. This ensured that all levels of the executive were aware of conditions imposed in the name of the Governor by his Inspector Commandant of Police. The proclamation for 1882 was first published in the press in November 1881, soon after the arrival of the official report. It was reprinted in the *Port of Spain Gazette* on 11 February 1882 following a deputation by thirteen Carnival bands. Their statement of

— ∽ —

ADVICE FOR THE
COMING
CARNIVAL
FOR THE YEAR
1882.

Ye brave Maskers of Trinidad, now is your festive season, perhaps the brightest Carnival that will be played by you all since its origin. May you all play with union, peace and loyalty to the Governor of the Island, who has so freely and independently given you freedom to play the Masquerade from the Sunday night at the hour of 12 o'clock till Tuesday night at 12 o'clock. I hope therefore that you all may unite on that bond of friendship to show that flowing loyalty which all Trinidadians can display at any time, and under any circumstances imaginable. Now, decent men and boys of Trinidad, you have been favoured with permission from His Excellency the Governor to play and have your annual amusement as before time; therefore let not any riotous or indecent behaviour on your parts stop to mar the pleasure of your sports, and by any uncalled for fight cast a stain on the Carnival of 1882. I hope you all may play in that decent mild and jolly manner that will characterize your sports as the best on record in the annals of the history of this Island, Remember the pains His Excellency took in coming to our market square last year to ask you to play peaceably and be loyal to the Government, and also by his Proclamation of last year, he begged of you all that when the Carnival of 1882 should be ended, that he shall have that satisfaction in your peaceably playing that will always give him pleasure in his allowing you to have your sports. So let all the bands of the island from far and near be united in one concerted action, which action is peaceful playing and temperate behaviour, so that we all that have not taken any part in the Masking, may be able to certify to the uprightness of your behaviour and the placid tone of your playing in this Masquerade season of 1882.

THE CHIEF BANDS ARE COMPOSED,

VIZ :—

1—Correl or the Liònness.
2—Baker or the New Cròwn.
3—Free Grammar.
4—Cannel.
5—English Boys.
6—Fire Brand.
7—Zulu.
8—Palama.
9—Danoit.
10—Jack-Spaniards.
11—Diamond.
12—Pin Carret.
13—Tambrand.

11 After the riot of 1881, and amelioration by the Governor, masqueraders were on their best behaviour the year following.

fidelity (freely circulated a fortnight previous in the Eastern Market) had been published by *Fair Play and Trinidad News* on 9 February:

ADVICE FOR THE
COMING
CARNIVAL
FOR THE YEAR
1882

Ye brave Maskers of Trinidad, now is your festive season, perhaps the brightest Carnival that will be played by you all since its origin. May you all play with union, peace and loyalty to the Governor of the Island, who has so freely and independently given you freedom to play the Masquerade from the Sunday night at the hour of 12 o'clock till Tuesday night at 12 o'clock. I hope therefore that you all may unite on that bond of friendship to show that flowing loyalty which all Trinidadians can display at any time and under any circumstances imaginable. Now, decent men and boys of Trinidad, you have been favoured with permission from His Excellency the Governor to play and have your annual amusement as before time; therefore let not any riotous or indecent behaviour on your parts stop to mar the pleasure of your sports, and by any uncalled for fight cast a stain on the Carnival of 1882. I hope you may all play in that decent mild and jolly manner that will characterise your sports as the best on record in the annals of the history of this Island. Remember the pains His Excellency took in coming to our market square last year to ask you to play peaceably and be loyal to the Government, and also by his Proclamation of last year, he begged of you all that when the Carnival of 1882 should be ended, that he shall have that satisfaction in your peaceably playing that will always give him pleasure in his allowing you to have your sports. So let all the bands of the island from far and near be united in one concerted action, which action is peaceful playing and temperate behaviour, so that we all that have not taken any part in the Masking, may be able to certify to the uprightness of your behaviour and the placid tone of your playing in this Masquerade season of 1882.

THE CHIEF BANDS ARE COMPOSED,
VIZ:–
1 – Correl or the Lìonness.
2 – Baker or the New Cròwn.
3 – Free Grammar.
4 – Cannel.

5 – English Boys.
6 – Fire Brand.
7 – Zulu.
8 – Palama.
9 – Danoit.
10 – Jack-Spaniards.
11 – Diamond.
12 – Pin Carret.
13 – Tambrand.

Despite fears of conflict, this advice was well received. Canboulay was peaceful. There were few fights, if any, during Carnival. The bands were on their best behaviour. Some were accompanied by 'men of influence' – the *Chronicle* (4 March) noted 'Mr. IGN. BODU of the Borough Council' and 'Mr C. A. FABIEN'. The police, out in force, did not interfere with the masquers. *Fair Play* (23 February) was pleased to report that: 'The gaiety of the two days was such as has not been witnessed for a long time past; from morning to night the streets were alive with constantly moving crowds of maskers playing music, dancing, jumping about and acting in keeping with the various characters which they personated'.

Familiar groups included the Venezuelan Army (who visited the Governor's residence, and were well received), the Zulus, a 'Coolie Hosé', Chinese women and bands of school children.

Vagabondage and bands, however, remained an issue. For example, despite their good account of Carnival, on 9 March *Fair Play* attacked the '*moral* aspect' of the festival. It noted that:

> The obscene songs and lewd dances of the Carnival are the same which are for months previously practised in yards, open to the public, and where the rehearsals for the masked Bacchanalia hold sway. The young men and young women who are subsequently ruined are often the ones who, attracted by the sound of the drum, become the witnesses of the corrupting scenes enacted at these dances. The fights which take place in all our streets but principally in our suburbs are the practices for and the precursors of similar and worse subsequent encounters at a season of licence.

That stickband confrontations marked out physical boundaries is further confirmed by a report in the *Trinidad Palladium* on 1 July. This identified the two principal zones in Port of Spain, one 'belonging to the "English

Band", the other the "French Band" *alias* the Bakers' and described a recent incident resulting from territorial infringement.

In line with Hamilton's recommendation, an Ordinance was passed on 1 July *'for Regulating the Festivals of Immigrants'*. This was to control Hosien and was based on similar legislation passed in British Guiana (Guyana) in 1869.

On 1 August, ex-slaves in Carenage held an elaborate celebration of the anniversary of Emancipation Day, an event that had been suppressed by the *curé* for six years. The French Dominican priest who described the occasion recalled there was an elected King who held court in a bamboo hut (named the palace). He 'was responsible for collecting money, buying food, issuing invitations, offering the holy bread [during the 'high mass', with which the feast began], and opening the dance'. These *'orgies sans nom, souvenirs de la vie africaine'* were accompanied by the *'horrible tambour africaine'*. By its description, this may have been a *Belair* drum dance.[16]

The Carnival of 1883 became the principal test of the truce between the pro- and anti-Carnival lobbies, and the diplomacy of the Governor. After official publication, the Governor's proclamation was printed in the *Port of Spain Gazette* on 13 January. It contained provisions similar to those of the year previous and the paper affirmed the Governor's view that: 'The same orderly behaviour displayed at the last Carnival will be observed'.

Unlike 1882, however, there were disturbances. Horns were blown to assemble the bands as early as 7.00 p.m. on the evening of Sunday, 4 February. This was five hours before official commencement of the festival. There was also stickfighting, provoked by a recently formed English-speaking band called the Newgates. They were on bail at the time of the Carnival. This did not prevent them attacking French-speaking stickbands 'who had turned out to play peacefully'. Notably, these were the Bakers, Daylions, and Maribones. The Newgates, who were 'unmasked, un-disguised' and well armed, took the drum of the latter; a calculated move to incite revenge by the most feared of the bands. In this, as *Fair Play* noted subsequent to the festival, there may have been foul play. A suggestion circulated that the anti-Carnival lobby, led by Captain Baker, paid the Newgates to cause trouble. It was observed that the police did not intervene to keep the peace until the second day. In addition, it was always the New-gates who instigated the fighting, yet they were favoured by the police. A correspondent, Anthony Guzman (who led the peacefully-orientated

Venezuelan Soldiers) described being incapacitated by the Newgates as his band assembled on Canboulay morning. He was told later that this was because he intended to present this fancy-costumed band at the Governor's residence, as he had in 1882.

The *Chronicle* reported another instance of interference. A troupe masquerading as a squad of police 'were . . . highly successful, until they were dispersed by the driver of a mule cart, who drove them out of the way of his vehicle by a vigorous application of the whip'.

In addition to fighting there were complaints about obscene songs and gestures, vulgar drum dances and the *pisse-en-lit* costume worn generally by men, dressed as women, but occasionally by women.

For the *Palladium* the highlights were 'a Coolie Hosien Temple' (constructed with great skill), a miniature steam engine, and a warship. The *Chronicle* saw 'facetiously inclined persons' who had 'rigged themselves out in quaint costumes' going 'dancing through the streets to more or less musical accompaniments afforded by improvised bands'. It was impressed by these costumes and complimented the maskers on the 'great taste and judgement' shown in their manufacture from 'poor materials'.

The violence appears to have decided Freeling that further legal controls on Carnival were necessary. He advised this intention to a meeting of the Legislative Council on 1 March. Although the anti-Carnival lobby achieved a partial victory, they did not attain abolition. Freeling noted that: 'In framing measures' he 'would endeavour not to deprive the community during the day time of the amusement they apparently find in masquerading.'[17]

At an earlier meeting of the Legislative Council (1 February), Henry Ludlow, the Attorney General, had introduced what became known as the 'Musical Ordinance'. Even the ultra-conservative *Port of Spain Gazette* viewed this as class legislation. Essentially all percussion instruments (played by black creoles, and people of East-Indian descent) were to be prohibited without police licence between 6.00 a.m. and 10.00 p.m. (They were controlled otherwise by Ordinance no. 6 of 1868). In addition, European musical devices such as string and woodwind instruments, were added to the stipulations. In line with the 1868 legislation they were to be licensed between 10.00 p.m. and 6.00 a.m. the day following.

The origin of the measure was said to be nightly drumming (one source says by East Indians) in the village of Peru, near the military garrison at St

James. As with Baker's 1881 measures against Canboulay, however, the *Port of Spain Gazette* (10 February) perceived the proposals as an attack on black-creole culture:

> To European ears the tambour and chac-chac produce nothing but the most discordant sounds, to Creoles, even of the higher classes, whose organs have been accustomed from their birth to this peculiar music, there is a cadence and rough harmony in their accompaniment of native songs which is far from disagreeable; and on the lower classes their effect is magical. We have only to look at a *round* of *Belair* and note the peculiar undulating motions of all present, as they follow with their heads, their hands, their whole bodies the peculiar cadence of the music, to be convinced that, to their ears, there is more, in the sound produced, than the discordant noise which alone strikes the European.

The *Chronicle* (14 February) was equally opposed to the catch-all clauses. They noted how 'the measure attacks at once the piano of the well-to-do classes, and the guitar or concertina of the labouring classes'. In addition they defended the drummers of Peru village, observing how 'the poor here have little enough recreation, and to attempt to deprive them of an amusement both harmless and humanizing is running directly counter to the interests of civilization and the dictates of humanity'.

On the same day that the proposed Ordinance was next discussed by the Legislative Council (1 March), *Fair Play* published a long editorial on drums and drum dances. It contrasted the construction of keg drums in the West Indies with those it had seen of African manufacture. The latter, it believed to be superior instruments. Past Trinidad drum dances were compared with a type of contemporary event that had long been criticised in the press:

> An open yard in some suburb of the town, sufficiently private for the proceedings not to be seen from the street but with no hindrance to the ingress and egress of visitors; a man in a dirty shirt and trousers, a bench and a drum; a few dirtily dressed women who serve as Chorus, a mixed crowd of dirtily dressed men and women who dance to the sound of the drum independently of each other, and a gaping crowd who are attracted to the spot by the noise; if it is not moonlight, a flickering flambeau to enlighten the scene – such is all that is required to constitute a drum dance! And what are the songs? Generally a few foolish sentences, composed by the leader of the Chorus to provoke some obnoxious person or band, and the sickening repetition of a

refrain which gives the greatest possible amount of exercise to the lungs compatible with the least possible disturbance of the brain. As for the dancing, it is nothing, but the most disgusting obscenity pure and simple, being an imitation more or less vigorous and lustful by the male and female performers of the motions of the respective sexes whilst in the act of coition. Not only the exercise, but copious draughts of rum warm their blood; quarrels ensue, sticks are freely used and the entertainment is ordinarily wound up by a fight. Performers and spectators then disperse with their passions excited to go and put into immediate practice the immoral lessons they have been greedily imbibing.

Fair Play believed such drum dances should be strictly controlled, but the measures proposed by Ludlow were impracticable and would not address these 'serious evils'. This was the persuasive argument opposing the 'Musical Ordinance', made by George L. Garcia at the Legislative Council Meeting. His speech led to the substitution later in the year of strict controls of drum dances in yards. These were contained in the *Summary Convictions (amendment) Ordinance*, no 11 of 1883 (10 July). The latter made the 'owner of any yard, where a drum dance took place, liable to a heavy fine, if a detective could prove that there was anyone present ... who had been convicted before the Magistrate for any cause'.[18]

An important indirect result of events such as the Canboulay Riot and the 'Musical Ordinance', is contemporary descriptions of musical activities by black creoles. Thus the *Chronicle* in 1881 confirms the actions of stickmen, accompanied by drumming, with extempore singing by chantwell and chorus in a call and response pattern.

Fair Play, in 1883, extends this pattern by implying that different types of drum dances would be performed at yard events. Its description indicates the involvement of male and female partners, who seem to have danced 'winin' style. The latter confirms the recall of Inniss, who identified the dances as '*calindas*'. Other sources such as *New Era* (October 1873), called the occasions '"Bel Air" dances' (a term Inniss reserves for songs). It will be recalled *bamboula*, *bel air*, *calenda* and *juba* are terms for creole drum dances developed in the French-speaking Caribbean during slavery and can each refer to a form of song as well as dance.

These old creole dances stood alongside others brought directly from Africa, which reflected more immediate contact with that continent. In addition, there were similar dances brought to Trinidad from other islands.

Thus, on 9 August 1883, in response to the *Summary Convictions (amend-ment) Ordinance*, the *Trinidad Review* sprang to the defence of 'songs and dances that are decent'. The 'indecent songs and dances' in Trinidad, it explained, were 'either importations or imitations of the lewd songs of Curaçao, from which island they were first brought over and practised here by one BIM BIM and her equally vile daughters, who every night, to the peculiar music of their Quelbays, went through the most lascivious antics, indicative of the sensuous vocation to which they abandoned themselves'. Noting the dance 'with the songs composed for it' could not 'be mistaken by the Police', it advised that it should be 'stamped out of the colony like a pestilence'.

Although their island of origin is unusual, like other comments in this period, migrants are blamed for social difficulties experienced in Trinidad. More specifically, *Quelbe* can be grouped with the new creole dances devel-oped in this period. The same is probably true for the 'abominable dance called Calypso' described to Abbé Massé in 1882. 'According to the old negroes', the dance was 'the cause of perversion of young men and girls'. This reasoning is similar to that given for the influence of 'Quelbays' by the *Trinidad Review*. More important, this appears to be the first use of the word 'calypso' in a musical context in Trinidad. Subsequent sources give a variety of reasons for the origin of this meaning. It is probably significant, however, that during the late nineteenth century, songs in Trinidad called *cariso* or *caliso* are said to have been performed to the accompaniment of the goatskin drum.

It would be wrong to suppose that the drum provided the only accom-paniment for musical recreations among black creoles. Confirming that there were 'many' dances, some 'very lewd', Massé described instru-mentation in 1879: 'the violin, the "landola" [and], the American accord-ion which is always accompanied by drums'. The last named were of several types. In 1882 he recalled in his diary how: 'Every evening I have my head aching for long hours either by an accordion or by the violins.' He noted how black people had 'a passion for music as they have a passion for dance'. He also reported how the 'Spaniards' (presumably migrants from Venez-uela, of part African- and Native-American ancestry) had a similar passion. They also played the 'Bandole'.

Massé's recall is confirmed by newspaper reports. For example, in November 1880 the *Trinidad Chronicle* indicated how instruction in violin playing for dance music was 'taking a large extension among the humbler classes'. It hoped that this trend would see the demise of 'the abominable African drum (a goat skin drawn tightly over a keg and tapped by the fingers)'. Similar observations were made in March 1882, following Carnival, noting how 'the fiddle is played by dozens, scores, of black and coloured youths this year, while clarionet, violincello, horn, piccolo and cornet are not quite neglected'.

Despite the *Port of Spain Gazette*'s defence of the *belair*, in February 1883, the elite were generally agreed that, whatever the name of the drum dance, virtually all dance movements and song lyrics were 'obscene'. This applied to regular drum dances by the 'societies or bands', as well as their songs during Carnival. For the latter, Hamilton obtained a description in 1881 that shows why they were considered objectionable: 'It is common during the Carnival for the vilest songs, in which the names of ladies of the Island are introduced, to be sung in the streets, and the vilest talk to be indulged in.'

Songs of this type were not the only Carnival vocal music. There were also the 'war songs' of the stickbands. Drumming, carrying of sticks, and stickfighting by bands, however, were the principal objections of the elite towards Carnival, especially during Canboulay. It was these aspects of the festival Freeling stated he would address in his message to the masqueraders of 1 March 1883.[19]

'The Carnival' was the subject of an editorial in the *Port of Spain Gazette* as early as 12 January 1884. This was almost one-and-a-half months before Shrovetide and in advance of government action to control the festival. The opportunity was taken to present its view of the perpetrators of violence. Once more it was 'the ruffianly bands, organised by the most desperate characters, men and women; thieves, vagabonds, prostitutes [who] took possession of the town from midnight of the Sunday preceding Ash Wednesday'. It noted how 'in former days no Police Force was required to control the *cannes-boulées*'. Blame was again apportioned to 'the large immigration of roughs from Barbados and other islands'. There was advice and comment, also: 'Let the Police patrol the streets in squads so as not to hesitate to arrest, at once, anyone violating public decency either by gesture or language. There are some costumes – the *pisse-en-lit* for example – which are so very indecent they should not be tolerated.'

Just over a week later, on 21 January, the Legislative Council met to discuss Carnival. The 'Governor's Message' of 1 March 1883 was reiterated and a draft read of the 'Torch Ordinance'. The following day a Proclamation was published (no 1 of 1884) which, for the first time, stated Carnival would not commence until 6.00 a.m. on the morning of Shrove Monday, and: 'The Procession generally known as the Cannes-brulées or Canboulay shall not be allowed to take place'. For the latter, additional regulations were to be promulgated. These were encompassed in the 'Torch Ordinance' which, when agreed by the Legislative Council on 25 January, became the *Peace Preservation Ordinance* (no 1 of 1884). The Governor was given powers to prohibit 'in any street, highway or public place' at times specified by Proclamation:

1.   The carrying of any lighted torch.
2.   The beating of any drum, the blowing of any horn or the use of
     any other noisy instrument.
3.   Any dance or procession, and
4.   Any assemblage or collection of persons armed with sticks or other
     weapons of offence and numbering ten or more.

This stringent attack on their traditional activities met with resistance by the stickbands, especially in the French-Creole speaking area of Belmont. Bands who assembled in this vicinity, 'to have their drum dance, &c' on 22 January, were dispersed by police, with only minor trouble. Four days later, however, there was a more concerted attack on law officers in Belmont Road. At a court case involving this assault, it was noted that: 'As soon as the policemen had passed they were assailed by the mob with stones, and several of them were hit, the pass word being *fonté li* – beat them – words said to be French, but which the Attorney General said did not form part of any language known to him. The police were forced to retreat'.

By 31 January, the *Trinidad Review* stated that 'attacks on the Police are daily reported from Belmont'. It noted how 'lawless bands' were acting with apparent impunity and described the rescue of a prisoner being escorted to police custody 'from somewhere about Sorzansville'. Bands of *'Diametres'* from the centre of Port of Spain were apparently involved in some of these fracas. Even the police on guard at the Governor's residence were assaulted.

A Proclamation was issued on 28 January (no 3 of 1884) that established even more severe conditions for the holding of Carnival than had been specified previously. The settlements of Port of Spain, San Fernando, Arima, Princes Town, St Joseph and Couva were singled out for special attention. A period from 7.00 p.m. on Saturday 23 February to 6.00 a.m. on Wednesday 27 February was stipulated in which the *Peace Preservation Ordinance* would be in operation. The latter was quoted in full, as were the relevant provisions of Ordinance no 6 of 1868.

The administration appear to have been acting as though they were under siege. Another explanation might be, however, that tactics were dictated by the Colonial Office, in an endeavour to control the Carnival and force the co-operation of the French-speaking community. In this respect the Governor issued a circular, asking for the swearing in of special Constables. There was, therefore, a moral obligation for French-speaking members of the elite to side with 'law and order'. The executive were also at pains to explain that legislation against the Carnival and drum dances applied only to Canboulay, and to the activities of 'rogues and vagabonds'. To emphasise this, two more pieces of legislation were passed, the *Licencing Amendment Ordinance* (revoking licences for selling intoxicating liquor at times of riot), and an even more comprehensive version of the *Summary Convictions (amendment) Ordinance* (to further clamp down on drum dances by the bands).

This legislation and proclamation did not go without comment in the press. On 14 February, both the *Trinidad Review* and *Fair Play* devoted editorials to the subject. The *Review* perceived the actions of the government to have become heavy-handed. Like objections to the 'Musical Ordinance' a year earlier, it believed 'all the facts of class legislation [were] in full play, namely, a harsh enactment, the hastiness of which when resented, is attempted to be softened by the arbitrary limitation of its provisions to a particular class'. It also considered that penalty for 'possession of any weapon, stick or other thing' raised a presumption of guilt against the innocent outside 'the fundamental maxims of the criminal law'. *Fair Play*, in an outline of official policy towards Carnival since 1881, thought the executive had over-reacted. It also raised a crucial question that portended tragic consequences later in the year: 'But should the Creoles part unresistingly with their "Cannes Brulées," will our immense Coolie population dispense as readily with *their* torch-light procession? And should they resist and be joined by disaffected Creole laborers, whose cause would be one with theirs, where would be the means to repress them before the perpetration of incalculable atrocities?'

During the period that legislation was passed for controlling Carnival, the unpopularity of government officials remained high among black creoles in Port of Spain. Ludlow, the Attorney General, was 'mobbed and pelted with stones, on the Belmont road, near the Queen's Park'. Some two weeks later the *Port of Spain Gazette* (23 February) reported 'the Governor was, a few days ago, insulted in the streets'. Freeling, however, was set to retire from his post as Governor of Trinidad at the end of March and insults from what was being termed the '*canaille*' would have been of little consequence.

With special preparations for Carnival in Port of Spain, apart from the breaking of a few lamps, there was no trouble. No attempt was made to hold Canboulay and, during the daytime on Monday and Tuesday, 'there was less masquerading in the streets than in previous years'.

There were Canboulay disturbances, however, at three of the other locations specified in the Proclamation of 28 January. All of a similar nature, they occurred at Couva, Princes Town, and San Fernando, on the night of Sunday, 24 February and early morning of Monday, 25 February.

At Couva, drums were played and parties assembled from about 10.20 p.m. on the Sunday. Bands comprising 200 people, carrying sticks, torches and drums, came as near as a few hundred yards from the police barracks. The riot act was read, but the police challenged and dispersed the assembly without resort to firearms.

A more concerted attempt at holding the ceremony, by 500 or more at Princes Town, ended with the police firing on the masqueraders. There were two fatalities, one said to have been a band ringleader. From 11.00 p.m. on the Sunday there had been horn blowing, loud singing, lighted torches, beating drums, and stick playing. Women danced and sang, mocking the police. Missiles, some containing foul-smelling substances, were hurled at the police before the riot act was read, and two volleys fired. The police were heavily outnumbered. The bands fled at the shooting.

At San Fernando, celebrants lit a bonfire and commenced their ceremony before being forced to abandon activities. The authorities, as in Port of Spain, were well prepared to disperse the bands.

Some held the opinion, according to the *Trinidad Review* (28 February), 'that the ringleaders of some of the most desperate bands in Port-of-Spain were wishful of holding in the Naparimas those orgies which were forbidden them in Port-of-Spain'. Their suggestion that this might explain the confrontation in Princes Town has not been confirmed.

For the administration, there was satisfaction at no major altercations.

Freeling published a notice in the *Trinidad Royal Gazette* on 12 March, thanking all those concerned, the military, the police, and the judiciary, 'for the moral support afforded to the Government in its endeavours to prevent and suppress the ruffianism of certain lawless bands and individuals'.[20]

The *Hosien* massacre – 1884

Following suppression of Canboulay, the problem remained whether to discipline Hosien. The *Port of Spain Gazette* (1 March) was in no doubt. It believed the festival should be kept to the plantations as in Guyana declaring: 'It is utterly absurd to pretend that the monster processions which, on a given day inundate our principal towns with thousands of fanatical drunken coolies, can form any necessary part of their religious ceremonies.' The real fear, however, was joint insurrection by black creoles and East Indians. The *Gazette* reported it had 'reliable information that the discomfited bands of ruffians, who, but for the vigilance of the Government, would have imperilled the lives and properties of the peaceable inhabitants of Port-of-Spain, are determined to avail themselves of the occasion of the coolie Hosien to make another attempt to carry out their nefarious designs'. Judging by subsequent events, this siege-mentality reflected the position of the administration. It can be seen as a direct continuation of their policy towards Carnival.

That the executive decided to take a more forthright attitude towards Hosien is shown by publication of festival regulations for the first time. These were issued on 30 July 1884, using powers established in the *Ordinance for Regulating the Festivals of Immigrants*. As advised by the *Port of Spain Gazette*, its objective was to confine the celebrations to plantations. This would re-emphasise the segregation of East Indians from black creoles, and mollify the elite's fear of widespread mutiny. The move was also designed to counter criticism of administrative inconsistency in banning Canboulay but allowing similar processions through towns by East Indians.

Like Canboulay, under the cover of darkness, Hosien included parades by different groups carrying torches and hakka sticks through the towns. Of Muslim origin (but shared in Trinidad by people of Hindu descent, as well as a proportion of black creoles) the festival 're-enacted the historical events leading to the death of the Prophet Mohammed's grandsons, Hassan and Hussain'. Known as 'Tajahs', model mausoleums for the two 'Shia' martyrs were carried from estates to the nearest town and deposited at night into the sea. Accompaniment was by tassa drums. For a few days prior to the celebration there was also drumming by torch-light, 'ending sometimes in quarrels, fights and bloodshed'. In common with Carnival, street parades sometimes involved hostile encounters between bands. Despite black creole involvement in the processions, according to official sources, confrontations were always between East Indians. The groups involved in Canboulay violence kept their conflicts for other occasions.

There was great dissatisfaction at the regulations among East Indians, especially in the area surrounding San Fernando. This was the region of the festival's greatest popularity in Trinidad. Petitions were made for the restrictions to be lifted, but these were rejected. On 30 October, therefore, participants chose to disregard the authorities and carry their tajahs towards San Fernando. Police, under the command of 'Captain' Baker, fired a hail of bullets to stop the advance, and this resulted in many deaths.[21]

At one stroke this attack on the East Indians maintained the divide between black creoles and 'coolies' (as they were called in derogatory fashion). The administration was able to govern Hosien by fear. Political circumstances, however, had led to the deduction that there was no scope for the complete suppression of Carnival. With regulation, this was to be left as the primary festival in towns. While there is no direct evidence, it is difficult not to suspect that the Colonial Office and Governor Freeling (who was responsible for instigating all the legislation), had acted with these aims in mind. Fear, engendered by the Indian Mutiny (1857) and the successful slave rebellion in Haiti (1804) would have been reason enough for this policy.

Incorporation begins – Carnival 1885–1887

In addition to the Hosien massacre, the Carnival of 1885 was held under the shadow of the Canboulay disturbances in southern districts the previous year. A similar proclamation to the one issued in 1884 was published in late January. Unlike 1884, however, there appears to have been little overt objection to its conditions. The festival (16–17 February), was the quietest seen in Trinidad for many years. According to all reports there were no fights (hostile bands being well disciplined by squads of police), and less 'obscenity'. *New Era* (23 February) noted, nevertheless, that 'it would be to the advantage of all parties, if men dressed up as women, and women in their bedroom costumes, could be induced to turn their propensities for fun to better account'. In contrast it also stated that 'comparatively large numbers of the respectable classes ... felt safe in venturing to disguise themselves this year for the purpose of amusement'.

Unlike the *Chronicle* (18 February), and *Port of Spain Gazette* (21 February), *New Era* also gave particulars of 'an elaborate plan for representing the *fracas* between the Police and Coolies in October last at San Fernando'. This had been quashed by 'Captain' Baker and the newspaper was indignant at his interference, reporting that 'trouble and expense, it seems, had been incurred in making the necessary preparations, without a thought having been given to the possibility of the Police being unduly tender in the matter'. Baker, however, was equally 'sensitive' to the political implications of such a Carnival representation.

In 1886 the *Port of Spain Gazette* (13 March) recounted that the Carnival was 'particularly remarkable'. There was an absence of stickbands, and a determined effort by the police 'to put down every attempt at immorality and obscenity whether in dress, speech or song'. The Venezuelan Army and Zulu band made reappearances. They were joined by a band of Naval Heroes who paid a visit to the Governor's residence. The newspaper was especially critical of the attitude of the police towards these fancily dressed bands. Despite the frivolous nature of their masques, technically they had been breaking the law. Each, therefore, had been apprehended by the constabulary and made an appearance in court. Unlike other cases, however, all three received a caution.

Masqueraders who received harsher treatment included three pierrots, sent to prison for fighting. Their attempt to escape arrest had been impeded by elaborate costumes, one of them having 'tripped over his tail'. Eight members of a stickband 'including two coolies', were fined, as were several men dressed as women. Four women, charged with singing obscene songs and making obscene gestures in the public street, were imprisoned. A similar group, four women and a boy, were penalised in the same manner. When arrested they were 'simply dressed in chemises and ribbons'. One case of obscenity was 'dismissed for want of evidence'. This involved two men who went about during the Carnival 'exhibiting "*Gombot Glise*" in a closed box and charging a few cents to anyone who looked into the box'. It seems 'one of the men was in the box' and the allegation was 'that those who looked in witnessed a very indecent spectacle'.

There is a general account of the Carnival in *A Guide to Trinidad* by J. H. Collens, first published in 1887. His description provides a little extra information not usually covered in the press. He notes how 'business is partially, if not altogether, suspended; masquerading and tomfoolery generally being the order of the day'. There were also 'the better class of Spaniards' who dressed 'themselves in fantastic costumes'. Such masquers were from families of long-standing, settled in Trinidad prior to 1797, or nineteenth-century migrants from Venezuela. They rode or drove 'about visiting their friends [and] showering small confitures upon them'.[22]

1887 – US Medicine shows

One external influence on the development of popular culture in Trinidad was yearly visits by 'Yankee Patent Medicine vendors'. This training ground for black and white entertainers in the United States appears to have stretched as far as the Caribbean. In 1932, Lewis Osborne Inniss recalled aspects of their money-making activities. These always centred around some form of divertissement. 'One fellow', he remembered, 'had a tent in Shine's Pasture, where he gave free entertainments to the people in the evening with two talking dolls by means of ventriloquism, the music being supplied by a Hurdy-Gurdy.' The show was concluded 'by a sale of his medicines, miniature specimens of which he had been distributing during the day'. There was 'another who sold Kick-a-Poo Remedies'. This vendor 'used to drive around the town in a gilded chariot, dressed in Indian Robes [and] extracted all the bad teeth of the public free'.

The Pharmaceutical Society, of which Inniss was a member, persuaded the Attorney General (Stephen Gatty) to pass a ' Medical Ordinance' (no 6 of 1887) 'which forbade the selling of medicines other than by Licensed Druggist in a Licensed Pharmacy'. This stopped the elaborate presentations, selling what were usually alcoholic cure-alls. Inniss noted, however, that vendors of patent medicine continued to ply their trade by 'scattering

... Almanacks, Dream Books, et cetera'. The same publications were popular among black people in the United States.[23]

It is not possible to gauge the full effect of medicine show performers in Trinidad. Their otherwise little documented presence, and eventual distribution of astrological literature, point to these North American trends reaching the Caribbean almost from their inception. Medicine shows, for example, evolved in the latter part of the nineteenth century, following the US Civil War.

Queen Victoria's Golden Jubilee

For obvious reasons, throughout the nineteenth century the principal economic and symbolic influence in British Caribbean islands was the 'Empire', in whose name they were governed. Imperial celebrations were of great significance, especially those revolving around the monarch. The 'Golden Jubilee' of the reign of Queen Victoria was no exception. Elaborate preparations were made in each island to commemorate this event at the end of June, 1887. An 'Alliance Musicale' was produced to mark the anniversary of fifty years rule by the Queen, including *West Indian Melodies* by John Urich. This is of great importance to Trinidad vernacular culture, for Urich notated a 'Bamboula', probably the first printed representation of the island's music. The publication further demonstrates a gradual change in attitude by the elite towards local tradition that was taking place in the latter part of the nineteenth century.[24]

Christmas

In his *Guide to Trinidad*, J. H. Collens mentioned that 'all classes ... celebrate Christmas with rejoicings, and let off gunpowder and superfluous steam in the form of fireworks'. At the time, it seems Christmas celebrations were regarded as harmless. This was not the view of the *Port of Spain Gazette*, when referring to Christmas 1887. It described 'the sad desecration of Christmas Day – a Sunday' by vagabondism (or, rather, the bands).[25] There seems to have been an attempt by stickbands to shift Canboulay and avoid the Carnival proclamation.

1888 – Carnival: Trinidad and Martinique in comparison

At the time of Carnival in 1888, the *Port of Spain Gazette* reported, a band 'assembled on the LaBasse on Sunday night with the intention of starting the *Canboulay* procession'. They were dispersed by police, four band members being arrested and fined by the magistrate. The same evening Sir William Robinson (the Governor) held a grand fancy dress ball at his residence 'in honour of the North American and West Indian Squadron, which had arrived in the morning'. On Shrove Tuesday there was also a Ladies Leap Year Ball at the Prince's Building, a principal location for 'society' events.

Grand balls were always a feature of the Carnival season, but appear to have dwindled in the 1870s and early 1880s. Some were held, however, such as a highly successful assembly in fancy dress given by Governor Freeling on 11 January 1883.

In 1888, Carnival parades in Port of Spain were witnessed by Melton Prior, an artist employed by the *Illustrated London News*. As well as publishing the only known nineteenth-century engraving, Prior provided a refreshingly open commentary from the perspective of a well-travelled observer. Drawing attention to the stringent conditions of the Governor's proclamation, he testified 'that there was nothing in Port of Spain to shock the most fastidious sense of decorum' in the 'attire and behaviour' of the masqueraders. The costumes 'worn by some of the negro people', he said, 'had a very picturesque effect'. They were 'mostly dressed in white'.

His engraving of a scene in Frederick Street shows greater variety of costume. In the foreground there are two devils, in dark apparel, the smaller of the two probably being a *jab molasi* (or little molasses-devil). Black women in white dresses with white masques otherwise predominate. Some of these may be men dressed as women. In the background there are a number of grotesques, a wild Indian, two be-turbaned minstrels (with banjos) and, probably one or two clowns, carrying air-filled bladders dangling from sticks. There are also black men dressed in white, with white masques and flat white hats.

Prior's drawing undoubtedly reflects some artistic licence, although several of the masquerade characters he depicts conform with contemporary and oral history references. José M. Bodu, whose *Trinidadiana* reported Prior's presence in Trinidad, was indignant at the illustration. He stated haughtily, 'in one [sketch], supposed to represent Frederick Street during

12 Melton Prior depicted Carnival in Frederick Street for the *Illustrated London News* in 1888.

the Carnival, the store of our esteemed fellow-colonist, Mr Arnold Knox, is transformed into a watch-making establishment'.

On the whole, the *Port of Spain Gazette* praised the Carnival: 'there was a greater prevalence of neat costumes and a better class of masks'. It complimented the dress of the '*Pierrots*' and mentioned also the familiar old women, and the Chinese, as well as representations of 'Coolies'. Dressed in red, there were 'devils in close fitting all-in-ones, with long tails', such as those shown in Prior's drawing. It also admired the depiction of the popular Chief Justice, Sir John Gorrie (or Papa Gorrie), and a band of Courtiers. Criticised were 'the shameless costumes in loose flowing night-gowns, all in white'. These were presumably *pisse-en-lit*. The newspaper seems to make a distinction between them and the 'men dressed as women and women dressed as men, *without masks*'. Particularly objectionable to the *Gazette* was the parading by men dressed as women through 'the whole City, from morning to night, repeating the same song, containing *doubles ententes* of the most obscene meaning, and dancing in the lewdest manner'. This practice may have had a social bias. The reporter described how in his 'presence, a small band of four of these, seeing a lady and her daughter at the window, sang an obscene distich of the most indecent character in the crudest words'. There was, he said, 'a burst of applause . . . amongst the bystanders – the confusion of these ladies may be imagined at being surprised and insulted in this brutal manner'.

Satirical and more overt insults in song were not exclusive to Trinidad. This can be demonstrated by comparison with Carnival in the French island of Martinique. Family connections between black creoles in Martinique and Trinidad have been emphasised. Songs and other cultural sentiments were shared between the two islands for much of the nineteenth century. Lafcadio Hearn, a most careful student of black-American culture in the late nineteenth century, witnessed the Carnival in St Pierre, Martinique in 1888. His detailed description allows exploration of similarities and differences between the two festivals.

In Martinique, the Carnival lasts from Shrove Monday to Ash Wednesday, and Hearn's observations were made on the afternoon and evening of Wednesday 15 February. There were two principal rival bands, the *Intrépides* and *Sans-souci* (or *Sans Souffrance* in another contemporary source). Hearn defined these bands as 'the great dancing societies'. They came towards each other from north and south along Grand Rue, indicating a likely territorial basis. Both were 'feminine associations' that had been 'established with a view to pleasure'. As with Trinidad, their rivalry seems to have led to 'scuffles'.

The bands usually sang satirical songs to creole airs – called *belairs*. Each group marched and danced, singing these songs to the accompaniment of drums, horns and possibly other instruments, together with the clapping of hands in chorus. By implication the chantwell provided the lead and mass voices the antiphon. While Hearn was listening to *Sans-souci* they broke into the latest song from France in vogue in the island. The musicians were all dressed as women or monks.

As in Trinidad, and elsewhere in the Caribbean, the principal masque of the multitude was of wire construction, painted white and 'having the form of an oval and regular human face'. Hearn noted 'they disguise the wearer absolutely, although they can be seen through perfectly well from within'. The predominant colours of the costumes were crimson and canary yellow.

The mock monks were dressed in Franciscan, Dominican or Penitent habits. Like the clergymen depicted in Trinidad in 1871, they satirised the attitude of the Church towards the Carnival and Carnival music.

There were few eccentricities or monsters and only a few vampire bats (a traditional costume not mentioned in Trinidad sources this early). The Congo band bore some parallels with the *nègre jardin* costumes, in that masquers were dressed in exact reproduction of clothing worn by workers on plantations. They were not stickfighters, however, and there was also a women's raiment in this class. The *Bébé* costume, or (*ti maumaille*), was worn by young girls in baby dress and described as 'really pretty'. They seem to have been less sexually overt than the school girls seen in Trinidad in the 1870s and 1880s. The *Ti Nègue gouos-sirop* (or little molasses negro), had a direct equivalent (*jab molasi*) as did the *Diable* (*jab*), but there appear to have been no bands of *Diablesses* in Trinidad Carnival. The latter represented the legend of the *lajables* who tempted men to follow her to their doom. This remains well known in several French-Creole speaking islands, including Trinidad.

At dusk in St Pierre, the masqueraders crowded into local ballrooms 'to dance strange tropical measures' that Hearn said, would 'become wilder and wilder' as the night progressed. The *Diable*, accompanied by his chorus, also made his final round of the unlighted streets, returning to his quarters only at the approach of midnight.

As well as collecting the music to three dance tunes, that were probably played at the grand balls where dancers wore fancy dress, masques, and other disguises, Hearn obtained the words and music for one example of each of two classes of Carnival song performed in Martinique.

Marie-Clémence he called a Carnival satire. He said that it had been composed not more than four years prior to 1890, when he published the words and music. Marie-Clémence was a seller of cheap cooked food. The song was sung to 'torment' her, although the embarrassment is not explained. Such derisive songs appear to be the *belairs* of the St Pierre Carnival newspaper report of 15 February 1888. Hearn noted that the composers and singers of these musical lampoons were the dancing societies. The lyrics were usually 'cruel satires' and the local meaning was 'unintelligible to those unacquainted with the incident inspiring the improvisation, of which the words are too often coarse or obscene, [and] whose burdens will be caught up and re-echoed through all the bourgs of the island'.

Loéma Tombe he described as a '*pillard*, or in creole *piyà*'. Loéma 'was a girl who lived near the Pont Bas and affected virtue'. The song was composed after 'it was learned that she received not one but many lovers'. The 'popular malicious custom' of performing this kind of song of insult may not have been confined to Carnival. Thus:

> Some person whom it is deemed justifiable and safe to annoy, may suddenly find himself followed in the street by a singing chorus of several hundred, all clapping hands and dancing or running in perfect time, so that all the bare feet strike the ground together. Or the *pillard-chorus* may even take up its position before the residence of the party disliked, and then proceed with its performance.

Hearn described an instance of the latter practice when the *Diable* and his chorus in their Carnival perambulations halted before a dwelling in the Rue Peysette and sang 'a piece of spite work' against someone living there. As with *Loéma Tombe*, the song was performed with a single voice (the *Diable*), improvising a line followed by the response of the chorus.[26]

On the scant evidence available, there appears to be a great similarity between the way in which Carnival songs were composed and sung in Martinique, and Trinidad. Thus the complaints against songs by the *Port of Spain Gazette* in 1888 mention a Carnival street song similar to those described by Hearn, and also a *pillard*-like song, performed by a small band in front of a mother and daughter at the window of their residence. The participation of rival bands run by women and devoted to dancing, recalls the Carnival in Trinidad of the late 1860s. Certain masques have also been shown to have been common in both islands. The circumstances of the two Carnivals, however, appear to have been very different.

Emancipation Day – Golden Jubilee celebrations

Descriptions of festivities during the Golden Jubilee of Emancipation augment understanding of the island's vernacular traditions.

According to *Public Opinion* (7 August), bands of music began parading through the streets of Arouca during the evening of 31 July. They serenaded the inhabitants throughout the night. Daybreak 'was heralded by the discharge of guns from several places'. Tolerance for the proceedings probably indicates music of 'gentility'.

On 1 August at Chatham (*Public Opinion*, 24 August), there was an evening 'ball in the school house which was kept up till the small hours'. Unfortunately, the type of music played is not identified. On the same evening at Mayaro, however (*Public Opinion*, 10 August), 'a Belle-air, or drum dance' was held from 7.00 p.m. in a tent where a banquet had taken place earlier in the day. The dancing lasted until 6.00 a.m. the next morning. A ball, of similar duration, was held the following day.

These events may be similar to an Emancipation Day 'Bel' air' at Arima attended by E. M. Encinas when he was a child. Organised by subscription, this was held in 'a large open timite-covered structure' with 'concrete palm leaves' enclosing the 'northern end'. There was a feast followed by dancing accompanied by 'tambourines'. The dances included 'the "pirouette," the quadrille, the "galleron," the snake dance, the pure unadulterated french curtsey, [and] the advance and retire of the French saloons'. The women were highly dressed and there was a Dowager Queen, King and Queen, Dauphin and Dauphine.[27]

Stickbands were not involved in this 'Bel' air', nor the Golden Jubilee celebrations. Black people with greater social mobility sustained the latter anniversary. Together with the white elite, the same group was to increase participation in Carnival as the century drew to a close. The character of the festival altered gradually in relation to their changing attitudes. A further component in this evolution was the cultural influence of the United States. This may have begun to increase among black people in Trinidad following the acceptance of high-class black-American jubilee and minstrel music among white inhabitants.

The visit of the Tennessee Jubilee Singers

Jubilee singing and blacks-in-blackface minstrelsy were highly significant in the spread of black-North-American culture in the late-nineteenth century. In the Caribbean the former style was introduced during two tours, respectively in 1888–9 and 1890–91, by the Tennessee Jubilee Singers.

Troupes such as this did not perform in the same way as the burlesques of 'plantation' music by white-in-blackface minstrels exemplified from the 1840s by the work of Dan Emmett and others. The Tennessee Jubilee Singers presented their music formally and included arrangements of black-North-American spirituals in the manner of the Fisk Jubilee Singers, that had become popular in the 1870s.

Mathilda S. Jones, or Sissieretta Jones, was the prima donna of the Tennessee company. From acclaim received during her first Caribbean tour she became known as Black Patti, in affinity with the famous Italian soprano Adelina Patti. The trip commenced on 2 August 1888, when the group left New York City by boat. There were three soloists, Mme Jones (soprano), Will H. Pierce (tenor), and Louis L. Brown (baritone). Two women (Hattie Brown, and Kate Johnson) provided a chorus singing Jubilee selections. There was also a quartette with operatic repertoire of whom two of the members were presumably Joseph G. Stevens, and John H. Woolford. Accompaniment was by a pianist (Professor A. K. La Rue).

The performers arrived at Kingston, Jamaica, on 10 August, and played their first engagements in that island. In the next three months, they worked their way south, giving highly popular concerts at each island they visited.

The Tennessee Jubilee Singers reached Port of Spain, Trinidad, on 30 November and 'gave their first performance ... the following evening'. José M. Bodu was full of praise for this '*troupe* of black artists from the United States'. They were, he said, 'different in every respect from the other musical combinations that had visited' the country. This seems to have assured their success among the white community.

The *Port of Spain Gazette* (5 December), also lauded them in a review of their first two concerts, especially the vocal ability of 'Madame JONES'. They were '*a new sensation*', with choruses of unexpected 'exhilarating and pleasing effect'. In these 'the happy expression of quaint, vigorous, original African feeling [was] control[l]ed, harmonised and refined under the powerful influences of civilised musical science'. Thus: 'In listening to and seeing the movements of the singers we find the spicy originality of negro-minstrelsy, made fit for the educated eyes and ears of the refined occupants of the drawing-room.'

These attitudes parallel the welcoming of 'refinement' and rejection of 'uncivilised' in Carnival. They were common among those who believed in the 'superiority' of white people (and European Christianity) and disdained the 'savagery' of Africa and other regions of the world. To counter these prejudices, black people of African descent developed two primary methods of behaviour (including performance). One, was an exaggerated 'cool, high style of self preservation'. The other was an equally exaggerated 'hot' rejection of the 'civilised' ideals of white elitists, communicated through dress, speech and action. Both can be viewed as forms of parody, although this was not always the intention of those who adopted these techniques.

The Tennessee Jubilee Singers were proponents of the former school and perceived as an antithesis of blackface minstrelsy. The latter, however, also reflected changing attitudes. Especially after the US Civil War, minstrelsy was shared between whites-in-blackface and blacks-in-blackface, both in some respects burlesques of each other. Black masqueraders dressed as blackface minstrels had become a feature of the Carnival by the 1890s, if not before. Known sometimes as 'comedians', this masque continues to this day.

The success of the Tennessee Jubilee Singers is significant in the light of these factors. Thus, the crowd gathered outside the Prince's Building where they performed were able to hear distinctly and 'concurred with the insiders in stamping them "very good"'. The *Port of Spain Gazette* believed this additional audience would 'no doubt [have] been of use as vocal advertisers of' the 'genuineness' of the troupe 'to their section of the Trinidad world'.[28]

Christmas

If vindication of exaggerated refinement can be seen in the acceptance of the Tennessee Jubilee Singers, the opposite was true regarding the action of the bands at Christmas. 'THE labour of years was undone' reported the *Gazette* (29 December). 'Night was made hideous with the shouts, obscene songs, and rioting of drunken revellers'. Thus: 'Save the wild glare of torches' it was as if Canboulay had returned. Several people 'were attacked in the streets and severely beaten with sticks'. The contrast with 'Christian civilisation' is drawn by the newspaper, which emphasised the feared 'barbarity' of the *diametres*.[29] These same contrasting 'ideals' representing 'euphony' and discord can be seen in the evolution of black-creole music in Trinidad.

1889 – Music and the vagabond bands

Excluding drum dances, the orchestration used to accompany other types of popular dancing in Trinidad is not readily discerned. A few clues are available, such as the report in 1882, which identified an increase in the playing of woodwind and string instruments among black creoles. Dance orchestras varied according to availability of musical instruments and those competent to play them. One influence was Venezuelan string band music. Across the Caribbean, percussion often included shac-shacs and a form of scraper (a notched surface scraped with a stick). The latter were sometimes called vira (probably from güira). These featured in a ball held in honour of the Commissioner for Tobago in January 1889:

> Dancing was kept up with great spirit. The musicians played in excellent time, but had evidently not studied their music by note, and many purely West Indian street airs were introduced. The instruments used were violins, a piccolo, a concertina, and a tin vessel scratched with a small iron rod, corresponding to the 'shack shack' of Trinidad and known in Barbados as a 'vira'. The arrangements otherwise were all that could be desired and the visitors were made to feel quite at home.

While this was Tobago, dances in outlying districts in Trinidad were also accompanied by musicians who played by ear. They used similar instruments. As Day had found in the late 1840s, black creoles in Port of Spain were the principal musicians running small formal dance orchestras. At large-scale events, the Police Band was the natural choice of the elite. This had been founded in 1870, but presumably did not employ black musicians during the early stage of its existence.

'Obscene songs' excepted, the music of Carnival bands in the late 1880s remains unreported. 'Rowdyism', however, continued as an issue. The *Port of Spain Gazette* (6 February 1889) drew attention to the forthcoming Carnival, noting 'that never before was Trinidad so over-run with open

violence and immorality, and with Obeahism and other secret abomi-
nations'. The culture of the vagabond bands still haunted the authorities.

No report of Carnival is available for 1889. In the same edition of the
Gazette, however, there is mention of another component in the evolution of
the festival's music, the *gayap* or work song. It noted that 'in bands of
sometimes more than a dozen called *gayapes*, African contractors help one
another in clearing contract land'. This term appears to have been used to
describe collective work, the song accompanying the work, and a gratuitous
feast given to those who freely helped in completing the task. The calypsonian Atilla the Hun saw in these procedures the origin of his style of
singing:

> Investigations have proven that it originated from the 'Gayap', a con-
> dition, vestiges of which can still be found in some of the remote dis-
> tricts, whereby a man would invite his neighbors to help in the prepar-
> ing of his lands for planting. On occasions when one man had more
> work than he could do, as he might have an extensive plot of land to
> cultivate, his friends would come around, and food and drink would be
> provided. These people would divide themselves into two groups, each
> trying to excel the other. The party doing the most work would then –
> led by their leader – sing to the less energetic party, ribald songs of
> derision and belittlement, foyening (reproaching is the nearest English
> equivalent I can find for this word) them for not having done as much
> work as the triumphant group.

The evolution of calypso is from a broader base of different kinds of
music. It is apparent, however, that collective call and response singing,
sometimes conducted competitively, was represented in a number of different vernacular musical traditions in Trinidad, as it was in the United
States.

Prevented from holding their drum dances, the 'vagabond' bands devised
new methods of musical recreation. *New Era*, on 13 September 1889, provides a particularly detailed description of these circumstances. Whether
the singing was by a chantwell and chorus is not explained:

> It is during bright moonlight, such as we have been favoured with
> during the past week, that the idle and dissolute enjoy their fullest
> fling. Seated on every door-step in certain localities, an assemblage
> may be seen of nymphs of the pavement and the male parasites who
> attach themselves to their fortunes. Guitars and concertinas are
> common, and on these instruments is played the accompaniment to the

lewd songs with which the vile wretches pollute the air. These parties are generally liberally provided with rum and as the fiery compound flies to their heads, the music (Heaven save the mark!) is suspended for the sake of a quarrel which, if it does not terminate in a free fight, is certain to be distinguished by the use of the most abominable language that the corrupt imagination can conjure up. Respectable passers-by are certain of molestation by these rowdies, who will keep up their quarrelling-concert until two or three in the morning, with a sublime disregard for the fact that an entire neighbourhood is being kept awake by their drunken antics. Another most objectionable practice is that bands of so-called musicians who make it a practice to go on moonlight nights to serenade(?) females of their acquaintance. The character of such females may be easily guessed at, and it is not difficult to imagine the class of music performed on such occasions. Fights, sometimes ending in the infliction of serious wounds, are the frequent outcome of such serenades and *al fresco* concerts, which should certainly not be tolerated after, say ten in the evening, an hour when most people are glad to be able to get to bed and rest after the labours of the day.

In 1885, the *Port of Spain Gazette* had identified 'the "Band" system' as one of 'secret societies or clubs, formed for the express purpose of open violence and gross immorality'. There were, however, other organisations of mutual help which did not include 'vagabond' elements. By the late 1880s, legislation had been passed to regulate these affiliations 'of popular origin', whose friendly-society function was praised by *New Era* on 8 November 1889. In addition to their promotion of 'thrift' and 'good fellowship' the newspaper described them as 'secret brotherhoods, with rituals and symbols resembling . . . those of the Masonic fraternity'. This was seen as a positive attribute when members 'met together in fraternal intercourse'. Of particular significance in relation to late-nineteenth-century Carnival bands, were 'banners which members carry on certain occasions of cere-mony, and the sashes and regalia with which they adorn themselves'. Nothing is known of the music of these organisations. An observation by old-time calypsonian Lord Executor may be pertinent. He recalled that before 1898 'the "more decent people" used to sing Martiniquian songs'.[30]

Stickney and Donovan's Great American Circus – balloon ascent and parachute descent

Lord Executor's observation is of great interest in that versions of a song about Stickney and Donovan's Great American Circus can be traced to Martinique and Trinidad. The lyrics concern the activities of 'Professor' Colby, whose stunt was to ascend in an hot air balloon and, on reaching a great height, make a parachute jump from the balloon basket.

Although *New Era* (8 November 1899) reported this Circus had arrived direct from New York, it is likely to have proceeded to Trinidad by staging performances island by island. This was a recognised pattern for performers of all sorts throughout the nineteenth century. Thus, Colby would have first presented his display in Martinique.

In the French island (presumably at St Pierre, on the Savannah, by the Fort), a wind squall disrupted his first attempt. On the second occasion Colby achieved his aim, dropping by parachute, landing in the sea, and being picked up by boat. An appropriate Carnival satirical song, entitled *Colby*, was composed. The chorus was:

Jusqu' Colby que lé badiné nous!	Even Colby is teasing us
Jusqu' Colby que lé badiné nous!	Even Colby is teasing us
Colby monté, Colby descende,	Colby goes up, Colby goes down,
Colby tombé dans d' l'eau!	Colby falls into the water
Colby monté, Colby descende,	Colby goes up, Colby goes down,
Colby tombé dans lan me!	Colby falls into the sea

Versions were recorded commercially by black migrants from Martinique in France during the 1930s and the song remains well known in the island.

Donovan's circus arrived in Trinidad on 4 November 1889. They set up on the patch of ground known as Shine's Pasture (now Victoria Square) in Port of Spain. Colby carried out his first aeronautical operation the following Thursday. As in Martinique, this was aborted, but on 11 November, the balloon reached a height of 500 feet, and there was a successful parachute jump. The exploit and song associated with it was recalled by Patrick Jones, in recorded reminiscences of past Carnival songs, made in 1956. His performance is directly related to the Martinique song about Colby's bravura.[31]

Further aspects of incorporation – Carnival 1890–1891

Colby is likely to have been sung at Shrovetide in Martinique and Trinidad in 1890. Atilla the Hun reports other songs that arrived from outside the island prior to 1890. He cites *L' Année Passée* from Martinique (the melody remained popular for over fifty years) and *Deedee* from Dominica. These stood alongside popular stickfighting songs from the 1870s and 1880s such as *Jour Ouvert Barre O'* (about confrontations between stickbands, or stickbands and the police), *Congo Bara* (about a prison turnkey), and *Joe Talmana* (about a stickfighter involved in conflict with 'Captain' Baker).[32]

Early in 1889, 'Captain' Baker was forced to relinquish his command, pending investigation for misuse of police funds. Later in the year the colonial authorities transferred him to Guyana. They brought Captain E. Fortescue (who was Inspector of Prisons in that colony) to Trinidad. The Carnival of 1890, therefore, was the first under Fortescue's control.

Presumably, he was determined to prove himself Baker's equal and there was great complaint at his harsh treatment of masquers (*New Era* 21 February). There had been determined 'interference' by the police with the 'amusements' of 'members of the upper class of society'. This appears to have been a clamp down on throwing 'bouquets of flowers, confitures, or flour' by this section of the community.

An Ordinance was passed just before the Carnival in the following year (no 2 of 1891) that made this diversion illegal. The police were successful in continuing their Carnival repression. On the final day of the festival the *Port of Spain Gazette* (10 February 1891) commented on the 'greater control of the Police over the mob than in previous years' and observed that the Carnival had been 'the quietest and least "patronized" on record'. It was shocked, however, that the police continued to permit 'certain public indecencies to go unchecked, such as the masquerading in men's clothes of many low women, when they came down so heavily on merely numerical transgression of the law'.

Court reports in the same edition give some indication of the stringent view taken by the police. Four members of a large band, two in costume, all of whom were carrying sticks, were apprehended on the morning of Carnival Monday. Four disguised masquers who had taken part in a dancing procession numbering thirteen persons were also arraigned. On the Tuesday a similar group were seen in procession in Charlotte Street. Five of them were arrested. 'They had "shack-shacks" and were disguised', the

police officer told the court. The crime of this band was 'they were ...
troubling the public and it was against the Proclamation'.

There was only one authority perceived by the under-privileged as being
on their side. This was the Chief Justice, Sir John Gorrie. On 13 February
the *Gazette* noted 'during the Carnival a band paraded singing "We are
Gorrie men"'. This resulted from a rumour that Gorrie had remitted fines
and freed those imprisoned for Carnival offences. Although this was not the
case, faith in Gorrie as a liberal in a repressive society was signalled by the
chorus of a song in French Creole noted in translation:

> Stollmeyer open the door,
> What a good man Sir John Gorrie is!
> What a good papa!
> He let us go free,
> Lewis is a bad man.

Further evidence of the mix of different vernacular traditions in Trinidad is a court case reported on 17 February. This involved crowds of people
assembling in Woodford Street, New Town, to see 'Angel Soucouyans'.
Soucouyan is a legendary male or female devil who has the ability to peel off
its skin and fly. It appears between midnight and dawn as a great ball of fire,
and sucks the blood of its selected victim. Versions of the legend are well
known in the French-speaking Caribbean. In 1891, a witness told the court
'he didn't know where [the manifestations] "deviated" from'. He said,
however, 'the spirits were there singing old time slave plantation songs.
They sung sweetly. He had told persons who came to hear the songs to
"desert" from there. The spirits stopped singing when the footsteps of the
police were heard approaching.' By implication, the sweetly-sung 'old time
slave plantation songs' came from North American repertoire sold as sheet
music. An example of the latter is '"Popular Music": SONGS as sung by the
Tennessee Jubilee Singers taken over from the manager and offered at
cheap price' advertised in the *Port of Spain Gazette* in January 1889, after
the departure of that troupe.[33]

The Arouca riot – Easter 1891

The evolution of black-creole culture in Trinidad is particularly evident in
the 'riot' which took place at the village of Arouca on Easter Monday and
Tuesday (30 and 31 March) 1891.

An application was made to the police by one Marquis to hold a drum dance on Easter Monday. Organisations representing peoples of both Yoruba and Congo descent were allowed to hold similar dances but Marquis was refused. This decision was made on grounds of 'previous misbehaviour of the people of Arouca over the same sort of thing in the district'. Those associated with Marquis were said not to have been 'members of any friendly society' but had created disturbances during Carnival and 'at the fête of a friendly society'. In short, they were classified by the police as rogues and vagabonds (or *diametres*).

This group decided, notwithstanding, to hold their drum dance or '*bamboula*' in the yard of Charles Odahou on Easter Monday. The participants were described subsequently as members of the 'two notorious bands' of Arouca. They were 'composed not only of the riff-raff of the creole population but also of Barbadians ... of the worst type'. The dance, which involved drinking and feasting as well as drumming, appears to have lasted for most of the day before the police approached the yard during late afternoon to quell activities. They encountered fifty to a hundred people drinking, gambling, and 'dancing in a most disorderly manner'. Singing and dancing was inside a 'tent' (almost certainly a temporary folk structure of bamboo, covered with palm fronds). The music was provided by chac-chacs and two drums. Fighting sticks were also to hand.

The police, having ascertained there were people present who had received previous convictions (and thereby were breaking the law), entered and stopped proceedings. The drums were confiscated and the police left without objection. As they went down the street, however, one of the stickmen, Henry Joseph, whose fighting name was 'Grammar', called out 'D–d if the Arima boys they would never allow the drums to be taken away' and another, John Jacob, whose fighting name was 'Simeron', shouted 'Sergeant, it is not right for you to take away our drums'. A fight ensued in which Sergeant Urquhart was injured and his helmet taken as a trophy. The bands retrieved their drums and went away to continue drumming and dancing into the night and early morning.

Between 8.00 and 9.00. on the same Tuesday morning, the principal stickmen came down the road and stopped in front of the police station. They parried their sticks, sang '*diamete* songs', and shouted 'sortee, sortee, come out and we will give you something', and 'if you come out today we will give your flesh to the birds'. This bravado lasted fifteen minutes, after which they retired to the yard of 'Simeron' and set themselves up with bottles and stones pending an expected fight.

Police reinforcements were dispatched from Port of Spain and, after their arrival, two parties were sent out '*unarmed*' to look for the stickmen. In the ensuing court case, one witness reported that the police carried long sticks (which seems likely), but this evidence was rejected. The party led by Superintendent Sergeant Fraser encountered the band at 'Simeron's' yard and were routed. Fraser was knocked to the ground and his blood said to have been drunk by 'Bulbul Tigre' (one of three fighting names adopted by Arthur Augustin). Fraser, however, escaped with his life.

Further reinforcements arrived from Port of Spain and, by 14 April, thirty-one of those believed to have taken part in the 'riot' had been arrested. Six more were still at large, including Simeron, who fled to Venezuela and was never caught. Most of the other principal stickmen received prison sentences:

Baboul/Bulbul Tigre/Nicho	Arthur Augustin	3 years
Bengy Moomoo	Benjamin Jacob	18 months
Codrington	Joseph Carrington	3 years
Grammar	Henry Joseph	3 years
Magamoutch	Albert Joseph	3 years
Nedzie	Nelsie John	3 years
Pappeto	Johnson Augustus/	
	Johnson Augustin	18 months
Ramsay	Augustus James	18 months
Soucatau/Soucantan	Henry Jacob	18 months

As well as high-lighting the regulations for drum dances – the police apparently received 'dozens of' applications 'by the week' from legitimate organisations – accounts of this 'riot' illuminate both the organisational context of drum dancing, such as its location and instrumentation, and the 'Dionysian aesthetic' of the *jamettes*. For example, 'Codrington' shouted to his compatriots when the drums were seized 'Bulbul tigre, Ramsay de feu', the 'reigning' names of these two stickmen; names adopted as a result of winning stickfighting contests. The *jamettes* were expressing 'solidarity without authority'. They represented revolt, obscenity (the flouting of taboos), fearlessness, and rejection (both a focus for defiance, and its introspective opposite). Underlying these was an unstated but assumed association with African magic, the devil and devil power, and 'blackness'. Thus, Anastasia Coombs recalled in 1951 that several of these men sang when brought handcuffed from Port of Spain to Arima to stand their trial:

An ou day se way	Let us unlock
An ou day se way	Let us unlock
Sonnie Broken	Sonnie Broken
Denou pou day ve way	Devil to go back
Ce mois tay connait	It's I who knew
Battaile sala takey way rein	This fight would happen
Mois say pois bouttè coul la mois	I can take the end of my cutlass
Pou la chan la via Sonnie Bo.[34]	For the chance of Sonny Bo's life

Sonnie Broken or Sonny Bo is probably another name for one of the stick-fighters and the last line calls for a chance to save his life.

The musical aesthetic of the stickmen incorporated pugilistic and self-reflective themes and probably took the name *kalenda* in this period. As the end of the century drew near, these sentiments were to fuse with other elements to form a new kind of Carnival vocal music that was first documented at the turn of the century as '*calipso*'.

Aspects of music and Carnival – 1891–1896

One month after the Arouca 'riot' a second visit was made to Trinidad by a revived Tennessee Jubilee Singers. Black Patti remained their principal singer. The new party appears to have been formed in March 1890 and again began its Caribbean tour in Jamaica. Newspapers show it stayed in Trinidad from the beginning of May 1891 until at least mid-June, undertaking popular presentations, including a Sacred Concert at the Wesleyan Chapel, Hanover Street.

Another outside influence on Trinidad music came from Venezuela. This is epitomised by the popularity of mainland dances, notably the *paseo* (a promenade) and *castilian* (a fast waltz). The latter was also known as a Spanish Waltz. A collection of them composed for the piano by J. Coggins, a Trinidad creole, was published locally in late 1891. One was entitled *Para Siempre Tuya Carnaval*. Such dance music would have been played by the Police Band when they provided music for a Venezuelan Ball held at the Prince's Building early in December 1891. Organised by the Venezuelan consul the ball was in favour of the elite (the Governor attended for part of the evening). Venezuelan dance rhythms and string bands were taken up by a cross-section of the populace, Carnival revellers included. The latter is apparent in an evocative recall of the festival by Dr George H. Masson. He remembered:

> The Carnival of the old days was a very different affair from that of to-day. The rival bands of men and women, the fights, the *dévergondage* of the men, the *abandonnement* of the women, the din, the heat, the choking dust, made a tour of the streets, with a horse between the shafts, an adventure; and yet, withal, there still remain lingering memories of the *paseos*, the music, the strings – guitars, bandols, quatros and violins, the basses and imposing double basses, the shrieking clarionets, the saucy piccolos, the soothing flutes, the noisy shak-shaks, the wonderful *tempo* of the *tout-ensemble*! A crop of quinsy, coughs and colds, an epidemic of lost voices, and a sudden rise in the attendance at the Tuberculosis Dispensary invariably followed the dusty passage of King Carnival: but what of that? It was part of the price the devotees of *Mon Seigneur* were prepared to pay for their fun and, after all, Masquerade would not come back again for a whole year. *Mais, quand même Papaillot*, the dust, *la poussiére!* Well, *que voulez-vous? C'est la volonté*; and is not the morrow of Mardi Gras, les Cendres? *Certes*, ashes to ashes ... Yes ... and dust to dust!

Unfortunately, Masson says nothing of Carnival songs but a tirade by Eugene Chalamelle shows scandal remained in the repertoire. He described the devastating effect of a derogatory Carnival lyric about a young woman (Miss P.) which, he alleged, was perpetrated in spiteful revenge by two young men. He warned that if 'the domestic affairs of respectable families ... leak and reach the ever expectant ... gossiper who hawks the "latest news" with the rapidity of lightning' then they are 'certain of becoming the subject of a "Carnival song" and thus the private doings of a decent household are made a matter for scandal among the lewd community'.

There were other subjects for Carnival verses. One that would have been commemorated first during the 1892 Carnival was the celebrated trial of Louis Camille for the murder of John Eligon (which took place in 1891).

Another song that seems to date from the early 1890s is *Capitan Gabar bas mois un passay supplay*:

Capitan Gabar bas mois un passay supplay	Captain Gabar give me a passage, please
Capitan Gabar bas mois un passay supplay	Captain Gabar give me a passage, please
Bas mois un passay just La Brea	Give me a passage to La Brea
Poui montrer yo ki la roi mois yay	To show them that I am a king

Transportation to La Brea would have been in a lighter.

The repeat of the first two lines and their two line resolution are in the form of the earliest popular English-language calypso *Governor Jerningham*, adopted by the majority of masqueraders during the Carnival of 1899.[35]

The Carnival of 1892 saw the first regulations to control Pierrots. Initially, they were banned from the streets. Interestingly, the *Port of Spain Gazette* (23 February) could not understand why ' "Pierrots" or masquers wearing a rich and ornamental dress' had been singled out. It believed them to be 'among the least objectionable of the masquers' in relation to 'indecent and unbecoming disguises'. After representations, the Governor decided to allow Pierrots on the condition each applied to the police for a permit, and furnished 'two sureties of good conduct'. This became a permanent annual requirement.

Pierrots still retained something of their previous prestige, although they seem to have separated from the stickbands. They could be found in every district 'but only a few since they had to master the "Universal Spelling Book" and a little history, in case called upon to give an exhibition of knowledge'. Two Pierrots not satisfied in verbal exchanges still resorted to physical conflict.

Complaining again of 'unbecoming disguises' the *Port of Spain Gazette* (1 March) believed there were fewer participants in 1892. It considered the most striking representation was 'the masquer who walked about the streets inside a large square box with the "People's Bank" in large printed characters outside and a few of the Munchausen tales credited to the bankrupt scheme by Sir John Gorrie'. This referred to an effort by Gorrie to establish a bank for the poor which failed in ignominy and led to his downfall.[36]

Bands of stickmen remained active, although their presence in Carnival was rigorously put down. A confrontation took place in Upper Prince and Charlotte Streets, Port of Spain, early in December 1891. This battle was between 'Canelle' (the English-speaking band) led by 'Gooty' and 'Typean' (a French-speaking band) led by 'Eli'. 'One Man' is another fighting name mentioned in the newspaper report. This may have been 'One Man Biscoe', whose exploits were commemorated in song. Biscoe was remembered in 1919 as a 'notable stick fighter' and in the 1950s as 'the greatest terror in Canboulay'. He was an exponent of Bajan stick (a similar sport to stick-fighting *kalenda*, from the English-speaking island of Barbados). This fact, and his membership of the 'Freegrammars' (in which he was recalled as having been its 'second king') suggests he was one of the many black migrants drawn to Trinidad from Barbados.

Court proceedings in newspapers hardly ever distinguished stickfighting names, or the origin of the stickfighters. Following Carnival in 1893, case reports in the *Port of Spain Gazette* classify apprehended stickmen as '*negre-jardins*', indicating their stylised costumes, and gave their proper names.

Other 1893 Carnival court cases concerned the new regulations for Pierrots. They were mostly for fighting, but one also held a permit in an assumed name. Another, in San Fernando, was found to have obtained a permit unbeknown to the police when he was arrested. One, convicted for being drunk and disorderly, appeared before the bar in costume. There were also cases involving musical instruments, such as the young lad who blew a bottle after ten o'clock at night on Shrove Sunday, or the man who shook his 'chac-chac' on Shrove Tuesday (14 February) after seven o'clock, though whether at night or in the morning is unclear.

Among prosecutions concerning women dressed in men's clothing was one where two women were charged with 'indecent behaviour' going down the street 'singing Ta-ra-ra-boom-de-ay which they accompanied by indecent gestures'. Their lawyer argued successfully 'that the song mentioned was by no means indecent, and was one which had often been sung in his drawing room'.

These cases indicate that police enforcement of Carnival legislation was gradually altering the shape of the festival. The *Gazette*, however, retained its moral antagonism. It called the season 'one of those relics of mediaeval barbarism, which should not have been permitted to exist under the enlightenment of the nineteenth century'. Once more it objected to 'the vulgar posturings and vile songs of the disguised rabble' and to the drums and fifes which accompanied some bands. Drums appear to have been allowed despite the ban. The newspaper hoped 'that the time' would not be 'far distant when the Carnival will be a thing of the past'. In contrast, the *Daily News* (15 February) evinced a revival among upper class masquers of 'the pre-1838 tradition of house-to-house visiting, with practical jokes and music'.[37]

While white-in-blackface minstrelsy has been mentioned, the international popularity of this style among white people bears repetition. The success in New York in 1846 of the Christy Minstrels was still significant in San Fernando in 1884. A 'Grand Christy Minstrel Performance' was staged there on 16 February. The local inhabitants who blacked-up on such occasions were almost certainly amateurs who had learnt the repertoire from printed sheet music and songsters produced in the United States.

The compositions of Stephen C. Foster were mainstays of the original Christy organisation. His *Poor Old Joe* was performed by a local amateur troupe who put on a 'Musical Entertainment' at the Prince's Building on Shrove Saturday, 11 February 1893. The *Port of Spain Gazette* (14 February) shows the troupe comprised two 'corner' men, two 'bones' men, two 'tambos' and an 'interlocutor' in regular US minstrel-show formation. Of extra interest is the music played by 'Mr Coggins' string orchestra' (Mr Bradfield, pianist) which included 'a pretty Spanish Waltz'. Both US and Venezuelan musical influence in Trinidad are demonstrated by this event.

String bands and minstrelsy were soon to be documented authoritatively in Carnival reports, the latter as early as 1894. In an action for premature masquing: 'a well-dressed black young man ... was prosecuted ... for appearing in disguise in Duke street'. He had dressed as a 'Christy Minstrel' and 'looked like an old man'. Unfortunately, the *Gazette*'s report (20 January) does not confirm that minstrel songs were performed but 'complaints from respectable residents' in the street suggest this was the case.

In the same edition, the editor renewed his campaign against the 'practices' in Carnival 'against which the better-thinking people have taken up arms'. These he identified as 'disgusting gestures, bad songs, women wearing men's clothes and *vice versa*'. This was continued two days later with another attack on 'men going about at nights dressed in women's clothes and *vice versa*'.

The administration took heed and agreed to publish an additional Carnival notice subsequent to their first, printed in the *Trinidad Royal Gazette* on 10 January). The former would be to prohibit 'the disgusting spectacle of women appearing in the streets as "pisse-en-lit"'. According to Chalamelle, who called it Pisanee, this was 'a disguise in which persons of both sexes were permitted to parade in the street in women's chemises or under-garments'. This class of masque, therefore, seems not to have covered all eventualities, for the *Port of Spain Gazette* commented on 23 January that it was 'to be regretted that the Government did not go a step further and prohibit women being dressed in men's clothes and *vice versa*'.

The full notice was published in the newspaper on 25 January and, although 'men dressing as women and women as men' were identified, only those found guilty of indecent behaviour were liable to penalty. From 1895, all transvestite dressing was prohibited.

Just before Carnival in 1894, members of the 'Typin' stickband appear to have been 'barring' people in Charlotte Street when five of them were arrested. All were classified as members of the '*diametre* class'. The band's leader was named as Emmanuel Dardian(e). Another of those arraigned was Abraham Ravin ('*alias* Shortest') who, on this evidence, took part in the clash between 'Canelle' and 'Typean' in December 1891.

Stickmen dressed as '*negres jardiniers*' also featured in a court case on the second day of Carnival. On Shrove Monday (5 February), two Pierrots were charged with 'being armed with a weapon with intent to commit a felony'. One of them, named Watson, appeared in court 'gaudily dressed, plumed, and accompanied by a tinkling of bells'. His crime was to hold in his left hand the traditional Pierrot's whip, and in his right a loaded stick, ready to fight his opponent.

The *Port of Spain Gazette* reported little else on the Carnival for 1894. During the season, however, it printed an interesting advertisement. This was 'The "Creole Pharmacy" Paseo', with lyrics to a song (in *paseo* rhythm) praising this establishment. The legend reads that the music, by Mr Albert Coggins, would be 'given away gratis to cash purchasers at the CREOLE PHARMACY' and is another demonstration of Venezuelan musical styles being absorbed into the cultural pool of Trinidad music.[38]

At Christmas 1894, stickmen in *nègre jardin* costumes were again on the streets in Port of Spain. They paraded and danced to drumming, once more avoiding restrictions imposed by the Carnival proclamation. On 27 December *Public Opinion* asked 'how is the moral advancement of mankind served by overgrown children parading in silly disguises and rendering day and night hideous by untuneful music'.

Slowly, zeal for Victorian ideals of 'Christian civilisation' apparently had an effect on Carnival. By 1895, in the wake of legislation, *diametre* elements began to withdraw from the event. This retreat, however, seems rather to

(a)

(b)

13 Trinidad Carnival music incorporated black Jubilee songs from North America, as well as sharing French-Creole songs from Martinique. *Colby* (popular in both islands in 1890) was recorded by Martiniquians in Paris in 1937.

have been a truce, probably occasioned by other social circumstances as much as by legal enforcement. Potential for violence remained, as is shown by a flair-up between masquers and the authorities at Cedros during Carnival that year, which is known as the Cedros Riot

The police seem to have been heavy-handed in overseeing the festival in this area of South Trinidad. On Shrove Monday masquers 'amusing themselves' were 'prevented [from] playing either on the road or in the yards'. Permission was sought from the Magistrate, 'but it was refused'. Thus, 'the beating of any drum was disallowed' and a woman was arrested 'for singing on the street'.

This challenge to their regular Carnival activities determined villagers 'to play on the street' on Shrove Tuesday. A correspondent in the *Port of Spain Gazette* (2 March), reported how masqueraders had paraded on the road between 'Fullarton and Bonas without making any row' but two 'Kings' of their Carnival bands had been arrested. 'At Bonas village', he went on, 'the police stopped them again, and there the riot began'. Police were attacked with sticks. The violence was quelled after remonstrations. Masqueraders were allowed on the streets on surety of quietude. Some 'rioters' were arrested on Ash Wednesday!

Despite tumult, negotiation had eventually been allowed by the police. The arrest of law breakers, however, maintained police authority. This further signals the changing official attitude towards Carnival in the mid-1890s, which was marked by a greater show of tolerance than in the days of 'Captain' Baker. Cedros was the exception in 1895. In 'Tacarigua, Arima and intervening districts' and in San Fernando there were quiet Carnivals. In Port of Spain, on 27 February, the *Gazette* observed how 'maskers' had been 'fewer in number and in many instances better and certainly more decently dressed than in former years'.

In addition to *pisse-en-lit*, the Carnival proclamation had finally prohibited men dressed as women and women as men and 'indecent behaviour in any street'. These were the last characteristics of the 'Jamette Carnival' to be brought under official control in the nineteenth century. At the same time, the 'Social Unions' that were to be a feature of the more mutually accepted Carnivals of the early 1900s began to appear in the celebrations.

In 1900, the White Rose Social Union, pre-eminent band of this type, advertised on its banner that it had been founded in 1895. If not 'friendly societies', this and similar fancy bands appear to have adopted the regalia and elected hierarchy of such organisations. In turn, of course, the voting for Kings, Queens and others in a retinue of European nomenclature can be traced to dancing societies in the slavery period. For black masquers in a world turned upside down these served to satirise the symbols of European power as well as to establish an African-American authority over them. Modified by the circumstances of creole culture, a pattern of past African hierarchies in masquerade and other traditions was maintained.

Lead singers (chantrels or chantwells) at the head of these Social Unions, responded to the choruses of the members as they paraded competitively in Carnival. In line with band hierarchy the songsters also adopted 'powerful' names as their sobriquets.

White Rose had apparently been based on a military format but changed their disguises to represent the English court. They absorbed popular late-nineteenth-century masques such as 'school girls'. Despite rivalry with others of their ilk they were different from the stickbands; their membership being mainly store clerks and similar socially mobile black creoles. String bands provided musical accompaniment.

A well-established band of the military type from which White Rose evolved was the Venezuelan army, who were still parading in 1895. The *Daily News* (27 February) reported how this band 'fought battles "with wooden swords and bamboo rifles and the General delivered patriotic speeches in the Spanish tongue to the victorious army"'.

It is possible that the Cedros 'riot' was sparked by what was remembered, by Joseph Clarke and Anthony, as a concerted effort to stamp out drumming (and, therefore, drum dances and stickfighting bouts). They recalled this happened in about 1895. 'Bamboo beating' was adopted as a substitute, especially by stickfighters. At this time, it seems these sets of tuned bamboo tubes (beaten rhythmically against the ground) were used to accompany activities in yards rather than in Carnival street parades. They were known as tamboo bamboo (sometimes bamboo tamboo) and may have been adopted from Venezuela, where a similar consort of bamboo stamping tubes are called *quitiplas*.

Changes in Carnival, represented symbolically by the gradual ascent of fancy bands and decline in street activity by stickbands, are demonstrated admirably by the Carnival of 1896. While a few stickmen were apprehended by the police, and four men were arrested for wearing women's clothes, the *Port of Spain Gazette* was, for once, well pleased with the festival.

From its comments on Ash Wednesday (19 February), this was due to self-satisfaction in that 'one of the pleasant features was the number from the upper classes who joined in'. Many of these masqueraders were 'young men' who 'drove about town in cabs clad in elegant costumes'. There was also a wheelmen's parade and competition by fancily costumed cyclists.

The *Gazette* was pleased to mention the usual disguises of animals, ballet girls, clowns, obeah men and pages, and to comment that 'all the guitars in town seemed to be in use and there was lots of music'. The latter included a successful Fancy Dress Ball on Shrove Monday in which 'excellent music was discoursed by the Band of Mr Coggins'. His services were required because the police band could not 'be spared from duty during the Carnival'.[39]

By 1896, all the elements were in place representing the first phase of incorporating Carnival into the mainstream of Trinidad society. Legislation and its enforcement by the police had reduced the *diametre* element to a rump of its 1881 pre-eminence. Canboulay had been stopped, bands of more than ten persons carrying sticks were prohibited, pierrots were obliged to obtain police licences, *pisse-en-lit* and transvestism were banned, as were obscene words and actions. Roads were paved and refuse (including bottles) was collected municipally – thereby depriving stickbands of sources of ammunition. At the same time, the elite began to demonstrate openly their participation in the festival, for example holding grand balls and masquerading in carriages driven through the streets. Bands representing socially mobile black creoles began parading in greater number than before. Likewise, this signalled a difference in musical values, with more genteel string bands taking the place of the drum that had also been banned in parades.[40]

It should not be assumed that this was a one-sided movement towards making the Carnival more acceptable to all sections of the community. There appears to have been a spirit of compromise among both the *diametre* and the elite that smoothed the path of transition. In essence, a mutual admiration developed between all sectors of society, the reasons for which are not easily distinguished. Carnival, hitherto despised by many in the hierarchy, suddenly became the ground on which it was possible to share values. This change in attitude was reciprocated by those who had expressed diametrically opposed representations designed to shock those with power into recognising those to whom power was denied. How these changes affected Carnival music will be examined in the next chapter.

4

'Iron Duke In The Land': banners, bands and music, 1897–1920

Carnival and the development of calypso – 1897–1920

The amalgam of traditional music and celebration represented in Carnival at the turn of the nineteenth century stemmed from many different social institutions. Slave dancing societies, with elected kings, queens and others, are a principal starting point for this evolution. There were subscription or bouquet balls, at which the king and queen of the evening wore a nosegay. Participants dressed in their best clothes, and both creole and African dances were performed. Similar practices continued after the ending of Apprenticeship, especially at *belair* drum dances. The structure of these organisations appears to have been founded in equivalent African and European traditions.

Carnival bands also had their kings, queens and other notables, whether depicting historical personalities and events, or denoting the prowess of stickfighting champions and the fidelity of their followers. In these, African and European elements also coalesced, as did cultural influences from the Orient and Latin America.

While the most persistent exchange of ideas was between African-American and European-American traditions, these extra influences sometimes featured in Carnival descriptions published during the nineteenth century. For example, in the 1840s 'wild Indians', or 'Indians of South America', were played by Spanish-speaking peons who had migrated from Venezuela. Similar influences apparent in the 1870s and 1880s were the '*bourrique*' and 'Venezuelan may-pole dancers'. By 1879, other migrant groups represented in Carnival included the Chinese, and bands depicting East-Indian 'Hosé'.

This pattern confirms the view that by the 1860s folk culture in Trinidad comprised four main strands. First were ex-slaves and their children (subdivided into French and English plantation traditions). Second were descendants of non-slaves of African and mixed ancestry. The third group was of free Africans. The final group comprised Spanish-speaking peons, usually of Native American and African genealogy. The principal language of all four was French Creole. Less ready to merge were migrants from China, Portugal and the Indian sub-continent. Separation of the latter resulted from coercion.

The British administration did not preside over a united colonial elite. There were continuing antagonisms between the French landed gentry, British settlers and officialdom. There was also competition between Roman Catholic and Protestant Christianity. The law, churches, schools, manners and customs of the elite, were all institutions to which folk culture had to adjust in order to survive. During the last quarter of the century the *diametre* formed themselves into self-perpetuating units. Such *bandes*, like plantation slaves before them, were divided into English-Creole- and French-Creole-speaking groups. In the 1870s, the English Creoles were principally migrants from Barbados who had come to Trinidad in search of work. While song lyrics throughout the nineteenth century were usually composed in French Creole, a few were performed in English.

The association of drum dances with particular types of song, most notably *belairs*, is apparent. This may apply to 'calypso' if Abbé Massé's 1882 description of a dance with this name can be relied upon.

Caliso, or *cariso*, the precursor of the twentieth-century song form known as calypso, was remembered to have been accompanied by goatskin drum and shac-shacs. Lord Executor (doyen of old-time calypsonians) also recalled that it was usual for the singer and his audience to dance during a performance. This is a positive link with Massé's 'calypso' dance. *Caliso* was sung in French Creole and was popular among 'the lower levels of Trinidad society'. It incorporated songs from other French-Creole-speaking islands in the Caribbean.

Whatever the provenance of the song and social status of its performer, *caliso* would have been affected by the legislation controlling drum dances. This, together with the banning of the drum in Carnival parades, slowly altered the culture of the *diametres*. The change was not without violent confrontations. Of those charged initially with participation in the Arouca riot in 1891, one was an East Indian known as Chinavaz, and another a 'Spanish boy' called Esperanza Gomez. Others were of French Creole ancestry, or had migrated from Barbados. This again demonstrates the mixing of cultural influences taking place in Trinidad. In addition, all the Creoles who were sentenced had stickfighting monikers. The latter were still remembered in the 1950s. They parallel the names adopted by chant-wells for Carnival performances. Alongside their given names, songsters sometimes had a pseudonym for singing and another for stickfighting. This attitude towards titles may date from slavery, when African names were altered to denote European ownership, or 'conversion' to Christianity. Some black people may well have viewed these changes as an additional form of masquerade in their relationship with white inhabitants.

By the mid 1890s, especially among socially mobile black creoles, licensed drum dances gave way to dancing to the accompaniment of string bands. In the same period, tamboo bamboo accompaniment was introduced for stick-fighting bouts among the *diametre*. These distinctions were not exclusive: 'gentlemen' stickfighters continued to participate in the sport, and string band music had widespread appeal.

Carnival bands adopted and adapted folk structures used for drum dances and rituals that became known as 'tents'. There are reports of vernacular constructions built for similar purposes in other islands in the Caribbean. Originally, these were temporary shelters made of bamboo and covered with palm fronds. They housed the drummers. This confirms the diversity of religious and secular traditions that came together in Trinidad Carnival celebrations.[1] They are especially evident in the organisation and activities of Fancy Bands. These dominated the turn-of-the-century Carnivals and were responsible for the fashion for singing 'calipsos' in English.

The true name of the Lord Executor was Philip Garcia. He remembered that the first 'tent' run by one of these bands 'was established on Rose Hill (east of the Dry River) by the "Rose Hillians"' and that 'Iere was a "Cobo-town" ... band whose meeting place was under a coconut tree next to the Fish Market'. Charles Jones, whose singing name was the Duke of Albany, described these constructions. They were:

> Built of bamboo, with coconut palms for a roof, lovely lace curtains, with ribbons to hold them in place and in the centre of the Tent, on a table set there for that purpose, a lovely bowl of Roses or other

Flowers. For seats there were benches made of bamboo set around the Tent or a few chairs. There were no electric lights. In place of that, lamps made of tin or large bottles called Flambeaux were placed all around the tent, giving a lovely soft glow to the surroundings.

In line with their ancestry from ritual structures, the area for performance appears to have been a circle in the centre with musicians on one side of the ring. Alternatively, Clarke and Anthony recalled that tents 'had a stage with chairs around, just as you have [in] the theatre, with the front row of chairs, and benches for the members to sit'. Some nineteenth-century drum dances were arranged with a raised platform for the musicians and king and queen of the dance.

The elected kings and queens of Fancy Bands were crowned at pre-Carnival ceremonies. Members paid contributions which went towards making costumes and other activities. Further financial support sometimes came from the French Creole elite. Much to the disgust of the pro-English anti-Carnival lobby and the police, they had earlier financed and otherwise aided stickbands. Commercial interests were another source of sponsorship for these masquerade groups.

Six to three weeks before the Carnival, depending on the date of Shrovetide, 'practices' were held by each band two or three times a week. Tents provided shelters for members. They met there to learn 'their songs or to discuss all and sundry, the affairs of the band'. The king and queen, together with the band's chantwell and musicians, would sit at one side of the ring, or on the stage. Songs were composed by the chantwell, and generally had topical themes. The chantwell sang the lead and the chorus was provided by women members of the band. Instrumental accompaniment was by an augmented string ensemble that usually included clarinet, flute, string bass, *cuatro* (a small four-string guitar), guitar and violin. Throughout the season, songsters would visit the tents of each other's band, assembling one night at one location, a second at another, and so on. They would compete against one another in song and in a group perform *picongs* or 'war'. These were duels in song in the manner of verbal contests between pierrots and others. In turn, singers would improvise 'stanzas in glorification of themselves and disparagement of their rivals'.

Sometimes the coronation of a band's king and queen took place several days before Carnival and sometimes it was held at midnight on *Dimanche Swa* (or Carnival Sunday evening). Otherwise, or following the coronation, 'Dame Lorraine' would be celebrated. This was a bawdy folk play with many different characters, overseen by *Met lekol* (Schoolmaster). Participants wore 'vulgar' costumes and sang and danced to string band accompaniment.

At *Jour Ouvert* (6.00 a.m., in accordance with the Carnival proclamation), individuals dressed in 'disreputable' clothes would participate in Old Masque (Ol' Mas'). It is likely elements of this activity were originally in honour of ancestors. Later in the day, bands would don more respectable costumes. They competed against similarly dressed units with the chantwells of each band challenging one another in song when they met on the streets. Full costume was reserved for parades on Carnival Tuesday (*Mardi Gras*). Some bands paraded with string band accompaniment.

It would be wrong to assume this pattern was fully established by 1897, or rather there is insufficient evidence to make a definitive judgement. Despite the inadequacy of contemporary reports, however, an analysis of Carnival accounts from 1897 to 1920, supports the recollections of old-time calypsonians and others.

Lord Executor said that the first full-scale experiments in which *caliso* lyrics were sung, part in French Creole and part in English, were in 1898. The initiator of the trend was 'Charlie "Don Don"'.

He recalled two other songsters with reputations for spearheading the movement to sing calypso in English. These were Henry Forbes, known for this pioneering as Inventor (later Senior Inventor), and Norman le Blanc, known as Persecutor (later Richard Coeur de Leon).

The terms used for Carnival songs in this period are difficult to distinguish. Most were composed using melodies in minor keys and singers and musicians used the tonic sol-fa to identify the keys in which they performed. Initially, it seems, calypsos sung in French Creole became known as 'Single Tone Calipsos', or, in one source, 'Single Tome'. This has four stanzas to each verse. Two strophes might be identical or two might be alternate, one solo and one chorus. Songs in English were called 'Double Tone Calipsos'. They had eight stanzas to the verse and first line repetition in the first verse. This was known as the oratorical pattern, or 'oration' style. The first evidence for the terms 'calipso' and 'double tone' appears in the *Port of Spain Gazette* in 1900. Carnival songs called '*calendas*' are first mentioned in the same newspaper in 1898. They appear to be synonymous with *lavways* sung in French Creole by *nègre jardin* stickmen and their followers (*Port of Spain Gazette* 1908). In 1906 the *Mirror* noted that 'the music which went up from the bands of *negres jardin* was as usual pitched in the monstrous minor which one may describe as the musical parody on the Gregorian composition'.[2] From 1900 to 1902, when Fancy Bands were at the height of their popularity, it seems that stickmen dressed in *nègre jardin* costumes played little or no role in the Carnival.

'Fancy Bands' and '*calipsos*' in English (the oration style with string bands) – 1897–1903

Newspaper reports between 1897 and 1903 give a much fuller picture of Carnival than their immediate predecessors. Although descriptions remained select, there was a greater willingness to identify masquerades and in particular the Fancy Bands.

Just before Shrovetide in 1897, Trinidad celebrated the centenary of British rule. One of the activities on the Saturday (27 February) was a procession of Friendly Societies. This was described by the *Port of Spain Gazette* (3 March) as 'perhaps the only event of the programme which partook the nature of a popular demonstration'. A considerable number of people participated and the newspaper commented how 'the banners, regalias [*sic*] and the dresses of the female members showed that care had been lavished to make a good display and to vie with one another in the attractiveness of the turn-out'.

A feature of the first day of Carnival (1 March) was the '*La Favorita* Band'. The masqueraders were complimented on their neat and becoming dress and the *Gazette* was pleased to receive them when they visited its office. Associated with the store called 'La Favorita' (run by J. R. Metivier and Co.), this band was probably composed of clerks employed by the firm. Other Fancy Bands had similar membership and also adopted the banners and regalia of Friendly Societies.

After Carnival the *Gazette* announced just twenty seven arrests, for only minor offences. Eugene Chalamelle was dissatisfied. In San Fernando, an old-time stickfighting champion 'General' Buckley had endeavoured to promote Canboulay at midnight on Carnival Sunday. This was thwarted by the police. Chalamelle was equally indignant at the activities of the ex-mayor and chief magistrate of Arima. During the Carnival, he had dressed as a 'Nègre Jardin' and 'before the day was out ... found the chance of having a free fight in the middle of the street with a character said to be lower than him'.[3] Stickfighting, therefore, was still an underlying component of the festival. Its appeal, although centred on the *diametre*, and those employed as carters, fishermen, tinkers and the like, remained a challenge of physical prowess and fighting skill for some members of the elite.

Prior to the Carnival of 1898 there were several newspaper accounts of music associated with the festival. On 15 February, the *Mirror* was unable to understand how participants in hot clothes, with their faces covered by masques, could 'go dancing and jumping through the hot dusty streets, with crowds of others, to the sound of squeaking clarinets and scraping fiddles, singing till almost choked with dust and heat the external "Hi-i-i-yi-yi"'. 'Old Fogey' wrote a letter published in the same newspaper on 19 February that explained the songs were 'almost always of a lewd character' and 'generally in Patois' but 'the hoarse voices of the semi-inebriate song-sters' were 'not very audible'.

The *Port of Spain Gazette* (17 February) warned: 'several songs' in rehearsal, 'with the view of their being sung during the Carnival', were of 'a grossly indecent nature' and 'the Police [should] be on the alert to put a stop to them'. They were 'all in *patois*'. Several days later (20 February), the *Gazette* commented on the 'great preparations' for Carnival being made by musicians. Practices were conducted late into the night but 'most of the music produced at these midnight revels was not altogether harmonious'.

Police moves to prevent the singing of 'indecent ballads' during the Carnival were to no avail. Reporting on Shrove Monday activities the *Gazette* (22 February) was indignant:

> DESPITE the fact that special men were told off to prevent the singing of indecent ballads in which the names of ladies and gentlemen were brought in, we regret to state that a plenty of these indecent and per-sonal *patois* medleys were indulged in. We hope the police will be more vigilant in that respect to-day.

On the same day, the *Mirror* gave a more general description of music in the first day of the festival:

> Large bands paraded the streets, singing songs and gesticulating in nondescript costumes got up for the occasion in all the colours of the rainbow. It was easy to distinguish the vulgar from the more refined masquers. The former were simply tolerated, but among the latter some of the musical efforts were appreciated as there were some good voices among them. Of course the flute and the guitar were in evi-dence, and there was a great deal of that weird music, peculiar to the Spanish descendants of the West.

The structure of the event remained similar to that established by news-paper reports in 1871. The music, however, indicates changes in instru-mentation and other aspects of presentation that were a feature of the time.

On the following day the *Mirror* reported how police prevented 'a desperate encounter' between two stickbands, Starlight (from New Town) and Junction (from St James). Adopting military terminology, each band was led by a 'Captain'. After being dispersed before fighting, the Junction contingent was 'remustered and stirred by the obscene patois songs' of their chantwell, Charles Pierre. Members were arrested as they strove to fight for a second time.

Commenting after the festival, the *Port of Spain Gazette* (26 February) affirmed these activities had become rare. It was quick to point out, never-theless, that 'driven from the streets' the 'open exhibition of . . . immorality' had 'taken refuge in the yards and houses of ill-fame which abound in Port-of-Spain and elsewhere'.

The *Mirror* (23 February) singled out the throng of street dancers on the second day of Carnival. 'Each band was accompanied by its own music – flutes, violins, or guitars, without drums'. They were unimpressed by a minstrel troupe called the New York Boys. The *Gazette*, however, credited them with good singing. The latter still viewed the Carnival as a vestige of an unsatisfactory past, especially the majority of the songs. It explained the method by which officers of the law were avoided:

> Occasionally an obscene ballad was trolled out in *patois*, but the Police could hardly be blamed for not detecting the offenders. They were so well known and immediately they hove in sight 'a change came over the spirit of the dream', or rather the song, and the ballad that reached the ears was demure enough.

In a subsequent résumé (26 February), it made further comments on the music:

> THE ancient and time-honoured amusement of *the people* is over for this time. The last *shack-shack* has been shaken, the last *Calenda* sung, the last *quatro* strummed, the last clarionet squeaked and quiet reigns once more . . . Many of the late masquers who have been the most assiduous in chanting the monotonous repetitions which do duty for songs during the carnival (such, for instance, as '*Penny a day, penny a day, penny a day to buy a dejuiner* [*sic*]' *sole et tutti and di capo ad nauseam*) have almost quite lost their voices.

The mixture of French Creole and English in the lyrics to this 'song of the season' (reported also by the *Mirror* on 23 February) confirm the year Lord Executor identified the populace accepted this development in Carnival choruses.

La Favorita is the only store band in newspaper reports, although traditional masques, such as clowns and devils, are mentioned. There were 'Venezuelans' and a 'Rajah' band. Snake charmers (like the Rajah's) probably represent the influence of the Indian sub continent.[4]

During 1898, the fate of the Port of Spain Borough Council became a principal political issue. Negotiations for reform took place between the Secretary of State for the Colonies in Britain (Joseph Chamberlain), his representative in Trinidad (Sir Hubert Jerningham, the Governor), and members of the Council. In August, Chamberlain decided to abolish the city's elected administration and replace it with a nominated Board of Commissioners. This caused great consternation and bitterness. Disbandment was effected only by an Ordinance, passed at the end of the year by the Legislative Council, under the hand of the Governor. The last meeting of the Borough Council was held on 18 January 1899, with great protests from its members.[5]

This event took place in the season of pre-Carnival 'practices' and the *Port of Spain Gazette* (20 January) was quick to observe its effect on preliminaries for the masquerade, at what appear to be the tents of Carnival bands:

> Already are preparations being made for this fête, as can be proved almost nightly on passing some of our back streets where will be heard rehearsals of the songs which form no small part of these proceedings. On this occasion the now defunct Borough Council of Port-of-Spain will come in for a large share of attention.

The 'noise' generated in the back streets, 'especially Duke and George Streets', was not confined to rehearsals, as the *Gazette* noted early in February. Rum was available at all hours, and rowdies gathered nightly. Further afield (St James Road), the Starlight stickband again featured in court: 'the king of the "No Surrender Band"' (disbanded by the police) endeavoured to take over Starlight, but was rebuffed. Stones were then thrown into their yard, striking 'those singing'. The newspaper still considered members of all Carnival bands to be 'roughs'. On 8 February, in a subheading, it castigated 'THE EXAMPLE SET BY SOME GENTLEMEN' in patronising band activities:

One of the bands which figured in the Court on Monday last bore the high sounding name of the 'No Surrender Band' and like similar organizations numbers of this band congregate, we understand, for the practising of ribald songs which are to be sung during the two days of the fête. These songs are for the most part intend to bring certain persons into ridicule, and if rumour speaks correctly some of the respectable persons do not think it either undignified or as setting a bad example, to attend some of these rehearsals and openly evince their approval and appreciation of these mountebank proceedings which were they lovers of order and public decency they would use every effort on their part to stamp out of our midst as a disgrace and scandal to our boasted civilisation. When men of intelligence and occupying some position in the community give their sympathy and probably substantial support to the carnival as carried out in Trinidad by the lower classes how can it ever be expected to improve or die out?

The *Gazette* returned to this issue in a long editorial on the history of Carnival published on 11 February, two days before Shrove Monday. It summarised the evolution of the festival from the time Governor Keate endeavoured to prohibit masquing in 1858. 'Gentlemen' had evidently complained and the newspaper was at pains to justify its criticism by refocussing attention on Carnival songs:

Our reference was to another feature of the Carnival which, harmless enough in itself, has often been made the means of insulting and annoying individuals. It has always been the custom for songs to be specially composed for this season, containing allusions to any notable events that have occurred during the year and some of these are frequently very witty and amusing. So long as they contain merely good-humoured satire they are perfectly harmless and it would be very ill judged on the part of the authorities to interfere, merely because the satire is levelled at persons of high position, but when, as we have reason to believe is now the case, the satire is mingled with gross and vulgar expressions of an offensive nature and coupled with the names of individuals, then it is the duty of the authorities to intervene whether those individuals occupy the highest position in the Colony or belong to its humblest classes. The remarks we thought it right to make and the sense of which we now repeat, were directed against this most objectionable custom and against those persons who, directly or indirectly, either by their presence, or by furnishing funds for the purpose, encourage the perpetration of this offence against decency and order. We trust that the Police Authorities are well informed on this point, and whilst we altogether depreciate any interference with the harmless amusement of the people we also hope that if songs of the kind we have described are heard in the streets on Monday and Tuesday next, that not only the singer but those by whom they are encouraged will meet with well deserved punishment.

One result of this concentrated attack on Carnival songs was that the *Gazette* made no mention of those performed during the festival. The *Mirror* (14 February) had no such inhibitions. It gave a graphic account of the song most popular on the first day of the celebration:

'JERNINGHAM de Governor, Jerningham de Governor', was the burden of a song sung by the first band of masqueraders which invaded the sanctuary of *The Mirror* office yesterday morning. As this was not exactly the latest news and as ancient history is not in our line, although it may be the strong characteristic of editors of another school, we politely requested to be informed what connection this fact had with their visit. This was met with the astonishing accusation:

> 'It is rudeness into you
> To break de laws of de Borough Council.'

We indignantly denied the somewhat ambiguous insinuation and requested further particulars:

> 'At a noble conference
> At de gran' Prince's Building
> Mr Laghlin, Mr. Agostini
> Mr Nanco fan de fire "pon dem".'

We were getting more mixed than ever, and our confusion was increased as the multi-coloured songsters whirled, stamped and howled more stuff of the same sort. It was no doubt very amusing to the people in 'the know as to what it was about', but as we were not in it we could not enter into the fun.

This then was the famous song (for we heard no other) from the singing of which so much untold riot and misfortune was to result. All day long we listened for more but with the exception of a band with a refrain, in which the words 'Board of Education' were distinguishable, this was the only reference made to recent events, thus again proving our assertion that the lower classes have no interest in matters that have formed the subject of animated discussion during the past few months.

Governor Jerningham was composed by Norman Le Blanc (Persecutor). It is recognised as the first 'calipso' in the English language to have achieved popularity. This acclaim set the trend for the future.

The *Mirror* described several other songs. One, which they could not comprehend, was performed by the 'Never Surrender Mirror Band' who 'invaded [their] office and were got rid of with difficulty'. There was also 'a bouncing black lassie, with a great deal of neck and still more leg [who] danced down the street, singing "March on! march on! we shall gain the victory"'. The popular song 'I don't love nobody; nobody loves me' was 'frequently sung by offensively affectionate young ladies with very low necked dresses and short skirts of the type worn by the premier da[n]seuse in the ballet'. Minstrels, dressed 'with cocoanut fibre hats' and other appropriate costumes, also entertained. In caricature 'the police band was well represented by a string band'.

On the second day of the festival the *Mirror* (15 February) noted songs 'were much the same as those sung on the previous occasion' and singled out the refrain of one more:

> Come and see me before I die
> The last day of Carnival.

There were several store bands, Bonanza, El Popular, Eureka, and La Favorita, as well as advertising groups. Three 'Fancy Bands' who were to dominate the Carnival in Port of Spain from 1900 to 1902 are identified for the first time: Artillery, Highlanders and White Rose. Golden Heart displayed 'a magnificent tinsel banner', a forerunner of the painted banners used by similar bands during the early 1900s. Masques as well as songs depicted the events of the previous year, including Governor Jerningham in caricature, a mock court case, the 'Hurricane which "blew dem Bajans away"' and 'Mr Chamberlain and his Private Secretary'. Traditional elements included black bats, boot blacks, clowns, cow-faced convicts, devils, doctors, naval and marine officers, and a woman with a baby 'which she presented to all her friends and acquaintance[s]'.

Another significant feature was the sanction given by the British administrative class in 'Viewing the Carnival'. This included the Chief of Police, Sir Francis Scott and members of his staff in an official capacity on Shrove Monday, and Scott and his wife 'among the sight-seers who drove about the town' on Tuesday (*Mardi Gras*).

Despite the *Port of Spain Gazette*'s continued antagonism, especially

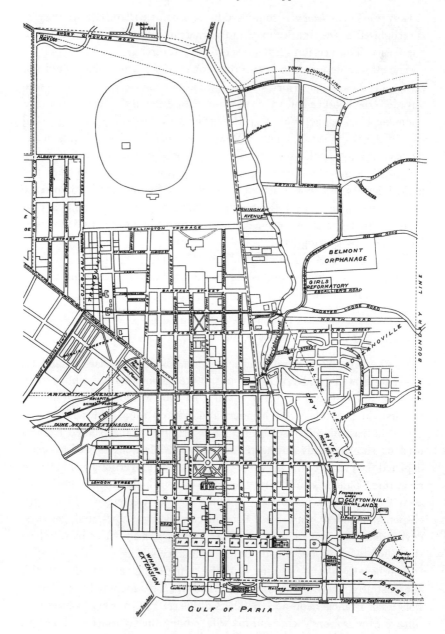

14 Plan of Port of Spain, *c*. 1899. Generally the French-creole element had extended
their territory to Rose Hill, Sorzanoville and Belmont.

towards Carnival songs and those who promoted them (17 February), this greater tolerance and open patronage signalled a major change in attitude towards Carnival throughout the island.

Comments regarding the street songs should be judged against observations that:

> At the start of the 20th Century the only calypsoes known to the upper and middle class were the 'le'gos'. And these 'le'gos' were not calypso in its full unadulterated glory but the short stanzas of its choruses stripped of all the humour and other commentary trimmings. As they usually dealt with the top-ranking scandal of the year – or the most recent one – those who failed to hear them in their original composition at the 'Carnival practices' also failed to appreciate their significance.[6]

Those who attended the tents, however, were fully aware of the political and social potential of the medium and it is hard to believe newspaper editors with long-standing connections in French-creole society were not party to this knowledge.

By 1900, with some reluctance, the change in attitude towards the Carnival altered the stance of the *Port of Spain Gazette*. Under the heading 'CARNIVAL SONGS' (20 January), the editor saw fit to publish the words of a 'calipso', the first full example of such a song and the first appearance of the word 'calipso' in print:

> THE following has been sent us with a request for publication as being one of the Carnival songs to be sung next month. For ourselves we fail to see either rhyme or reason in it; but doubtless its composer and his party appreciate it.

1900 MASQUERADE CALIPSO
Sunday afternoon going round the Circular
Circular stimulator *brulé la main moin*   [burn my hand]

28 December in the year 1899
Trayline and great Little Diamond *brulé*
    Savan la   [burn the Savannah]

Run Mordecal run, run them round the Circular
Mohawk Prince you don't know that
    Trayline *selera, San Humanité*   [is fearless]

People all, People all, I am going to the battle field,
Battle field of Sir Jerningham, 1900, *San Humanité*

Barracks! Barracks! Artillery you don't know the law,
Artillery you don't know the Barracks *fire*
   arm báca devirer   [fire arm doesn't come back]

Climbing up, climbing up, climbing up Majouba Hill,
We are all a contingent and foremen Calipso

Tell the people for me we coming up, *San Humanité*
We coming up, we make up we mind to sing
   the double tone, *faire yo devirai.*   [make them come back]

A few words in French Creole remain in this 'calipso'. In some performances this pattern was to be followed for the next thirty years or so,
especially the phrase '*san humanité*', from the stickfighting corpus. This
represented the disdain of warriors towards their opponents. Two other
versions of 'without humanity' might be used as an ending in '*cariso*' songs:
san de manite or *san te manitor*. The latter was regarded as a 'higher expression' or rather 'expressive of a higher class of stick player'. The phrase 'we
make up we mind to sing the double tone' may be a reference to the decision
to perform in English rather than French Creole.

Seven days later the *Gazette* reported regular rehearsals for the Carnival,
and a large number of bands, including one (presumably a minstrel troupe)
'getting up a repertoire of Jubilee and Plantation songs for the occasion'. On
7 February the newspaper went so far as to give details of certain bands,
praise their preparations, and rejoiced that 'all the singing will be patriotic
tunes in English, a decided improvement on the old *patois* style'. This
confirms Lord Executor's recollection that the switch to 'calipsos' in
English was sudden and overwhelming. Several bands would be displaying
elaborately painted banners (those for Artillery, Brigade and White Rose
were mentioned) and the masquerade themes were to be many and varied.
Judging by the twenty-five bands named, British Imperial loyalty and the
Boer War provided significant topics.

While there was a special attitude of allegiance towards Britain in Trinidad, some opposition to Imperial grandeur was maintained. This is exemplified by the 'Laventille Boers' who specialised in 'rowdyism' and had re-
christened their hideout 'Majuba Hill'. On the same day the *Gazette* drew
attention to the Fancy Bands, it also reported with indignation how two of
the 'Laventille' group were arrested on Rose Hill and, *en route* to the police
station, rescued by their compatriots. A police constable was injured in the
'rescue'. The 'Boers' boasted 'of their having defeated the British'. Such

vestiges of stickband-like bravado seem to have been rare. The *Mirror* (12 February) noted only 'seven persons had applied for permission to disguise as "Pierrots"' and the 'issuing of licences' was likely to 'be extended for a few days more'.

With a view to establishing a Carnival that lived up to the elite's romanticised expectations, a prize was offered by Ignatio Bodu (Papa Bodi), the former City Councillor and surreptitious supporter of stickbands. By 23 February the *Mirror* recorded 'various bands, many in number, are undergoing vigorous preparation for the prize offered' in this competition. Their reporter had listened 'to the practice of the "White Rose" on Wednesday night' and commented 'judging by the manner in which they are trained and conducted by their leader Mr Henry Julian, one should predict for them great success'.

In retrospect (on 1 March), the *Port of Spain Gazette* noted how 'the *fête* really began fully a fortnight ago, when single maskers and bands dressed in full carnival costume, except masks, paraded the streets nightly accompanied by bands of music'.

Bodu's competition for a cup to be awarded to the best dressed band was scheduled to take place in Marine Square (now Independence Square) on Shrove Tuesday. Reporting favourably on the first day of Carnival, the *Gazette* (27 February) looked forward to this event with great anticipation.

Musical activities on Carnival Monday involved the 'crude *a la* Gregorian tunes' of the majority of the masqueraders, an imitation Police Band (as in 1899) and the Iere band playing 'Spanish airs' that were 'aimed at a purely Terpsichorean effect'. Other string bands were the Excelsior (led by Mr Martinez), the Red Cross Society, and the Liberty Band. The Minstrel troupe (the *Mirror* reported) attracted 'considerable attention by their well rendered songs as well as provoking laughter by their grotesque facial contortions'. Stilt dancers (Moko Jumbie) 'stalked through the streets to the strains of drum and fife'. One was 20 feet high.

With the Boer War and Imperial patriotism as principal themes, on the day of the cup competition the *Gazette* published a composition by the White Rose Social Union as a sample of songs performed the days before:

Britain has held her own from the time of the Conqueror
Britain has held her own from the time of the Conqueror
And is prepared to hold it again in the Transvaal, *sans humanité*

France should know she is dead, since brave Napoleon fell
Whose policy is rotten and Government a mere farce
Yet claims that [*sic*] the title as the World's greatest nation
But will never again be the nation that she was, *sans humanité*

She should glance and reconnoitre into her past history
The land which gave birth to the men who were brutes
She should seek to amend the crimes committed *sans humanité*
And remember Robespie[r]re, Danton and Basson, *pasco sans*
    humanité   [is doing something]

France who gives shelter to anarchists of Italy
France who harbours the villains of the world
Who lives in conspiracy with the Russian bear
Should be excluded as a power *sans humanité*

See the big Russian bear only dreaming of expansion
Seized Port Arthur whilst we were politically engaged
Creeping like the snail from Circassia into Persia
When we are at war with the Boers, *sans humanité*

The great Prussian territory land of our grandsons
Should avoid being in colleague with two such worthless nations
But should join hand in hand with Uncle Tom our cousin
And must remain the world's conquerors, *sans humanité*

In the event of hostilities our plan of campaign is laid
We will send the North Sea squadron to the Baltic Sea
And the Mediterranean to the Archipelago
And then will strain the big white Bear *sans humanité*

The Channel Squadron will then guard shameful France
And the North American and West Indian will come to aid
Then the Powerful, Indefatigable, Terrible and Renown
Will patrol the world's waters *sans humanité*

Then rule Britannia, Britannia must rule the waves
Then the Colonies will come in for a share in the pie
Then hip hip hurrah, for Great Britain *pasca devera*   [is not turning back]
Then Trinidad will claim the skin of the white Bear, *sans humanité.*

    With his reputation as 'a singer of the most intellectual songs,' almost
certainly this was written by Henry Julian whose singing name was Iron
Duke, known otherwise as Julian White Rose or Whiterose. The White
Rose masquerade band employed two other chantwells. In 1900, one of

these was Pharaoh (Joseph, or Andrew Bernard), another well known songster.

While traditional masques are described, the emphasis in reports of the second day of the festival is on the Fancy Band competition. The *Gazette* (1 March), noted the novel 'adoption of the idea of combination into "Bands," each with a distinctive banner bearing a title or motto, and accompanied by a brass or string band of more or less creditable pretentions'. Of these the *Mirror* (28 February) singled out Brigade Union, White Rose Social Union, the Artillery Company and Cock of the North Highlanders (known also as Gordon Highlanders, or Scottish Highlanders). The *Mirror* mentioned the patriotism of the songs and the *Gazette* gave further particulars (1 March).

The Brigade Social Union was headed by David Scott (its leader and songster) and accompanied by a 'clarionet and string band'. Their song 'which was really well performed,' was 'a fair history of the Transvaal from 1876 to date; and gave evidence of wide reading and no small knowledge of the history of the time'.

Rose Hill Social Union contributed 'a long version in verse of the glorious reign of "Alexandrina Victoria"' and 'was fully up to the usual merit for loyalty'. This band was probably headed by another famous singer, Mentor Dominique Trimm.

There was also 'the war song' of the Artillery Band 'with a wild and pathetic chorus of "Far far away!" and the bold one of "Fight Britannia fight" ... eminently suitable to the season'. The newspaper was impressed also with the skills of the band's songster, Henry Forbes, the Inventor, stating that 'with an ingenuity which did the soloist considerable credit, within a couple of hours of receipt of the news of the surrender of General Cronje and his 8,000 at Paardenberg, on the 27th, a set of home made verses in celebration of the event were being sung to the usually curiously weird characteristic chant'.

White Rose appear to have performed the song published by the *Gazette* on 27 February (although Patrick Jones recalled two others sung *en route* to the competition).

The Scottish Highlanders do not seem to have had a song, but marched to the accompaniment of a guitar and cuatro band.

The competition was heavily subscribed and a decision on the winner put off. After parading, and under sanction of a mounted police escort, White Rose proceeded to the residence of Ignacio Bodu in York Street, where they had been invited. 'Several songs were rendered' for Bodu and his friends, after which members were 'liberally treated to refreshments' and speeches made. Artillery subsequently visited Bodu's house and were given a similar reception.

Although White Rose won the cup, which they received at a presentation on 19 March, in the opinion of both the *Mirror* and *Port of Spain Gazette* the best band had been Brigade.

As with the surrender of Cronje the day before, news of the relief of Ladysmith reached Trinidad on the day the siege was lifted in South Africa. Thus, on 28 February there was spontaneous rejoicing on the streets of Port of Spain, and elsewhere in the island. Without masques, many of the bands began parading dressed in costumes of the previous day. The police allowed extra celebrations because of the occasion. The *Gazette* (2 March) considered the merits of Brigade Social Union were vindicated in the afternoon when they 'went up in a procession to Government House' and 'were received in the Legislative Council Chamber'. The members 'ranged themselves around the horseshoe table; and to the accompaniment of their brass and string band sang a specially composed song of triumph for the occasion; the tune being the same peculiar, wild and almost plaintive chant so characteristic [and they considered] so suitable to the present war'. The song may be one called *Ladysmith* (attributed to 'Scott' Brigade) remembered in the 1950s:

> 60,000 Boers surround Ladysmith
> 60,000 Boers surround Ladysmith
> Lord Roberts with his *manima*
> The bayonet charge is the rod of correction
> Oh, the bayonet charge is the rod of correction
> *San humanité.*

In addition to their tolerant attitude towards patriotism at the relief of Ladysmith, members of the elite (including the Governor and his wife), took time to view the Carnival in Port of Spain. This general accord between all sectors is further exemplified by the limited number of arrests in the city. Even an anticipated appearance by the Laventille Boers came to nothing. They remained in their Rose Hill lair, fortified to resemble Majuba Hill in miniature! The celebration in virtually all country districts was also peaceful. The *Mirror* (1 March) reported that bands in Arouca strove 'hard for the empty glory [*sic*] of being considered the premier band ... – "the marksmen in Calypso"'.

The Boer War encouraged a similar spate of patriotism in Britain, reflected in Music Hall songs of the period. In Trinidad, this sentiment was again encouraged after the capture of Pretoria by General Roberts on 5 June. A 'Pretoria Celebration' was held a few days later, but lacked the popular spontaneity of the demonstrations following 'Ladysmith'.[7]

Although close harmony between bands and patronage by the elite was again the objective for the Carnival of 1901, continuity was broken by the death of Queen Victoria on 22 January. White Rose immediately postponed their practices (*Mirror*, 23 January), and Artillery, Rose Hill and Brigade mirrored this suspension (*Port of Spain Gazette*, 24 January). In San Fernando, Moral Diamond deferred their ball in respect for the dead monarch (*Mirror*, 25 January), and bands, such as the Aurora Borealis in Arouca, held solemn wakes for Victoria in their tents (*Gazette*, 7 February).

There was great debate as to the propriety for holding Carnival. Ignacio Bodu suggested a delay until Easter (as in 1827, although the precedent was forgotten). His endeavours met with opposition from the bands, and led to his estrangement from Carnival. After arranging for principal band leaders to consult the Governor, they refused and Bodu attended alone. Judging by correspondence in the newspapers, the bands seem to have fallen out amongst themselves. Henry Julian defended his position, claiming he had been forced to side with Bodu. Other band leaders identified in the press at this time were:

Reginald Plummer	Iere Social Union
Mentor Dominique Trimm	Rose Hill Social Union
F. Toussaint	Rose of England Social Union
James Inniss	British Heroes Social Union
David Scott	Brigade Social Union

In the end it was decided to hold Carnival at Shrovetide as usual. Song rehearsals were resumed at 'practices' such as those in Sangre Grande (*Gazette*, 8 February) and Tunapuna (*Gazette*, 10 February). The latter included a visit of 'leading songsters from the city connected with the "White Rose SU" of Tunapuna'. One was 'the well-known "Chanter" A. Julien' [*sic*] who 'afforded much pleasure with his recitation of the customary songs'.

The Carnival took place on 18 and 19 February. On the first day Russell and Company held a clown competition. The masqueraders sang 'calipsos'

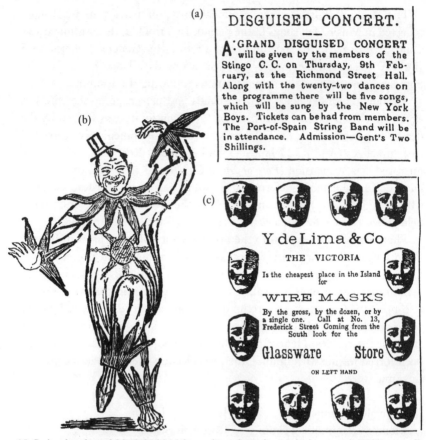

15 String bands and black in blackface minstrels took part in 'concerts' (1899) as well as Carnival parades, alongside clowns (1900) and participants in wire masques (1901).

and 'Carnival songs upon the reign and death of Her Majesty' but, the *Gazette* (19 February) felt that 'in many instances' these 'were in very poor taste'. Fancy Bands, again with elaborate costumes, banners and music, took to the streets on *Mardi Gras* and received the *Port of Spain Gazette*'s approval (20 February). Three days later, the newspaper published one of the patriotic lyrics:

THE following, which in a fair sample of the memorial verses sung at the late Carnival, has been sent us for publication:

In memory of Her late Majesty – In Sol Major
[By G. R. PLUMMER – Duke of Iere]

Chorus.

She has gone to rest – Peace be with her departed soul
She has gone to rest – Peace be with her departed soul
She has gone from time – To sweet eternity – She has gone forever
She has gone from time – Poor Queen Victoria Bless her in her grave

Toll the Bells and mourn and lament for our noble Queen
Who throughout her glorious reign successfully has been
A kind protector, a noble patron, and a mother, to one and all
Who has won her subjects love and affections Bless her in her grave

Chorus – She has gone to rest, etc.

A noble Queen to whom one and all have shown their loyalty
In accordance with our wish may she have sweet immortality
And rest with Saints and Angels above for our Sovereign we had loved
So may she rest in peace and sweet eternity Bless her in her grave

Chorus – She has gone to rest, etc.

We must sympathise and mourn and the glories of her name adorn
Bless her for the wisdom that has guided us o'er many a storm
So in sympathy and condolence with the Royal family
We mourn her loss with great sincerity Bless her in her grave

Chorus – She has gone to rest, etc.

Plummer, as has been noted, was leader of Iere Social Union and came from Guyana.

The Carnival in country districts was of a similar pattern to Port of Spain with few arrests and a preponderance of Fancy Bands. The songs at Princes Town were described as 'memorial sonnets' for the late Queen. Her death was the subject of songs at Tunapuna, where 'the South African war' provided another topic. At this location bands 'paraded the thronged streets singing their *Callypsos* to the accompaniment of guitars, quatros and shac shacs'. 'Noble tones in Calypso' were the order of the day at Caura.[8]

A signal of the approaching Carnival in 1902 is an announcement in the *Port of Spain Gazette* (25 January) that 'the Eclipse String Band will play tonight at the Queen's Park Café from 7 to 10 p.m.' This was the season of masquerade balls. Court proceedings (*Gazette* 31 January) revolved around defining facial disguise when walking to these functions in fancy costume. The black man charged was Joseph Bernard (known to the police as Andrew Bernard). He was almost certainly the calypsonian Pharaoh.

At the time of his arrest Bernard had been:

> with others in similar costume to the defendant's, that of a prince of the Elizabethan times, short hose of brilliant hued velvet, elaborately trimmed, a jacket to match and a long silken cloak, and broad trimmed flowered and feathered hat, caught up on one side in imitation of the CIV. He wore no mask, but his features were completely disguised by a deep covering of powder.

His offence, said the magistrate, in an action that had strong racial overtones, was his white powdered face. As his lawyer pointed out 'gentlemen' disguised likewise had attended 'the Ball of the previous evening at the Queen's Park Hotel' without molestation. Pharaoh was convicted, but even the *Port of Spain Gazette* (31 January) castigated the magistrate and police for bringing the case.

Dancing was a popular pastime in Trinidad, as was discovered by Algernon Aspinall, Secretary to the West India Committee (the planter's lobby in London). He was particularly impressed by the 'dreamy Spanish waltzes' enjoyed by black and white inhabitants. The programme of a ball to which he was invited (but did not attend), held by black creoles at the Prince's Building, included lancers, mazurkas, paseos, polkas, two steps and waltzes. The titles of some were *A Green Swizz* (waltz), *Oh! Madam looks sweet. By the Maid* (lancers), *It's Time to go a flirting* (two step), *Whiskey and Soda to the crowd* (paseo), and *You must be brisk John* (polka).

These entertainments sometimes took place in the tents of Carnival bands. In 1902, pending the crowning of a new Imperial monarch in Britain, a *Gazette* correspondent described a San Fernando band's coronation ceremony (5 February). Together with dance repertoire, this indicates activities and music with which Fancy Bands were associated:

> Last Friday night at the Marquee of the *Standard Social Union* at High Street, San Fernando, a rather novel and interesting scene was witnessed in the coronation of the newly elected Sovereigns of the *Standard Social Union*.
>
> The Marquee was tastily decorated with a profusion of cocoanut boughs and other ornamental foliage draped here and there with coloured cloths, while on the wall were hung numerous patriotic

pictures of the South African heroes and scenes of the war. At about 9 o' clock the ceremony of the coronation commenced when Joseph Perreira and Doodoo Baptiste were crowned king and queen of the ... Union by the prince and princess, Tomy Perreira and Pinky Grantham assisted by their secretary; amid the acclamation of their subjects. The Sovereigns then occupied a throne on a chair at the rear of the Marquee while the *Maitre Chantrel* sang several suitable ballads (calypsos) specially prepared for the occasion by a local poet.

The health of the King and Queen of England was then proposed and drunk while the *National Anthem* was rendered after which the health of the newly crowned Sovereigns was drunk during the singing of *Rule Britannia*. The usual carnival calypsos were then sung by the band up to 10 o'clock when the band adjourned to a recherché luncheon which continued, with songs etc., up to the early hours of the next day. The ceremony was very unique and created quite a sensation in the district which might be judged by the hundred of persons who gathered to witness it.

Ignatio Bodu seems not to have been directly involved in the Fancy Band competition in Port of Spain. This was held at the Queen's Park Savannah grandstand, on Shrove Tuesday (11 February). Describing *Lundi Gras* celebrations, the *Gazette* noted the usual bands had 'paraded the streets, with music, singing and dancing'. Reporting on the second day they attributed 'one of the principal causes of the marked improvement' in the Carnival to 'numerous string bands', some of which had given 'very good' performances '[that] bore evidence of long and careful practice for some days before'.

Principal Fancy Band rivals were the same as in 1900 and 1901: Brigade (whose 'King' in 1902 was Allan Sealy), and White Rose (under 'Lord Iron Duke' – Henry Julian). White Rose were first to arrive at the Savannah. The *Gazette* (12 February) thought their music was a 'disappointment' in comparison with other bands. 'After some singing', it stated, 'White Rose gave way to the Brigade Union'. Once the latter had grouped themselves:

> The leader from a position immediately in front of the stand sang to an accompaniment on guitars and cuatros a most patriotic '*callypso*' and brought down thunders of applause which was redoubled on the singing of the chorus by the other members.

They continued:

For some time these two were the only bands on the ground and they
formed in regular order and marched side by side along the grounds
singing against one another.

The theatricals were performed with great elan. White Rose were awarded
the cup for best dressed band, and Brigade a silver bronze clock for best
painted banner.
Then:

> Some time after the award had been made the two bands assembled
> separately in front of the stand and led by their chief 'chantrells' spirit-
> edly sang callypsos, the words of which unfortunately were not heard
> by all; though judging from the cheers following each verse seem to
> have been very popular.

Similar bands presented themselves to the judges at the grandstand.
Finally:

> At the conclusion of the competition the bands paraded the city in-
> dulging in their various songs and exhibiting their gorgeous costumes
> and banners to the satisfaction of the onlookers.

In San Fernando, Fancy Bands (including the Standard Social Union)
also paraded on Carnival Tuesday 'singing their strange monotonous
calypsos to the clash of cymbals and the picking of guitars and cuatros'
(*Gazette*, 13 February). Reports in the *Mirror* (same date) show less elaborate competitions and music were a feature of Carnival festivities in country
districts.

The *Port of Spain Gazette* was so impressed with the change in Carnival,
their editorial of 14 February proposed a further Fancy Band competition
as part of the coronation celebration for Edward VII. Bands would parade
on the Queen's Park Savannah and be awarded prizes for dress, singing and
best banner. No evidence has been found that this competition took place.
The King was crowned in London, on 9 August, the event having been
postponed from 26 June because of illness.[9]

There was a greater emphasis on Carnival in country districts in 1903. As
early as 22 January, the *Gazette* reported activities in the 'gaily decorated
and brilliantly illuminated' tent of the Brigade Union in Arima. Next day
they noted how bands in Arouca and Tacarigua were busy 'rehearsing songs
for the Carnival'.

Tents in Arima again received attention on 30 January, their construction and decor being described alongside rehearsing 'songs with stringed instrument accompaniment'. Bands in Tumpuna had begun their practices. On 1 February 'two very respectable carnival bands' in Maracas were 'practising their native songs and choruses to the musical tinkle of the mandolin, the twang of the Spanish [guitar] . . . and the regular beat of the cuatro'. At Sangre Grande there were four local bands preparing to compete for best costume and song. Iere, led by Eddy the Confuser, was to have music by the Julian Francis String Band.

On 5 February the *Port of Spain Gazette* noted a change in the approach of the White Rose Social Union of San Fernando:

> The music of various 'calypso' etc. is an improvement on last year's and a noticeable feature is that the songs are not composed in order to ridicule any person in the community, as is the case with other bands, but the words are merely based on local events of importance and in praise of their union.

They also announced the coronation of the king and queen of this band on the 11th of the month.

In the first three weeks of February the *Gazette* announced or described coronations of kings and queens of Carnival bands from several locations. At Arima there was a diversion by rival bands outside the tent of the Trafalgar Union during the coronation. Following the ceremony 'the band proceeded through the streets to the dwelling of the Queen to the song *Cheer boys cheer*, and the dancing was kept up till morning'. A counter attraction was created by Brigade Union when the Rosehillians staged a coronation at their tent in Tacarigua. The latter were also let down by 'the *Beginner*', who was to have performed the ceremony. In Tumpuna, following the crowning of their king and queen at the White Rose tent in Brazil village, the king gave 'a grand reception' at his residence 'ending with a ball, lasting into the small hours of the morning'.

This activity in country districts, based on the model set for the past three years by Fancy Bands in Port of Spain, was in marked contrast to the conduct of Carnival in the capital. While some bands (such as Melbourne) remained active, the majority of the principal singers and band leaders did not participate. This was on account of post-Carnival criticism of the banners in 1902 and, it seems likely, other points of conflict between the hierarchy and the populace.

It is evident from prior correspondence and reports of the Carnival in

1902 that genuine local origin and the judging of banners in competition were disputed. In addition, Patrick Jones remembered 'the ministers of religion got themselves together and criticised the banners', saying they were 'more suitable to religious processions and so on'. Lord Executor recalled 'King Pharaoh' had 'offended public morals by using religious symbols on his banner'. As a result, Jones said, 'the bands the following year resigned', together with the 'songsters,' and 'calypso went away'. Executor put down the scattering of singers to 'competition', remembering 'Norman le Blanc was first to leave the capital, for St Joseph, where he carried on the "White Rose" band'.

There is no evidence in 1903 reports of Carnival in Port of Spain to support Executor's assertion that 'banners were abolished by "the government"'. The *Port of Spain Gazette* (25 February) went so far as to express surprise that 'several of the leading bands owing to some reason or another had dropped out' and comment on 'the absence of banners'. The *Mirror* noted 'small flags' were used as a substitute.

These bulletins substantiate the demise of Fancy Bands in the capital and the *Gazette* (26 February) confirms the presence of Norman le Blanc in St Joseph. He was crowned king of the local White Rose band while others 'accused them of having included among them members of White Rose from the City'.

At St Joseph, and elsewhere outside Port of Spain, the competitions for Fancy Bands usually had two or more categories. Principal prizes were for dress or presentation, and singing. Bands paraded the streets with well-rehearsed music and sometimes engaged 'in friendly competition in song'. Some traditional masques and activities are reported, such as pierrots in Maracas and Tunapuna, house-to-house visits by bands in Tacarigua, and in Tunapuna door-to-door singing by Christy Minstrels. 'Men dressed as women' also evaded the police at the last location. There was no stick-fighting. When it was threatened, as in St Joseph and Tunapuna, the police either confiscated the sticks, or barred the stickmen from entering the village. In Port of Spain, however, there was a reappearance of 'the dangerous practice of free "stick-licking" . . . by certain bands of roughs known in the masquerade world as *neg Jardine*'. This turn of events was also recalled by Patrick Jones. The *Gazette*, which noted this presence of stickmen on the second day of Carnival, also observed the reappearance of another aspect of *jamette* culture. On Shrove Monday they were affronted by 'women dressed in more or less indecent costumes' – known either as 'matadors' (high class or retired prostitutes) or *jamet/diametre* women.

Although it mentions neither '*neg Jardine*' nor 'women' the *Mirror* published the fullest account of Carnival in 1903. Participants on the Monday included string bands, masques such as 'the peacock', strolling acrobats, boxers and even a giant 'puss in boots'. Unlike *Lundi Gras* in 1902, when some skirmishes appear to have taken place on the edge of the festival, the behaviour of the masqueraders 'was very good'.

On *Mardi Gras* in 1903, the *Mirror* singled out twelve Fancy Bands for mention, five of which had appeared in previous Carnivals. A minstrel troupe (the Royal Minstrels) 'sang some excellent songs including "Honey", "I can't tell why I love you" and "Love's old Sweet Song"'. There was a decline in the standard of costume worn by 'the "queens" and "kings"' of the bands. Discipline may also have begun to break down. In Tragarete Road 'two rival queens who had centred their affections on the same king, and disregarding the fact that they were attired in all their regal robes, pitched into each other in a very determined and unqueenly manner'. Fighting was quelled by intervention of 'the two kings and their subjects'. Late in the evening there were several arrests for flour throwing.[10]

The 1903 Carnival in Port of Spain reflects a general change in social attitudes. The spirit of compromise that maintained support for friendly competitions had gone. Since 1902, actions by different sectors of the hierarchy had alienated many, especially in the French-speaking community. Disaffection was current in all classes. The elite, denied a forum since the abolition of the Borough Council, took issue over plans to place controls on the supply of water. This provided a flashpoint for resentment and, on 23 March, resulted in what is known as the Water Riot. Sixteen were killed, forty-three wounded and the Red House (seat of the Legislative Council) was burned.[11]

This event caused great resentment throughout Trinidad and prevented further accord between the majority and the colonial administration. The annual celebration of Carnival was to reflect this difference for several years.

The return of stickbands and stickfighting *kalendas* – 1904–1907

The Water Riot raised serious questions about the way in which the colony was being governed. A Royal Commission was appointed to investigate the disturbances. They arrived in Trinidad in April 1903, and reported to the British Parliament in July. This was followed in Trinidad by a trial of twenty-two persons indicted for riot. One was Johnnie Blades (known as Johnnie Zizi). Of stately build, he was a famous drummer, stickman and dancer of the *kalenda*. Zizi received five years while Lolotte Borde (a *diametre* woman of corporate stature) may have escaped incarceration because the jury could not agree a majority verdict. This is the likely source of a satirical single tone *caliso* sung presumably when Zizi was released from gaol.

Se vwe, se vwe, lajol dajewe	It's true, it's true, jail is dangerous
Se vwe, se vwe, lajol dajewe	It's true, it's true, jail is dangerous
Johnnie Zizi *alle lajol*	Johnnie Zizi went to jail
I soti gwo ko Lolotte Borde.	He came out as big as Lolotte Borde

Women from the *diametre* had played a prominent part in the assault on the Red House – dancing and singing in the street as they approached the building, before throwing stones.

In December 1903, four influential personalities in the intelligensia were tried for inciting the riot. The case was dropped against R. R. Mole. J. C. Marresse-Smith, H. N. Hall and the radical black lawyer E. M. Lazare were found not guilty. A member of the Rate Payers Association, and former leader of the Port of Spain branch of the Pan-African Association, Lazare had written an indignant letter to the *Mirror* in 1902, complaining at the injustice of 'Pharoah's' conviction for premature masquing. This indicates possible links between songsters, Carnival bands, the black elite, and a radical political commitment found in some contemporary songs. Atilla reports one by Fijonel:

> The Brave, the brave
> The Brave, the brave
> Hundreds were sent to eternity
> In the riot of 1903
> The people say no taxation
> Without representation
> The police answered with bayonet and gun
> And brutally started to shoot them down.

The *Port of Spain Gazette* was fully aware of the likely content of songs and portrayals in caricature that would appear in the masquerade of 1904. Before the Carnival it was apprehensive of police attitudes, especially after the massacre of the previous March. The festival was to take place on 15 and 16 February and in a well informed editorial, published on the 10th, they noted:

As is only reasonable to expect after so eventful a year as that which has elapsed since last February, the Carnival of this year bids fair to be much fuller than customary of local references both in action and in song. We know for example that the water ordinance, the riot, the commission of enquiry, the trial of the Ratepayers, that of Sergeant Holder, and the forthcoming departure of his Excellency the Governor, will all be subjects of 'songs' at the Masquerade of next Monday and Tuesday; and more than probable is it that several personages in high position who have in the course of the past year rendered themselves more than usually obnoxious or pleasant to the general public will also come in for their share of notice, favourable or otherwise.

Among those killed in the Water Riot was Eva Cavallo who was shot by her former paramour, Holder, though he was found not guilty at his trial.

Atilla has noted several songs that fit these categories. Reports of the Carnival also establish that there were similar masques devoted to repercussions of the riot.

Some of the 1904 masqueraders represented international issues. There was a band of Japanese reflecting the Russian-Japanese confrontation, and masques personifying the Anglo-German blockade of Venezuela (December 1902 to March 1903). The United States, also the subject of a masque, had consolidated the Monroe doctrine (their sphere of influence in the Americas) in the protocols of peace. The British and Germans raised their blockade on 11 March 1903 but Castro, the Venezuelan president, did not cancel his counter blockade of Trinidad until just before the Carnival in 1904. This was the subject of a calypso recalled by Patrick Jones:

> I asked Castro open blockade
> Castro would not hear
> I asked Castro open blockade
> Castro would not hear
> I asked Castro open blockade
> Castro would not hear
> You see this thing, strangers seeing misery.

Although their presence was becoming less significant, several Fancy Bands appeared in the Carnival of 1904. Some had participated in previous festivals. Traditional masques included bats (in two bands), Christy Minstrels, clowns, mock policemen (one of whom was mistaken as an official by a regular member of the force), a mock trial, and wild Indians.

The police, whose actions in the Water Riot had been much criticised, were given special instructions 'not to interfere with the songs and take no notice of them even though they contained allusions to Public Officers'. The *Mirror* (17 February), reported that at a late hour on the final night of the festival not one arrest had been made 'due to the forbearance of the Police' and the *Gazette* (18 February) went out of its way to praise them. There were a few fights between rival bands. On 17 February, the *Gazette*'s principal censure had concerned 'that rougher element known as *negre jardin* and their partisans'. They had assembled 'in parts of the town less frequented by the police and indulged in stick-fighting [and] bottle and stone throwing', Colonel Swain recalled, in 1916, that he had seen 'about six hundred men with sticks marching about in disorder'.[12] The police sustained good order in a period of social disquiet but stickmen and their entourages had re-established themselves as an antithesis of colonial propriety.

Joseph Belgrave provides a vivid recollection of stickbands in this era. He identifies names, geographical locations, costume, songs and musical accompaniment of these bands and notes:

> As well as stickfighting, these men danced about the streets to the strains of this form of music ['Calenda' chants, 'sung in patois,' accompanied 'by the beating of bamboos and bottles with a spoon']. It was a kind of drill-dance, carried out with grace and symmetrical exactness. As they marched along one could see the excitement which anxiety brings to those eager to meet the foe in battle.

This drill-dancing to rhythmic accompaniment has its parallel in Lafcadio Hearn's account of two rival (non-stickfighting) bands in the Carnival of 1888, in St Pierre, Martinique.

A description of *nègre jardin* bands, published in the *Port of Spain Gazette* just before the Carnival of 1908, augments Belgrave's observations. It quotes from a leader in the *Teacher's Journal* (the organ of the local Teachers' Association) that criticises several forms of masquerade:

> Others, less disposed to run, jump and skip about in grotesque forms and habiliments, may be seen in bands dressed '*a la negre jardin*' parading the streets with fearful-looking gasparee sticks in hand. These last are generally not many – eight or ten men composing a band; but what is very remarkable is the great fascination they exercise by their senseless parading, for whereas eight or ten are actively engaged in taking what they choose to call their pleasure, there is always a large crowd of a hundred or more following and bellowing with the utmost

power of their lungs the ridiculous *lavway* by which the principal actors are distinguished.

It is the business of these *negre jardins* to use their gasparee sticks with great freedom and *éclat* on the heads of members of rival bands wherever the Police are not in evidence or whenever a favourable opportunity presents itself. This is the way they amuse themselves – battering each others' heads, and making skilful flourishes of a pugnacious nature with their lovely gasparee sticks.

The *lavway* in this description is synonymous with the *la voix* (war song, or oath of challenge). Identified by the *Mirror* in 1906 as the 'monstrous minor', this was the 'Calenda' chanted in 'patois' to the accompaniment of tamboo bamboo and bottle and spoon.

These reports set the scene for the Carnivals of 1905, 1906 and 1907. Lieutenant Colonel Brake (the Inspector General of Police), and his Deputy (G. D. Swain) had to devise methods to keep the peace and rebuild confidence among black creoles alienated during the Water Riot. Swain had not been present during the disturbances, having taken up his appointment in September, 1903.

In its pre-Carnival editorial of 10 February 1904, the *Port of Spain Gazette* believed Swain (as Deputy Inspector General) was of a 'thin-skinned disposition' and likely to over-react at what he might perceive as impropriety in aspects of the masquerade. It appears to have misjudged his character. In 1916, Swain reminisced that on arriving in Trinidad he was warned against visiting 'the back yards of the town'. He ignored this, 'went to the yards, and everybody took off their hats and spoke to him with the utmost politeness and civility'. Swain eventually withdrew the staves, with which the police were armed, first in daytime patrols, then at night.

This combination of trust, courage and determination was to ensure that in tandem Brake and Swain would find means of reducing Carnival violence to a minimum without physical conflict. The second move made by Swain was to post police in pickets at particular locations. Stickbands were dispersed, and stickmen arrested. This procedure was first employed during the Carnival of 1905.[13]

Reports in the *Gazette* show the pre-Carnival period in Port of Spain was somewhat turbulent. There was a disturbance at a Carnival tent in Charlotte Street on 3 February, and on 11 February 'Sophia' Mattaloney was assaulted by Carry Watson (in self defence). Remembered by Atilla as a singer of *calisos* Mattaloney had been involved in the confrontation at

Charlotte Street. She egged on Joseph Johnson in an attempt to gain entrance without a ticket. A stick fight between two men in disguise, 'Man Cocoa' and Theopas Mason, took place in Duke Street on 21 February and on the following day a band of thirty or forty men dressed in costume, 'with mimic swords and other weapons, and blowing cow horns', were apprehended. These may have been dressed as wild Indians, as was another band stopped by the police in St Paul's Street. A dozen men, accompanied by followers (not in costume), 'rushed about the street shouting out Indian cries, and waving about their play swords and thrusting about their lances'. Each of these occurrences was the subject of a court case.

The Carnival took place on 6 and 7 March and reports of the first day in the *Mirror* and *Port of Spain Gazette* show stickfighting bands were curtailed by the police. A band of Venezuelan soldiers (comprising, it seems, mostly women), staged a mock battle using imitation rifles, once it was ascertained the replicas were 'not harmful'. Many of the early morning *'jouvert'* groups, the *Mirror* noted, 'were attended by bands of music, more or less discordant, which, added to the songs peculiar to the season, helped to usher in the brief reign of the Lord of Misrule'.

In its coverage of the second day the *Mirror* pinpointed 'an excellent band of music' that accompanied a 'very conspicuous' band of masqueraders dressed in yellow and black (led by Mr H. Valére) and also complimented the attire of the Sweet Morning Bells. The *Gazette*, however, observed that 'there was a marked absence of regularly organised bands – better known as "social unions" – and those that made their appearance seemed not to have laboured with the intention of vieing with one another in a point of costume or other distinctions'. This newspaper complained also about the 'carnival songs':

> Although it is not expected that the effusions of the carnival bards should excel in literary attainment, yet in many past instances, they have abounded with at least some degree of originality and local pointedness: which cannot fairly be said to have been the case with those under review. Despite the labours of months devoted to the various bands to the practicing [*sic*] of what is known in the masquerade world as 'calypsos' the entire carnival muse seemed to have degenerated in to meaningless fragments of verse, occasionally broken by the refrain of 'one bois' – a sentiment which we learn found its origin with a masquerade celebrity on being defeated in a course of stick fighting.

Almost certainly this song was about the famous stick fight between Eugene Myler (of the Belmont stickband) and Fitzy Banray (of the Typin stickband, based in George Street). The instant Fitzy 'carayed' (posed with his stick), Myler won the confrontation with one wood (or blow) – 'one bois' – which was commemorated in a *kalenda* chorus remembered by Atilla:

Fitzy *caree*, Myler *reve*	Fitzy carayed, Myler dreamt
Un bois faire yeux devire	One blow made them turn back
Les Fitzy *tombe*	When Fitzy fell
Tout des yeux despere.	All of them lost hope

Charles Jones stated this confrontation took place in 1894. Topicality, and the account of the song's performance in the *Gazette*, however, suggests the clash was in 1905. Myler, described as 'head stick-fighter of Trinidad', was charged with wounding one William Peters at the corner of Prince Street and Henry Street on Carnival Tuesday in 1905. This probably does not directly relate to the tussle with Banray but it does indicate that Myler was active in this period.

Several injuries from stickfights and a number of court cases were reported following the Carnival. On Shrove Tuesday, Colonel Brake prevented a clash between the combined Corbeau Town and Woodbrook bands, and the Belmont fraternity. The Corbeau Town group made a determined effort to do battle with their rivals. Some, who had been in Charlotte Street and Duke Street declaiming 'a song in which the words "No Surrender, no surrender" were constantly repeated', were 'prosecuted for having been in a band of more than nine armed with sticks'. Another case involved a band of devils who attacked a devil in a costume of a different colour.

Following the Carnival the *Gazette* (9 March) expressed surprise at 'the sudden rise once more into the position of an organised set of bands of what are known as the "negres jardines" of the several districts', and their 'unusually predisposed determination to fight each other'. Reports in the *Mirror* and *Gazette* show a great variety of traditional masques. On Carnival Monday there were Ol' Mas' characters such as boot blacks, bull fighters, dancing bears, fishermen (presumably with nets), itinerant courts of justice, and stilt masquers (Moko Jumbie). A covey of male and female bats were seen on Shrove Tuesday and there were several vehicles with masquers from the elite dressed as clowns, fortune tellers, or strange animals. Sweet

Evening Bells won the cup, awarded by Stephens & Scott Ltd., for the best (Fancy) Band. There were also bands of wild Indians (one in blue, the others in red), who competed for a prize for the best dressed group, offered by the La India hostelry.[14]

Just before the Carnival in 1906, *Penny Cuts* (a weekly trade union orientated publication) compared past glories with a less enticing present:

> The long expected days of this feast – if I may so term it, is fast approaching, and any one walking the streets of our city will realise the fact – blinded though he might be – – – by the number of premature Masqueraders who nightly parade the streets bedecked in their various disguises. Only one short week again and the city of Port-of-Spain, together with the other out districts of the island, will hum with the tones of King Calip; accompanied by the gestures and gyrations of masqueraders. It is a well known fact that you may deprive a Creole of everything else, but give him his Carnival. Preparation for these two brief days takes up weeks without speaking of the dollars expended for these sports. In former years at this time it was a regular practice of respectable folks to traisp [*sic*] up Majuba, thence to Duncan street, from there to Henry street, then to Charles street, to listen to the extemporaneous compositions of such well known Calypsoic Bards and Composers as Iron Duke, Marlborough, Lord Executor, Prince Henry of Artillery and Plum[m]er Duke of Iere. These great freshwater Nobles were engaged thrice weekly in treating their patrons, well wishers, and partisans with their so called compositions. To-day owing to the counter attractions of the Quaker man, the successors of these chiefs find their ranks so thinned that it is only sheer love of their own ability and worth which causes them to persevere in their noble task. As one remarked – 'That man prevent the people dem from hearing me tone? Man if you here [*sic*] me double-ray on the Cricketers.' Apart from these chiefs we must not forget such barbarous chiefs as Myler, Fitzy and Muscovy with their loyal Clan of hardy batoneers [*sic*] who armed with huge *poui* parade the city in a body ready to greet each other with the well known cry of 'Boi! Boi!' and to extend the well known 'One Boi facination' [*sic*] if need be.
>
> It is to be hoped that these days will pass off quietly and peacefully and that the Beak will not have occasion to facinate any one with fines or imprisonment, but that he from his exalted position will in viewing the Masquerading pageant, be so carried away as to find himself repeating loudly – 'A si day la hay. Sar ah ban arah'.

Several important songsters from the early 1900s are singled out, some for the first time in contemporary sources (The Duke of Marlborough was Jamesie Adilla and Prince Henry another name for Henry Forbes). A 'double-ray' is a double tone calypso in re-minor. The counter attractions and identity of the 'Quaker man' are not known, but 'the Beak' was common parlance for a magistrate. The predominance of stickfighting bands and their leaders is confirmed, as is the currency of 'one bois' in their repertoire of songs.

Patrick Jones recalled that the Carnival began to 'improve' again in 1906, the year in which he and Gilbert Scamaroni founded the Khaki and Slate devil band. Newspaper evidence points to this significant change having taken place in 1908 (including the first mention of Khaki and Slate). As in 1905, however, the *Mirror* identified a few groups in the tradition of earlier Fancy Bands who paraded on Shrove Tuesday (28 February 1906). They competed at the Ice House (hotel) where prizes were offered for dress and artistic apparel. The Sweet Morning Bells Social Union came first. On the same day the *Port of Spain Gazette* noted the presence of Tennessee vocalists (minstrels), 'who discoursed well rendered musical items in different parts of the city' and a 'troupe of musicians well dressed in blue Louis XIV costumes', as well as a band of Ethiopians.

Alongside the music of the '*negres jardin*', the first day of the festival saw 'several bands discoursing really good selections of the Terpsichorean order'. Together with the adaptations of blackface minstrel music from North America, these descriptions demonstrate the three principal strands of Carnival street music in this period: songs performed in minor keys by *nègres jardin* and their followers, dance music (played by neatly dressed string bands), and harmonised minstrel songs, performed by blacks in blackface (or, sometimes blacks in whiteface).

At least two advertising masques took part in the 1906 Carnival; one in favour of Hoster's beer, the other La India gold medal rum. Another prominent feature was the 'young fellows dressed in immaculate bathing suits with towels around their necks'. The *Mirror* complained of 'the *negre jardin*, and the sinuous female with the unprintable name who usually accompan[ies] him', as did the *Port of Spain Gazette*. The latter was also indignant at the fishermen with nets who waylaid 'passers by and under threat of ill-treatment' obtained money from their 'victims'.

The feud between the Corbeau Town and Belmont stickbands continued. There was a clash at the corner of Chacon Street and Queen Street on Carnival Tuesday which was quickly put down by the police, although not without injury to one fighter (who appears to have been of the Belmont fraternity). Albert Watson (a leader, presumably of the Corbeau Town group), was arrested and charged with taking part in the fracas.

1906 may also have been the year of a legendary fight equal in its status to that of Eugene Myler's defeat of Fitzy Banray. This involved 'Feddy Mungo' (or Freddy Manga) of Belmont and 'Caynan', a leader of the Corbeau Town Band. Reputedly, it took place on Shrove Monday. Mungo disabled Caynan with a blow on the mouth that struck out two of his teeth. Subsequently nicknamed 'The Dentist', Mungo's true name was Frederick Maginot. At his death in 1933 it was recalled how he had been a member of the elite Belmont band named Peema, under the leadership of Eugene Myler. Patrick Jones (as Chinee Patrick – his stickfighting name) is said to have been the composer of a *kalenda* on this victory:

Feddy Mungo, *batonier pour vrais*;	Feddy Mungo, a stickfighter for true
Feddy *c'est undentist l'annee sala*	Feddy is a dentist this year
Parceque e tiray deux dents en Corbeau Town	Because he took out two teeth in Corbeau Town
Sans Humanitay.	San Humanité

Another popular song in 1906, according to Atilla, was *Pauline* (or *Estomac-li-bas*). Originating in Guadeloupe, he recalled it was sung by 'Sophie Mattaloney'.[15]

In 1907 Sophie Mattaloney again featured in a pre-Carnival court case. On this occasion an action was brought by Amelia Holder against Mattaloney and a woman named Estel. They deliberately collided with and attacked Holder at a dance in a house on Frederick Street on 26 January. From this and her involvement in previous cases it seems likely Mattaloney was of the *diametre* and might have been a 'matador'. A subsequent case (*Mirror*, 23 February 1909), in which she maliciously wounded a man, adds weight to the former supposition.

Newspaper accounts concentrate on the *diametre* aspect of the festival. They mention only a few advertising masques, a troop fancily dressed as British sailors, and a well-produced caricature of Colonel Brake. An upper class parade of decorated carriages at the St Clair Oval ended in a fiasco. In 1906 this had been a great success, but bad organisation and poor funding in 1907 brought about its demise. Comments in the *Port of Spain Gazette* of

12 February sum up the general attitude towards the masqueraders and their music:

> There was a noticeable degeneracy in character as well as in song, and current topics which have been accustomed to afford opportunities for the local song maker were entirely discarded and in place thereof was substituted a monotonous chorus of ribaldry, and meaningless jargon to the strains of which the maskers of the feminine sex in particular, wrought themselves into contortions sufficient to explode the already accepted theory of vertebrae and human machination.

On the same day the *Mirror* gave details of the 'somewhat bold attempt to arrange a stick-fight between the famous Belmont and Corbeau Town Bands'. During the afternoon of Shrove Monday 'an unholy mob of some 400 men' met one another on the Queen's Park Savannah but were persuaded by Deputy Inspector General Swain not to fight. Swain led the mounted police who escorted 'the Corbeau Town contingent' home. As they marched they sang:

> Inspector Swain:
> Super Bell in five minutes
> I'll blow down the town
> *Ba mois temp*   [give me time]
> Pon blow down de town.

The combined stickbands who assembled to fight Belmont were identified in a court case, reported on 13 February: Corbeau Town (possibly known also as Man o' War), Rose Hill (or Rosehillians), St James, New Town (or probably Woodbrook). On Shrove Monday morning this combination had defeated the 'Typing Band' at the corner of Henry Street and Queen Street. Arthur Betty, one of about six 'head men' dressed in *nègre jardine* costume was convicted of having taken part in a procession contrary to the Carnival proclamation. Regular stickmen were not costumed. The sticks '"miraculously" disappeared, on the arrival of the police'.

On Shrove Tuesday, the police began what proved to be one of the principal methods of controlling Carnival stick fights. They systematically took away the sticks.

The only other song that can be associated directly with the 1907 festival is the 'monotonous masquerade refrain, in which the "Bonanza's" motor van afforded a universal theme'. This disdainful description formed part of the *Port of Spain Gazette*'s report of Tuesday's Carnival (13 February). One

(a)

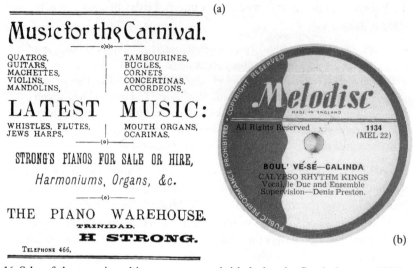

(b)

16 Sales of sheet music and instruments were brisk during the Carnival season (1904).
A stickfighting *kalenda* about Myler's defeat of Fitzy Banray (*c*. 1905) was recorded in
London in 1950.

day later, it complained not only of the stickfighters but 'worse than all, the
indecent behaviour of the women in the streets who seemed to imagine that
because their faces were hidden they had unbridled licence to misconduct
themselves'. It bemoaned how 'the people have harked back to the same old
thing' with 'usually meaningless' songs and 'common placed' and 'monotonous' music.

Such criticism returns to the attitudes of the last quarter of the nineteenth century, as does a report in the *Gazette* concerning Christmas festivities in 1907. This complained of the 'baccanalia' and how 'even the conduct
of church services on Christmas Eve was more or less disturbed by the
vulgar vapourings of bands of persons who, without the slightest compunc-
tion, wended their way along the public streets amidst the most disgusting
scenes which their feelings evidently prompted them to indulge in'. They
recommended Carnival-like regulations for the Christmas season, although
none were introduced.[16]

In the event, 1907 proved to be the peak of the revival of *diametre* culture
in Carnival. From 1908, reports of the festival and other evidence indicate a
slow change in the way in which the masquerade was celebrated.

'Hackneyed' refrains, tamboo bamboo, and Devil Bands – 1908–1912

Two factors in the administration of Carnival changed in 1908. First, G. D. Swain succeeded Colonel Brake as Inspector General of Constabulary. Second, Bonanza (Smith Brothers) organised a well-supported competition for the best dressed band. Bonanza, whose 'motor van' had featured in the street songs of 1907, were joined by Wilsons (another Port of Spain retailer), who ran a parallel competition.

Just before Carnival, the *Port of Spain Gazette* (1 March) published one of its tirades against the celebration. As with earlier complaints, this provides useful contemporary evidence for the festival and its music. After hoping for improvement following the provision of prizes by 'three or four of the leading firms', they turned their attention to Carnival songs:

> Next year, prizes should be offered for good part singing which should result in making the people learn to appreciate a better class of music than those who usually wind up with the hackneyed *sans humanité* refrain pitched in the minor key. Music is one of the arts of which people are particularly fond and that they have the facility of acquiring skill in this art is generally admitted; but such music as is heard at Carnival is not of the kind likely to give a visitor a very favourable impression of the musical talent of the people. It has, of course, its distinctive features and the Venezuelan impress is very strongly marked in the basic parts; but its chief failing is the lack of the charm of variety.

Complaint against singing in the minor tone was to be repeated time and again, as was the campaign against the stickfighting phrase *sans humanité*, used to conclude each verse. The identification of a Venezuelan component in the music confirms the trend begun in the late nineteenth century.

Summarising activities on the first day the *Mirror* (3 March) expressed a similar view of the musical ability of Carnival bands. These units made 'their round of the stores and offices entertaining the employees of those establishments with songs, dances, instrumental selections and other more or less funny business' accompanied by 'guitars, banjos, and quatros'. From this, and a description of a 'Yankee coon band' that 'regaled the staff [at the *Mirror*'s offices] with a couple of plantation ditties sung in good style and added a sort of clog dance', it seems they were a minstrel troupe.

In its report of Shrove Tuesday the *Mirror* criticised the music. They complained that '"God save the King" and "Rule Britannia"' were the predominant songs (in European-style), a 'brave' exception being 'the stirring notes of the "Marseillaise"' played by a band 'led by M Louis Arenal, the French globe-trotter'. This criticism appears to have been aimed at the compromise presented by bands competing for awards for best costume. It is indicative of a superior attitude towards the festival that, at times, was adopted by virtually all sections of the hierarchy as a means of sustaining their belief in values of European 'high' culture.

The first three prizes in the Bonanza competition were taken by Tiger Cat Social Union (sponsored by a liquor store in Belmont), Khaki And Slate, and Crown Lion Social Union. (Crown Lion was another Belmont liquor store). Tiger Cat also took first prize in Wilson's competition, with Crown Lion placed in second position.

Regular masques included clowns, court luminaries, a giant-headed individual, soldiers, and a spate of 'Yankee sailors' (occasioned by a recent visit of the 'US Pacific fleet'). There were also numerous people dressed in the costume of a king's jester. Possibly at this time, Colonel Swain prohibited the '*Moko Jumbie*' which he had found 'to be indecent'. Police confiscation of stickfighting weapons was very successful. Good relations with masqueraders and the general populace were maintained.

The oratorical pattern which, since 1900, had become the fashion for calypsos sung in English, was not confined to performances in tents. Eloquent speeches on contemporary topics were featured by other inheritors of the wordsmith tradition. The 'pierrot's' twentieth-century antithesis (in terms of costume) was the shabbily dressed Pierrot Grenade. This masque may represent two 'nondescripts' who visited the offices of the *Mirror* on the morning of Shrove Tuesday. One, dressed 'in a swallow tail coat, beaver hat and yellow knee breeches' (which did not match either the hat or coat) 'proceeded with a most graphic, harrowing and-oh! it was an 'orrible tale of the assassination of poor King Carlos'. The King and Crown Prince of Portugal had been killed while driving through the streets of Lisbon on 1 February. Topicality, therefore, featured in masques, individual orations by masquers, and the songs of Carnival band chantwells.

Word play in singing was not exclusive to Trinidadians. In 1908, the Golden Star band of San Fernando had as their songster 'a native of Little England' (Barbados). The *Mirror* (4 March) noted how 'this son of Bimshire had more adjectives and adverbs at his disposal [in comparison with other singers] – no matter whether they were misused or not'. With this advantage, Golden Star won the singing competition.[17] Similar tournaments in Port of Spain, with prizes awarded by benefactors, are not mentioned in the press until 1911.

The lack of organised song competitions in the capital did not affect masquerade groups singing *fatigues* or *picongs* against one another whilst parading. This tradition originated in the nineteenth century. With the advent of Fancy Bands, however, sung insults were not intended to arouse the ire of opponents with a view to physical conflict. Several stanzas from the early 1900s are recalled in which leading chantwells graciously disparaged their rivals as they marched through the town. Newspaper reports of Carnival verses and the recollections of Atilla, show the practice continued into the 1910s.[18]

The *Mirror* noted that Carnival of 1909 commenced 'with cries of "*jou ouvert*"'. This was probably the same phrase heard by Lafcadio Hearn during the Carnival of 1888 in St Pierre, Martinique, sung by a group of *diablesses* (female devils):

'*Jou ouvè?*' (Is it yet daybreak?)
[chanted by the 'tallest among the Devilesses', who always walked in
front of the band, to a response by the rest of the contingent]
'*Jou pa'nco ouvè?*' (It is not daybreak).

In parallel, Charles Jones ascribed the cry to 'the band of Old Mask called "Jour Ouvert"' who chanted this call and response phrase 'as the bells struck six on Monday morning'. 'Dressed as the proverbial witch' they 'wore tall hats, long black robes and carried long sticks to lean on'.

In 1909, the *Mirror* continued, Ol' Mas' also included 'the usual hideous and dirty looking maskers making the greatest noise on old tins, graters and other discordant instruments'. Other characters 'early on the warpath' were 'the fishermen, bailiffs and similar gentry who [made] Carnival a commercial affair'.

There were three competitions on Shrove Tuesday. One, run by the La India establishment for the best dressed wild Indian band, was won by the Blue Indians of Belmont. The other two were for the best dressed band. Cups in both instances were awarded to Khaki and Slate. This group, reported the *Mirror*, was attended by:

minstrels in the shape of a string band, which was decidedly refreshing
in its departure from the conventional tune [sung by most of the other

groups] and giving a new one to which the members of the band sang
the following:

> 'Monarchs and warriors come one come all,
> Monarchs don't you hear the bugle blow,
> It is time to satisfy King Lucifer waiting at the gate'

repeating the last line in a different key ... All the members were
uniformly dressed as also were the musicians, and they walked in time
to the tune they sang.

The *Mirror* stated that

> there was an absence of organised singing despite the last six weeks of
> regular practice,
>
> > 'You can't beat the Saylor Boy'
>
> being the universal refrain with but slight variation.

'Saylor Boy', a successful Trinidad race horse, was celebrated by a
Belmont-based masquerade band, the Saylor Social Union. The *Mirror*'s
reporter heard them '"Singing Gloria" to themselves and saying they were
"bound to rule the day"'.

A few more 'of the doggerels sung about the streets' were also printed by
the *Mirror*:

> 'Merry Sandy yon dunno
> You can't beat they Saylor Boy, you can't.'

and to the same tune:

> 'I didn't tell you so,
> They can't stand we fire brand, they can't',

and finally, sung by a picturesque little band in cream and blue colours;

> 'I didn't want to bother, but I must go (*bis*)
> And claim the cup Mardi Carnival.'

The *Port of Spain Gazette* remained unenthusiastic about the songs and
the festival, although it gave a fair report of the second day's proceedings.
In a post-Carnival editorial (25 February), its complaints harked back to
late nineteenth-century attitudes.

Despite being disguised, Percy Joseph (alias Gold Chain), was arrested
by the police on the first day of the Carnival in 1909. The king of a masquerade band, 'Gold Chain' had beaten his 'chantwell' Joseph Assam for

not singing loud enough at a practice on 3 February. A warrant, on a charge of assault and beating, was issued two days later. He was convicted and sentenced to three months hard labour. It is tempting to believe that Assam might be the correct name for one 'Ashton' against whom, Atilla the Hun remembered, Moro the Rebeller sang a *picong* during the Carnival of 1910:

> But look at Ashton going down the road
> But look at Ashton going down the road
> King Corbeau Master Booker A Doll
> Finger Smith *quid genre au yay*.[19] [Finger Smith, who are you?]

In its report on the first day of Carnival in 1910 (8 February), the *Port of Spain Gazette* was consistent in criticising 'the same ribaldry, indecent gestures, and meaningless jargon (doing duty for song)'. The *Mirror* took a slightly different attitude. While not complimentary, it provided a detailed description of some of the refrains heard on Shrove Monday. In the early morning 'J'ouvert' parade, when 'the dirtiest shabbiest and most grotesque costumes imaginable' were worn, the song of a group of prisoners was:

> Hold your cup for the ginger tea
> Hold your cup, the matron behind you

Other verses heard during the day included one reflecting the crackdown on stickfighting by Eric Blackwood Wright, a magistrate who had taken up his appointment in Trinidad in November 1909:

> As far as could be gathered there was hardly any fighting, which is easily explained by the following refrain:
>
>> 'I don't want to fight,
>> 'Cause I 'fraid Mr Blackwood Wright.'

The report continued:

> The races, as usual, seemed to have been the chief topic of the monotonous ditties, the following being the most popular, in celebration of Sangschaw's victory:
>
>> 'Come down with your Sangschaw *manema*.'

The Barbadians sang:

> 'Houghton ran away, and
> You can't find the Saylor Boy.'

To which the local patriots replied:

'Houghton win the race, but
We still love the Saylor Boy.'

The cricket was the next subject of their song and a fine band of cricketers, representing the Trinidad eleven, with implements, umpire, silver cup, &c., &c., went about singing some very original appropriate refrains, such as:

'Hurrah! hurrah! Trinidadians gained the victory
Barbadians ah! You fell like Lucifer.

Constantine, Constantine
He can play the cricket fine
Mr Hart took up his bat
Mr Small sent down his ball
Cipriani bowl the men
And he gained the victory
Sans Humanité!'

The recent fire at Alston's lumber yard was alluded to in the following manner:

'Going round the town, I heard the alarm
Alston burning down. (DC)
Insurance Company has to pay the expenses.'

The almost forgotten romance of the nun and the leper was also touched upon.

There were many other similar refrains which could not be easily caught, but on the whole the singing was a trifle better than last year's.

Groups representing the racehorse Sangschaw, and the All Trinidad Cricketers participated in the competition for the best dressed band, organised by the 'Bonanza' store on *Mardi Gras*. The cup was won by Red Dragon (a devil band).

On the basis of Atilla's evidence, 1910 is probably the occasion that a *picong* was composed against the winners of the previous year, Khaki and Slate, whose 'Lucifer' had been imprisoned for theft. This was an era of devil bands and Atilla recalled several *picongs* from the period, performed one band against another. Lyrics were part in French Creole and part in English. Atilla also remembered two songs from Barbados that entered the Trinidad repertoire at this time: *He Is A Dude* (or *See My Little Brown Boy*) and *Payne Dead* (or *Murder in the Market/Stone Cold Dead In The Market*).[20]

The *Mirror* (28 February) once again provides a useful summary of the music performed on the first day of the festival in 1911. There were more spectators than participants but 'small hustling bands of masqueraders' appeared as the day progressed. They:

> jumped all over the streets, shouting at the pitch of their voices their various senseless chants. The meaning of them was shrouded in patois, but others were distinctly obscene.
>
> Saylor Boy and Mickey Cipriani, however, were the principal themes though the Barbadians with Houghton also occupied a very prominent position.

The paper went on:

> There was a gratifying absence of several forms of objectionable masks, such as 'nasty-masks', fishermen, etc. The negres jardins and pierrots were few and on the whole in this direction there was a great improvement. With regard to the others, they wore the usual disguises, but a pleasant feature was the increase of string bands and the decrease of tinpans, bamboo, graters and bottle and spoon bands.

The use of bamboo stamping tubes in Carnival parades is first confirmed in this account, although it shows that they had become a familiar sight.

On the same day the *Gazette* complained of masqueraders 'from every nook and corner of the city and its surroundings' who repeated '*ad nausoam* [*sic*] the meaningless refrain of: ["]Oh, poh me one, too much uh dem pun Sailor boy" the solitary variation being the chorus of:- ["]Too much Babajan in de lan['] de most uh dem is cartah man".' *Po' Me One* was remembered into the 1950s. Another popular calypso from 1911 was recalled by Egbert Moore (who took the name Lord Beginner, when he became a calypsonian in the 1920s). Composed by Norman le Blanc, the song described the death of a Canadian jockey named Charlie Phair, killed riding West Dean in the Turf Club races at the Queen's Park Savannah, on 2 January. Beginner also confirmed that many of the Carnival chants in this period were sung in French Creole and included songs from the nineteenth century.

The year 1911 is the first for which a Carnival song competition can be confirmed in Port of Spain. Organised by the '"Jubilee" establishment', the cup for 'the most original song on a local topic' was won by a band named Peep of Day. Second were Fighting Cocks. The *Port of Spain Gazette* (1 March) reported that the cup for best dressed band (presented by 'the Petit Glacier Establishment') was won by the Red Lion Band. The Red Dragons came second. For the third consecutive year La India sponsored a competition for the best band of wild Indians. This was won by the Belmont Wild Indian Band. Traditional masques included bakers, Barbadian cooks, clowns, devils and sailors.

Post-Carnival court cases featured several men of East Indian ancestry indicted for being armed with sticks. One, named Tambie, was probably the Chin Tambie recalled in the 1950s, and may be one of the 'Tumblin Brothers' whom the calypsonian Wilmoth Houdini said had taught him stick play.[21]

The reminiscences of such as Houdini (Frederick Wilmoth Hendricks) and Beginner, together with those of Atilla the Hun, confirm newspaper accounts, and show the interrelated nature of calypso and other Carnival music in this period. This is especially true of the string bands who played different classes of music for different social functions.

Reports of black dance orchestras in the late 1840s, and mention of the Creole band in the 1860s, are likely to refer to string-based units. During the 1890s a Spanish (or rather Venezuelan) impress became a significant component in their repertoire. Local 'Spanish' compositions by J. and Albert Coggins (who may be the same person), and performances by the Coggins String Orchestra are noted between 1890 and 1896. At the time of the Carnival of 1898 the *Mirror* could single out flutes, violins or guitars, without drums, in parades. The music played was associated with people of 'Spanish' descent. In the same year the *Port of Spain Gazette* indicated the popularity of the *cuatro* and clarinet as well as the ever present shack-shack. These instruments all became associated with the accompaniment of calypso singers when they performed in the tents of Carnival bands.

This complement, together with the piano, provided music of all types. Thus, in 1902, the Eclipse String Band played at a pre-Carnival dance and also paraded in the streets during the two days of celebration. The string band led by Mr Martinez was engaged similarly on occasion. There was also 'Belasco's Renowned String Band', who appeared at a Fête Champetre (1903), Carnival Ball (1904), a pre-Carnival Agricultural Show (1905), and a Carnival Concert and Fancy Dress Ball in Princes Town (1907). Denis Walton ran another of these units.

According to a report in the *West India Committee Circular* (7 May 1912) an all-string aggregation with a slightly different purpose was founded early in 1911:

17 This photograph of the 'Trinidad Banjo, Mandoline and Guitar Orchestra' was published in London in 1912.

The amenities of social life in Trinidad have been added to by the formation of the Trinidad Banjo, Mandoline, and Guitar Orchestra organised on January 11th, 1911 by Mr D. E. Hyndman in co-operation with Messrs E. Durity, M. Bornn, W. Woods, D. Figeroux, J. A. Joseph, G. Durity, A. McIntosh, and J. D. Donawa. Its object has been to afford pleasure. Under the careful direction of Mr D. E. Hyndman much progress has been made. The repertoire of the orchestra includes classical as well as popular music and its services are in constant demand not only for Home Concerts but also for amusing the inmates of the different Government Institutions. During last year an inaugural 'At Home' was held at Greyfriars Hall, Frederick Street, Port-of-Spain, on May 29th, in the presence of some of the leading musicians of Port-of-Spain and an appreciative audience.

Other concerts followed with a view to raising funds for the purchase of 'musical instruments for the band'. A photograph shows that the orchestra had an all-male complement, comprising black and 'coloured' creoles and one individual of Chinese ancestry. There were two banjo players, four mandolinists, a cuatro player, four guitarists and two players whose plucked cordophones are not distinguishable. (Only nine of these performers were named in the *Circular*).[22] The broad base of their repertoire gives an indication of the versatility of string musicians in this period.

Musical diversity and its relationship to the Carnival is exemplified further in a pre-festival report published by the *Argos*, on 15 February 1912:

> For the past month persons were seen in gorgeous costumes wending their way through the City, some bound for the spacious and commodious ball rooms that the City boasts of, some for the decorated tents (made of bamboo) where they assemble to practise carisoes (masquerade songs) and regulate other transactions.
>
> Music is generally supplied by those [band] members who possess a little of the coveted art. They arm themselves with guitars, quartros [*sic*], shac shacs, veeras [*sic*], and two short pieces of bomboo [*sic*] which they strike one against the other. Occasionally, a stray violinist is seen among them. The chantrels (leading songsters) assume the highest titles possible, such as 'King Pharaoh', 'Prince Bismark', 'Duke of Wellington', 'Lord Ironside', etc. Some of them are very amusing, for while singing a competition (careso combat) they try to outclass each other by exhibiting the amount of scholastic training they possess. By far the best of our City chantrels is 'Executor', at whose command the others surrender verbally.

Other activities mentioned in this dispatch included wild Indians (and their special language), stickfighters, and house-to-house visits (culminating in dancing – waltzes, paseos, cake walks, etc. – to 'harmonious strains'). There were also pre-Carnival dances in ballrooms. By implication, ensembles generally featured string instruments. Larger more sophisticated orchestras were employed in the dance halls. The instruments specified to accompany 'chantrels' in the tents of Carnival bands show a mix of string and percussion. (The two pieces of bamboo struck one against the other are known as *qua qua*). The article is also the earliest contemporary reference found for the tradition of *picong* or 'careso combat'.

The Carnival of 1912 (held on 19 and 20 February) was not well received by either the *Mirror* or the *Port of Spain Gazette*. The former's report of the first day expressed disgust at:

> the masquers as they paraded the streets, creating a din, with tin pans, graters, bottles, spoons and bamboos, with here and there the tinkle of

a discordant cuatro, guitar or flute &c. A shriek here, a yell there, a long drawn droning chant, a fierce warwhoop [were also singled out].

As usual, the *Gazette* complained of 'indecent gestures' and 'carnival' ditties [that] were equally ribald and meaningless'. The 'money mendicants' received opprobrium but there was consolation that the 'net catchers' (fishermen) had been stopped. In addition, 'sticks were taken away from roughs, although [the weapons had been] dressed up like broom sticks to escape detection'.

Teams of masqueraders playing bamboos accompanied by percussion seem to have become a prominent feature of early-morning parades. Their emergence in the festival may not be coincidental with the rigorous control of *batonnier* bands but another counteraction to suppression by the authorities. Stickfighting *kalenda* and tamboo bamboo represented the defiant and sometimes violent extremity of black creole society, that did not conform with colonial ideas of decorum.

More acceptable to the *Gazette* (and, by inference, the *Mirror*), were the '"Yanks" with their banjoes and tambourines'. The double play of blacks masquerading in black (or white) face was lost on the colonial hierarchy.

Both newspapers continued to express dissatisfaction with Carnival songs in reports of the second day. The *Mirror* identified clowns, devils, drunken sailors and wild Indians as the most popular costumes. Results of two competitions were announced in the *Gazette*. That run by the Tiger Cat establishment (for the best dressed band) was won by Navy Dock, with the Imperial Syndicate coming second. The first prize in the La India competition went to the Dry River Wild Indians.[23]

1912 – *Trinidad Paseo*: the first commercial recordings by a string band

At the end of April 1912 the *Port of Spain Gazette* announced enthusiastically that Lovey's Band – one of the island's foremost string bands – was soon to embark on a tour of the United States. The visit was a result of 'intense delight' in their performances 'expressed by the numbers of tourists, chiefly American, who [had] lately visited' Trinidad. The Americans had 'strongly advised' the Band to make the trip.

Lovey's ensemble had sustained 'an all-conquering existence [for] over twelve years'. Founded in the same period calypso began to be sung in English, it might have been the 'Port of Spain String Band' who played at the 'Grand Disguised Concert' given by the Stingo Cricket Club just before Carnival in 1899. Creole dance music – 'Spanish Valses and Paseos' – was Lovey's speciality. 'The particular time and plaintiff minors characteristic of this style', the newspaper noted in 1912, could not 'fail to meet with the approval of those who [heard] it'.

Like the 'professional band of Port of Spain', encountered by Charles William Day in the late 1840s, 'the majority' of Lovey's band had 'no technical knowledge of music and for the most part play[ed] by ear'. Each musician, however, was 'a master of the particular instrument he play[ed] and at the same time [could] play with considerable skill half-a-dozen other instruments'.

The reliance on playing by ear indicates this was a long-standing tradition in creole music. It almost certainly dates from the time slaves began to adapt musical instruments of European design for their own purposes. This also demonstrates the underprivileged position of the majority of black musicians in the island. They probably had little opportunity to learn European music formally, even if they had so wished.

Lovey's ensemble epitomised string bands in Trinidad during the first years of the twentieth century. Their primary instruments were:

braga	Cleto Chacha
clarinet	W. Edwards
cuatro (or quatro)	C. Eugene Bernier
	F. A. Harte
double bass	Patrick L. Johnson
flute	P. Branche
guitar	D. Black
	L. Demile
piano	E. B. Butcher
tiplet (also listed as mandolin)	Louis Schneider
violin	George R. L. Baillie (Lovey) – first violin and leader
	L. Betancourt – second violin

(The exact design of the *braga* has not been determined. It is assumed the *tiplet* is a form of mandolin on the basis of the *Mirror* listing Schneider as playing the last named instrument).

Described as the 'Trinidad Dance Orchestra' for their American tour, the twelve members were fitted out with uniforms for the first time. They were scheduled to depart on the Royal Dutch Mail Steam Ship *'Saramacca'* on 7 May.

The evening before they left a farewell concert was organised at the Prince's Building under the patronage of the Governor of the Colony, Sir George R. Le Hunte. Funds were raised to help pay local expenses during the trip abroad. Appearing in their new uniforms, the Orchestra played a Spanish Waltz, Two Step, Waltz and Paseo from their latest repertoire, which were received with zest. Other musicians also took part, including G. Durity, the banjo player with the Trinidad Banjo, Mandoline and Guitar Orchestra. On the morning of 7 May 'music enthusiasts' besieged the Queen's wharf in Port of Spain in order to give a grand send-off for Lovey's ground-breaking expedition.

The *'Saramacca'* reached New York on 13 May. While in the United States, the band made commercial recordings for the two principal competitors: the Victor Talking Machine Company, and the Columbia Phonograph Company. On 20 June 1912, eight titles were recorded for Victor. They comprised five Trinidad Paseos, two Spanish Valses and a Tango Argentino. Some of the composer designations were to members of the band. The recordings were released in four consecutive couplings in Victor's Spanish American series. Credited to 'Lovey's String Band' on record labels, in the Trinidad and Venezuela sections of a 1922 catalogue they were described respectively as by 'Lovey's Mixed Band' or 'Banda Mixta Lovely'. This may be a reference to the mixed-creole ancestry of the band's members, evident in a photograph published in a Columbia catalogue. The black and white image is not distinct enough to distinguish the band's special instruments but the trim of their uniform conforms with a description in the *Port of Spain Gazette*. This states the costumes were 'made in the form of a dinner jacket suit of a dark green material, with a crimson roll collar and trimmed in gold'. Each member wore a white shirt, bow tie, and a peaked cap.

Much less is known of the session the band undertook for Columbia. It is believed this also took place in June 1912. As with the Victor releases some composer credits were to members of the Orchestra. The group was described as 'Lovey's Band, Trinidad, British W I' or *'Orquesta Tipica de Trinidad reconocido por Banda de Lovey'* on record labels. These records seem to have been issued in a special series for the Trinidad market and, in some instances, Columbia's popular Spanish-American catalogue.

The rhythm descriptions indicate that Vals and Spanish Valse, together with the Tango Argentino, were generally allocated to titles expressed in Spanish. The Paseos (designated 'Pasillos' in Victor's 1922 catalogue) were usually creole titles. Some tunes, such as *Mango Vert*, are recognised Trinidad folk melodies, although they might also be cross-fertilisations with others from the circum Caribbean.

The 1912 recordings by Lovey's Band present a useful cross-section of popular dance music in Trinidad. They also give some indication of the way in which this music had evolved from a complexity of influences both inside and outside the island. The 'Spanish' element in the Orchestra's repertoire allowed record companies to market their music in several countries.

It is not known when the Band returned to Trinidad. Advertisements for their recordings for Victor began to appear in the *Port of Spain Gazette* from 17 August. These were placed by Strong's Piano Warehouse (a local agent) and Waterman The Hatter (who claimed to have been the first in Trinidad to have received the records).[24]

'Songs without words' and the demise of the *diametre* bands – 1913–1914

'Lovey's full String Band of 14 men in Costume' were one of the attractions at a Concert in the Prince's Building on 28 January 1913. This was just before the Carnival. In a pre-festival editorial, the *Port of Spain Gazette* (2 February) attacked 'The Crying Shame of Trinidad' on grounds of immorality. Of greater interest is a list of past suggestions for the Carnival's 'betterment'. None, they claimed, had been put into effect:

> prizes awarded on voting tickets: prizes for bands, male and female characters, local songs and local music, obscenity or vulgarity in dress or costume to disqualify any competitor; the confining of the carnival procession to a few streets of the town; prizes for best decorated vehicles, floral tournaments, organised competitions, etc.

Several of these ideas were to be incorporated in the festival as the century progressed.

Following the celebration in 1912 the *Argos* pinpointed the main costume that caused 'offence' to the prudish in the elite. These were men and women dressed as *Diametres*. Since the demise of the stickmen, these

(a)

FAREWELL CONCERT

—IN AID OF—

LOVEY'S BAND

—AT THE —

PRINCE'S BUILDING

—ON—

Monday 6th May

AT 8.30 P.M.

Under the distinguished patronage of
His Excellency Sir GEO. R. LE
HUNTE G.C.M.G.

Last Appearance in Trinidad,
and First in Uniform.

Prices of Admission —3/- 2/ & 1/
☞ *TICKETS can be had at Wilson's
Ltd. (Corner Store.)*

(b)

(c)

WATERMAN
THE
HATTER
CLOTHIER AND OUTFITTER.
15, FREDERICK STREET.

VICTOR

LOVEY'S STRING BAND RECORDS.

A Well Known Fact.

We were the first in Trinidad to receive the world-renowned Victor Records of
Lovey's String Band. We are playing daily to large crowds and are taking orders.
The very best Spanish and Creole Paseos and Waltzes. Come and hear and book
your order at once. Large shipment to arrive. Victor Machine from $10.00 to
$200.00. Large shipment of Records to select from.

WATERMAN—Agent.

18 Before embarking Lovey's band was sponsored by the Governor. They recorded for
the Victor Talking Machine and Columbia Phonograph Companies in the USA (1912).

costumes were one of the last vestiges of late nineteenth century Carnivals. The *Argos* believed dry goods merchants held the key to reform:

> For instance, instead of having their show cases dressed with samples of 'diametre' men and women and such like monstrosities, might not the Frederick Street merchants substitute figures of continental peasants, Spanish toreadors, milkmaids, Danish women etc.

Merchants were encouraged to offer prizes 'for the best dressed band of a certain costume exhibited in their show cases'. The Government was advised to prohibit the *Diametre*.

Reports of Carnival in 1913 reflect this general attitude. Held on 3 and 4 February, there do not appear to have been any organised competitions.

'A rotten show!' was the gist of the description of the first day in the *Port of Spain Gazette* (4 February). No 'obscene songs' were heard, but 'indecent gestures' were seen in 'plenty'. The *Mirror* (of the same date) gave further information on the music:

> As to the 'singing', this department was always considered absurd and by s[o]me even disgusting but in spite of that there were still one or two grains of sense to be picked out of them, but this time it is impossible to apply any epithets to the 'songs' for there are none; all that is heard being the twang of instruments or the beating of bamboos. In some isolated instances one gets a hint of something relating to Reform and another song which is extremely obscene but on the whole the carnival refrains are songs without words.

A similar sentiment was expressed in the *Gazette* on the following day, noting how the bands 'sang (?) the same "meaningless nonsense"'. They hardly mentioned the costumes. Coverage of the second day of Carnival in the *Mirror* provided some particulars:

> There was the same throwing back of the shirt and dress which characterises the diamette man and woman. There were a few bands which deviated from this course, however, but these could be counted on the fingers of one hand. The chief of these were 'Navy Dock,' 'Demonites' and 'Dragons' who were all disguised as demons. There was a goodly sprinkling of Wild Indians and clowns, the former of which seems to be the substitute of the 'negre jardin', which has been put down by the police, the swords of the Indians forming effective weapons in a general mix up.

One of the songs of the season, was almost certainly Lord Executor's *Mr Pointer the Labour Member*. This reflected on the visit to Trinidad in October 1912 of Joseph Pointer, Member of the British Parliament for Attercliffe (Sheffield, Yorkshire). Elected on the ticket of the fledgling Labour Party, Pointer had come at the invitation of the Trinidad Working-men's Association, for whom he lobbied in the House of Commons. According to Atilla, the *Port of Spain Gazette* attempted to lampoon Pointer and Executor composed a double tone calypso in response:

> Hand me [the] *Port of Spain*,
> And read the *Mirror* once more again –   } (Repeat)
> Zee gee dee, zee gee dee marble stone
> Ah, what a burning shame
> They sang a schoolboy quotation
> To a man of education.

This became a famous riposte.

Strong's Piano Warehouse advertised Lovey's recordings for Victor as 'Masquerade Music' in the *Port of Spain Gazette* during the Carnival.[25]

Singing 'obscene songs' (and old-time lyrics in French Creole), beating bamboos in procession, and the presence of bands dressed in *Diametre* costumes indicates the masqueraders' strength of resistance to continuing calls for reform. This is true also for those dressed as wild Indians who took on something of the mantle of the suppressed *nègre jardin*.

The defiant stance of the *Diametre* bands in 1913 – when they flaunted themselves causing great offence – led to the masque being banned. The costume was prohibited in the Constabulary Notices for the Carnival of 1914. There was an immediate response by masqueraders. Some bands changed their vestments at once to close equivalents such as the Million-aires Union and Tourist Syndicate, both of whom participated.

The call was heeded for renewal of competition sponsorship. Two were organised by the proprietors of the Humming Bird Bar of New Town and Green Coconut Tree of St James. An advertisement placed in the *Port of Spain Gazette* on 14 February indicated these hostelries were:

> offering PRIZE CUPS (one each) for the best dressed Carnival Bands attired in the most original costumes, each band to be composed of 25 or more members. Six bottles (at each establishment) of the famous 7 YEARS OLD SPECIAL RUM [were to] be awarded for the best

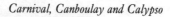

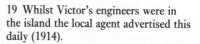
19 Whilst Victor's engineers were in the island the local agent advertised this daily (1914).

song or chorus in which the merits of the drinks sold at these establishments forme[d] the theme.

There was a special condition that the 'songs or choruses *must not* include
the meaningless *sans humanité*'. The majority of songsters and masquerade
choruses continued to ignore this interference. The *Gazette* (25 February)
was to confirm this in its report on the second day of the festival:

> none of the bands sang any properly composed songs, most of the
> songs having a jingle of words uttered with lightning-like rapidity and
> ending with the monotonous *sans humanité*.

They were also disappointed with the 'Yankee troupes', of which there were
only one or two. None sang 'anything lively as in former years'.

The day before, the *Mirror* declared the first day of 'Carnival was not
worth looking at': 'The disguises were poor, the singing wretched and the
weather bad'. There were also one or two fights, including a confrontation
involving a King and Queen of a Red Indian band and a bystander who
attempted to take on the whole band. Lovey provided the music for the
'Hermitage Dance', at the Prince's Building.

In its report of the second day the *Mirror* (25 February) was much more
positive. There were 'many good bands, well organised and dressed, with
string instruments'.

The competitions at the Humming Bird were won respectively by
Cavalry (singing) and Sons of Evil (dress). The last named (a devil band)
also received a special prize at the Green Coconut Tree. Similar com-
petitions were held at the Surprise Parlour. In these Athlete won the
singing prize, and the Columbine Yankee Band the prize for best song on a
'Yankee Shaker'. Red Dragon took the award for dress. At the Souls in
Purgatory Hall prizes were given to the Demonites, Millionaires Union and
Imperial Syndicate (in order of merit).[26]

The revival of sponsored competitions (in particular the introduction of
categories for singing), together with the advent of recordings by local performers, were to have a profound effect on the evolution of Carnival music.

1914 – *Iron Duke In The Land* and *Bagai sala que pocheray moin* (the first commercial recordings of '*calipso*' and *kalenda*)

It is believed the Columbia Graphophone Company visited Trinidad in
about August 1914, to make further recordings by Lovey's Band. Few

particulars are available. The records that have been recovered indicate dance rhythms remained much as before. Composer credits link them to leaders of other Trinidad string bands – *La Caja* by J. A. Coggin, *Centenario* by Dennis Walton (Valses), and *La Criolla* by Coraspe Martinez (Paseo).

While Columbia's early operations in Trinidad remain shrouded in obscurity, this is not the case for the Victor Talking Machine Company. Alerted by the success of their 1912 recordings by Lovey (and those released by Columbia), in mid August 1914, they sent Theodore Terry to organise sessions in the island. Their engineers, George K. Cheney and Charles Althouse, arrived on the SS *Matura* on 27 August, and by this time Terry had made arrangements with a number of performers. The *Port of Spain Gazette* (28 August) described this as a 'special trip to Trinidad for the purpose of recording a complete repertoire of Trinidadian music including the Pasillos Spanish Waltz and Two steps by well known Bands; also Carnival and Patois songs and East Indian selections by local talent'. The *Mirror* published a similar account and provided a few extra particulars: 'We understand that Mr Henry Julian, formerly of "White Rose" has been practising assiduously for the above purpose and that several other bands and performers have been engaged.'

Excepting 6 September, recording sessions were held every day between the 3rd and 16th of the month. Victor's principal artist was the pianist and well-known string band leader, Lionel Belasco. Henry Julian (Iron Duke/ Julian White Rose) recorded under the sobriquet J. Resigna. The other participants were Jules Sims (whose *kalendas* were sung in French Creole), S. M. Akberali and Gellum Hossein (of East Indian ancestry), and the Orquesta de Venezolana de Chargo (probably made up of Trinidad creoles, some of Venezuelan origin).

Many of the recordings were not released. The 'Trinidad Paseos' (or 'Pasillos') and the 'Calipsos' and *kalendas* ('Carnival and Patois songs') will be considered. One of the melodies in the first category was *Po' Me One* (Victor 67029). Performed by Belasco's Band, this was almost certainly an instrumental of the song popular during the Carnival of 1911. The composer credit was to 'J. Whiterose' (presumably the singer, Henry Julian). The Band's recording of *La Bonanza* may be the melody for the song about ' "Bonanza's" motor van' reported during the Carnival of 1907. Described as 'Albert's Paseo', this could be a reference to 'A. Vincent' who received credit as composer (Victor 67031).

Both were released in the first batch of the Victor Company's 'New

Creole Records' that went on sale just before the Carnival of 1915. *Saylor*, a later Belasco release, was presumably the melody for one of the songs about the racehorse 'Saylor Boy', reported in the festivals of 1909 and 1911. The composer credit for this record was again to 'J. Whiterose' (Victor 67388).

Unissued recordings of this type include *Papa Gorrie* and *Nobody's Business* (possibly the theme known first from folk song collections in the United States and, subsequently, in Jamaica and West Africa). Belasco's 'cousin', the violinist 'C[yril]. Monrose,' received the credit for *Nobody's Business*. He was the 'composer' of several other items.

A number of unreleased tunes were recut by Belasco as piano solos in New York in August 1915. Victor issued these, suggesting some of the original recordings were faulty. Several were described as 'Trinidad Paseos' in 1914. Two emanated from Barbados, *Buddy Abraham* and *Little Brown Boy*. The last named is the song Atilla called *He Is A Dude*. The words for two other melodies concern the reaction of Trinidad creoles to migrants from Barbados: *Bajan Girl* and *Not A Cent, Not A Cent*. *My Little Man's Gone Down De Main* was the tune for a calypso about Trinidad migrants seeking work in Venezuela:

> I have a little man and he gone down de Main
> To work for money for me
> I have a little man and he gone down de Main
> To work for money for me
> Aye *bandoola*, aye *bandoola*
> Aye *bandoola*, aye *bandoola*.

These instrumentals represent a broad cross-section of songs popular in Trinidad from the last quarter of the nineteenth century. They also give an indication of the pattern of migration to and from Trinidad in this period; as do the Spanish American rhythms. In addition, Belasco performed four piano solos. *Anita* (a Vals Espanol) and *Nora* (*Pauline*) (a Trinidad Paseo) were released (Victor 67399) but his renditions of two black North American ragtime compositions were not: *The Junk Man Rag* (by Lucky Roberts) and *Maple Leaf Rag* (by Scott Joplin). Each is the earliest known recording of these piano rags by a black musician in the Americas.

It seems the Victor Company's engineers did not take down titles of the vocal performances. Only descriptions of the kinds of music were printed on record labels, or in company catalogues. There were five Single Tone Calipsos, one Double Tone Calipso, and two Native Trinidad Kalendas.

One of the Single Tone Calipsos was not issued. Titles for all the other performances have been located in contemporary newspapers:

Single Tone Calipsos (performed by J. Resigna)
Belle Marie Coolie   Victor 67035
Hooray Jubal Jay   Victor 67375
Iron Duke In The Land   Victor 67362
Ringing A Bell   Victor 67035

Double Tone Calipso (performed by J. Resigna)
Bayonet Charge By The Laws
   Of Iron Duke   Victor 67387

Native Trinidad Kalendas (performed by Jules Sims)
Bagai sala que pocheray moin   Victor 67377
Ou belle philomen(e)   Victor 67033

The 'Calipsos' had 'Chorus and accompaniment' (a guitar and *cuatro*) and 'Kalendas' 'Chorus and bamboo accompaniment' (the chorus was female). This conforms with precedent. In the '*kalendas*', clash of bottle and spoon augmented the stamping tubes, just as it would had the bamboo band been in a Carnival procession.

There is a little documentary evidence for the 'calipsos' recorded by Henry Julian. A verse of *Belle Marie Coolie* (Beautiful Marie, the East Indian) is printed in the 'Foreign Section' of Thomas W. Talley's famous pioneering collection: *Negro Folk Rhymes* (New York, 1922), with lyrics in French Creole and English translation. The song concerns black-East Indian male-female relations.

Nothing is known of *Hooray Jubal Jay*, but *Iron Duke In The Land* is a song of self-praise from the doyen of the Fancy Bands that dominated Carnival in the early 1900s. Julian details some of the positions he held in the band's hierarchy before he became Lord of Resigna, the Iron Duke, whose White Rose Union was 'superior' to all others. In his third verse he comments:

> At my appearance upon the scene
> Julian come down with blazing sword
> And [see him] shouting an order
> Calling, screaming, to all the agony
> And see his magnetising mantle

> See it glinting, gleaming and swaying
> Jumping this way bawling
> 'Clear de way White Rose, *joli diable ré-ré-o*'.   [pretty devil, re-re-o]

The chorus also served as his first verse:

> Iron Duke in the land, Fire Brigade
> Iron Duke in the land, Fire Brigade
> Bring the locomotive, just because it is a fire federation
> Bring the locomotive, just because it is a fire federation,
> *Sans humanité*.

The final verse runs:

> It was a modern manifestation
> Of that elder civilisation
> That in the Carnival celebration
> Of the Social organisation
> Which causes the minds and extension
> Of all the population
> I Julian singing a Social recording
> With White Rose Union
> *Sans humanité*.

A review of 'Julian White Rose's' first Victor 78 rpm coupling, published in the *Mirror* on 8 February 1915, implies that *Ringing A Bell* was one of his 'compositions in creole' and its subject was 'Carupano Rum'.

It seems likely that the 'Double Tone Calipso' *Bayonet Charge By The Laws Of Iron Duke* was the song Patrick Jones said was performed by Pharaoh as the White Rose Band marched to the Carnival competition in 1900:

> Pharaoh bend the ankle on them
> Is to blow them down, is to break them down
> Pharaoh bend the ankle on them
> Is to blow them down, is to break them down
> And the bayonet charge, by the command of Iron Duke
> Mardi Carnival
> And the bayonet charge, by the command of Iron Duke.

Of the *kalendas*, the words to *Bagai sala que pocheray moin* (in French Creole) have proved very difficult to transcribe. No information has been located for *Ou Belle philomen(e)*.[27]

There was a strong element of tradition in the songs and 'Trinidad Paseos' recorded at these sessions. Older lyrics and melodies retained an attraction for the performers as much as they did for recording engineers seeking music to market as nostalgia. Local self respect was equally significant – pride that the prestigious Victor Company had come to Trinidad to make recordings of indigenous music. H. Strong's Piano Warehouse ran daily advertisements in the *Port of Spain Gazette* from 5 to 22 September (omitting the 7th), stating 'New Victor Records Are now being Made by the Victor Experts in Trinidad'. These ended five days after recording had been completed.

In common with the repertoire of Lovey's Band, the sessions included a representative sample of Spanish American dance rhythms (especially those from Venezuela) and extras, such as the ragtime pieces, from North America. There was one conventional waltz, *Ne m'abandonne pas* by Belasco's String Quintet (Victor 67397).

Outside influences can also be illuminated by advertisements placed by retailers during the Carnival period. A random sample from 1902 to 1913 offers musical instruments (string in particular), sheet music and (by 1911) 'Gramaphones' [*sic*] plus a wide range of records (in the languages of migrant groups in Trinidad – 'English, French, German, Spanish, Portuguese, Hindustani, Chinese, & Syrian'). In 1913, at the same time that Strong's were advertising 'Masquerade Music' by Lovey's Band, they also had stocks of 'Popular Piece Music'. Singled out were the 'Latest Ragtime Successes'. In general, these were not rags but Two Steps from North America. British-produced sheet music also circulated, as did British gramophones and gramophone records.[28]

How this impinged on Carnival music is unclear, especially in the light of the black creole commitment to traditional forms. Carnival music had been recorded commercially, however, and slowly began to change the status of both local music and musicians in Trinidad.

The Kaiser: Carnival and the First World War – 1915–1918

VICTOR RECORDS.
MR. BELASCO'S BAND FINE
DANCE MUSIC.
CREOLE SONGS BY JULIAN WHITE
ROSE.

– reads a headline in the *Mirror* on 8 February 1915. Underneath it states '(Passed by the Censor)', a reminder that since 1 August 1914 the British Empire had been at war with Germany.

The arrival of the first batch of Victor's recordings of Carnival music was received enthusiastically. Praise was lauded on the selections by 'Mr. Lionel Belasco's string band' and the quality. A large stock was 'on hand' and they were recommended as 'just the thing for drawing room parties'. This was the pre-Carnival season and it is evident a market for dance music was expected among those in the elite who had money to purchase both records and machines. Record sales were brisk.

The vocal items also received favourable audition:

> A novelty in creole music is afforded in calypsos after the rendering of 'Julian White Rose', the celebrated chantrel, whose voice has lost none of its sweetness. His compositions in creole on 'Belle Marie Coolie'[,] 'Carupano Rum' etc., are good; while the Bamboo Band 'Kalendar' is a new feature which will appeal to lovers of originality.

'A large supply' of these was 'expected soon'.

Five days later the *Mirror* (13 February) published Victor's press notice signalling official release of the records. (There were eleven couplings, including three by S. M. Akberali, chanting verses from the Koran). The Victor Company's approach indicates how they perceived markets for their local records and the popularity of the performers whom they had recorded:

> The records which we are today placing before our many friends in both Trinidad and Venezuela were recently recorded by one of our best experts, who was sent to the Isle of Trinidad with a special recording outfit. This, of course, put us to a great deal of expense and much work. Everybody will no doubt appreciate how fortunate we were in being able to obtain a repertoire of such beautiful local selections by Belas[c]o's Band, which organisation is under the able direction of the popular and eminent leader, Lionel Belasco, whose fame has spread to the smallest hamlets of Trinidad and Venezuela. The list comprises the best-known paseos and waltzes in these localities and produced by composers of acknowledged merit, such as Gomez, Belasco and Cedeno. The popular singers Jules Sims and J. Resigna contribute with some typical melodies of Trinidad which are sure to please all people who are fond of this class of music. An important addition to the collection is a small number of sacred Mohammedan chants by the eminent artist S. M. Akberali.

At the same time that Victor and their agents were trumpeting the arrival of these records:

Muir, Marshall & Co. (the exclusive importer) were advising purchasers to:

– and to:

In one advertisement it was stated:

The availability of recordings of Carnival music probably had little initial impact on the festival. Lord Beginner remembered the principal influence on contemporary calypsos was the advent of the war. There was a renewal of patriotism for England which sparked another fashion for singing calypsos in English. 'But what made this more so,' Beginner recalled, was 'the big-shots began taking an interest in Carnival'. Prizes were offered and competitions judged by the English elite, who had previously stood aloof from the celebration. This discouraged the use of French Creole on two counts. First, the 'big-shots' maintained that they 'couldn't speak patois' or at least pretended they could not, in order to sustain a distance from 'the man in the street'. Second, calypsonians began to employ 'big English' (high-sounding words and phrases) to impress the 'big-shots' and reciprocate for the interest shown in their music. Beginner's view was not the whole story. Emphasis on high-sounding words had been a feature of black culture throughout the English-speaking West Indies. In Trinidad, word play was one of the attributes of the *pierrot*. The use of the technique in

20 Lovey's band recorded a large number of sides in 1914 which were advertised in competition with Victor's new releases during the next Carnival.

calypso can be seen as a continuation of this tradition. In line with Beginner's recollections, however, the trend towards sponsored competitions for song as well as dress gained momentum in the mid-1910s.

The Carnival of 1915 was held on 16 and 17 March. Daytime activities on Shrove Monday hardly received mention in the press. In response to the serious situation in Europe, during the evening a Grand Allies Dance took place at the Prince's Building. This was covered by both the *Mirror* and *Port of Spain Gazette*. Proceeds were distributed to the widows of soldiers and 'wives of those . . . in the firing line'. The music for this successful event was provided by Lovey's String Band with, according to the *Gazette*, 'the result that enjoyment was writ on the faces of all, even those who did not trip the light fantastic toe'. The band, noted the *Mirror*, played 'select pieces, there being a complete absence of carnival airs, which met the appreciation of the dancers'.

Traditional masques were in evidence in street parades (presumably on both days of the festival). These included some clowns and bats (although the *Mirror* noted an absence of the former), demons, dragons, sailors and snake charmers. Cowboys, the precursor of the masque known as Midnight Robber, are noted for the first time.

Yankee or 'coon' bands performed in their usual number, as did string bands. The *Gazette* was pleased that there was 'an entire absence of vulgarity so prominent in years past'. It also commented on the music:

'Tipperary' and other patriotic airs superseded to some extent the senseless refrains usually indulged in. The 'Kaiser' in the latter songs came in for rough handling.

On Shrove Tuesday, both Humming Bird and Surprise Parlour ran competitions. Cavalry won the cup presented by Humming Bird for the best dressed band. At the Surprise Parlour the Punjab Regiment (also referred to as Gurkhas) won the cup for the most original band. Their representation in the masquerade was sparked by the war and, presumably, the island's East Indian community. Surprise ran two competitions for singing, both designed to marginalise traditional road marches. Four Roads Social Union won the cup for the best patriotic song to the tune of *It's A Long Way To Tipperary*, while Wake Up Yankee Band won the ice pitcher for the best song on Yankee Shakers.[29]

Despite the severity of the war in Europe, a Carnival was held in 1916. This took place on 6 and 7 March. By this time the Victor Company had released several more vocal recordings from their sessions in 1914. Just before the festival, the H. Strong Piano Warehouse was pleased to advertise these in the *Port of Spain Gazette* as:

EXCLUSIVE
VICTOR RECORDS
—— OF ——
Carnival Music

Reports in the *Mirror* show that the Carnival of 1916 maintained its regular pattern. Thus, in their account of the first day of the celebration, they commented:

The majority of masqueraders were half disguised in old clothes or last year's costumes.

The music also received attention:

There was practically an utter absence of intelligible singing or of instrumental music, bamboos which predominated.'

Some masques were identified:

Indians and yankees and rough riders were more numerous than
clowns.
There was absolutely nothing attractive except perhaps a peacock.

The newspaper also carried an advertisement for a competition of the
type Lord Beginner remembered. This offered prizes 'for the best original
Song on the present war on the first day, and on the second day the best
original Costume'. The judges were two 'prominent gentlemen in the community'. Who won these prizes is not known.

Although disappointed at the 'preponderance of devils and dragon bands'
the *Mirror* was more enthusiastic about the second day's proceedings:

> Before noon there were a number of orderly bands to be seen dispor-
> ting their gay costumes and chanting their songs with a gusto which is
> peculiar to the second day demonstration.

For it:

> The best bands were The Punjabies representing the well known
> Indian fighters.

One group of 'Punjabs' won the prize for the best band representing the
Allies in the competition at the Surprise Parlour. Other winners were the
Belmont Tourist Syndicate (for the best song on the Yankee Shaker). The
Union Belgium Boys received a special prize, subscribed by the judges. A
cup for first place at the Red Lion Establishment was won by the Gold
Medal Syndicate. The Chinese shopkeepers of Charlotte Street awarded a
prize to the Tempting Creatures (dragons).

Other similar bands are mentioned by the *Mirror* as well as traditional
masques, some of which had been seen the day before. It also described the
music:

> The songs were a decided improvement although there was too much
> of the general refrain 'Tina loose she Baby' and such rot. There were a
> few good compositions on the War, the Kaiser and the Contingents.
> The following are a couple:

> > Sound the bugle the Kaiser cried
> > On to war, my only pride;
> > But to this Old England replied
> > We must reach to Berlin or die.

> > SINGLE REFRAIN
> > The West Indian Contingents going away
> > Old England forever to rule the day.

21 By the Carnival of 1916 Victor completed release of recordings made two years earlier. Unusually, titles of 'Calipsos' and 'Kalendas' were not identified on record labels but in newspaper advertisements.

'Tina loose she Baby' was probably the song Lord Executor remembered as the first 'leggo' sung in English:

> 'Teena where you been?'
> 'I been to tie me goat in the bamboo.'

Songs about 'the Contingents' refer to the formation of the British West Indies Regiment, founded to facilitate participation by black West Indians in the war. The first Trinidad Contingent had left for Britain in October 1915 and were in training. Thus, on the same page as its report of the first day of Carnival, the *Mirror* (7 March) printed a photograph of 'MEMBERS of the Trinidad Contingent reading the *Argos* in camp at Seaford, England'. On the departure of the volunteers, the crowds had been greater than those during the Carnival, according to the *Port of Spain Gazette* (8 March). Theodore Roosevelt, however, observed onlookers forming 'a dense mass on the sidewalks' on the afternoon of Shrove Tuesday. (The former US President was on a tour of the Caribbean).

Atilla recalled that several calypsonians saw service in the war: Albany, Douglas, Hero, Kandahar, Miller and Wellington. Prominent stickmen also volunteered for service, as did Sam Manning, who subsequently made a career as a vaudevillian, and interpreter of calypsos and other folk songs from the English-speaking West Indies.

The presence of 'kith and kin' on the front line in the war against Germany formed the core of an attack on Carnival in the *Port of Spain Gazette* on 8 March. It scorned the '"Higher Society"' who 'had enjoyed themselves ... in a manner which hardly fell short ... [of] what [was] customary at carnival season among them' and, despised the activities of the 'poorer section of the population'. There was, it said, 'simply naught but the objectionable and indecent and immoral element of [the festival] on the streets'.

Leaving aside a more positive account in the *Mirror* (which seems much closer to reality), the *Gazette*'s view of the street celebration in 1916 provides a useful contrast with their conciliatory attitude during the Boer War some sixteen years earlier:

> there was an entire absence of any organised effort at carnival. The usual musical bands were hardly in evidence at all; the old time 'bands' with banners flying, accompanied with singers and dancers giving specially rehearsed exhibitions, were practically non-existent; and even the decorated cars, carts and cabs were surprisingly few and poorly got

up. Groups of rowdies, some with sticks, which the police very properly and promptly confiscated, and accompanied by a few kettle drums
or fiddles, paraded the streets [yet, the writer believed, interest in the
festival had waned as a result of the war].

In essence, this was the swan song of the Carnival as it had been played
during the first sixteen years of the century. Three primary factors changed
the event: the war, the retirement of Lieutenant Colonel Swain as Inspector
General of Constabulary (in August), and the appointment of Major Sir
John R. Chancellor as Governor on 1 June.[30]

Swain, in his farewell speech to the constabulary, drew attention to the
'improvement' in Carnival during the thirteen years he had spent in Trinidad. It is evident that his firm, but understanding, policing methods had a
profound effect (although he claimed no special credit). This grasp of local
affairs was lost on his departure.

Swain's wisdom was no longer available, a new Governor was in post
(inexperienced in the ways of Trinidad), and there were the terrible circumstances of the war in Europe. The anti-Carnival lobby therefore persuaded
the authorities to further limit the festival in 1917. Chancellor issued a
Gazette Extraordinary on 12 January containing a constraint additional to
usual provisions. This stipulated: 'Persons will not, during the Carnival, be
allowed either alone or in bands to walk or drive about the public streets
masked or to walk or drive about in bands in disguise'. Chancellor
published a special message explaining his decision was based on the great
sacrifices being made by those serving in 'His Majesty's Navy and Army' in
defence of the British Empire.

A 'Constabulary Notice' reinforced Chancellor's Proclamation, making
clear that 'during the approaching CARNIVAL the wearing in public of
Masks of any description will not be permitted' and 'Processions or Bands
of Persons in Disguise or Fancy Dress is also forbidden'. Dated 8 January
this was signed by Lieutenant Colonel Geo. H. May, the new Inspector
General of Constabulary.

The days of Carnival were 19 and 20 February. The new restrictions
appear to have been observed by all but a handful of people (whom the
police treated with tolerance). A few bands in fancy dress, and one or two
others, made merry in the streets but none wore masques. Dancing was
confined to houses or lodge and society halls. Only one slight disturbance
received attention, at Carpicharima on Carnival Monday. The outcome
of the new arrangement met with approval. The *Port of Spain Gazette*

(21 February) believed the restraints had been accepted by 'the lower orders' and recommended the ban on masques should become permanent. Indirectly, this was a return to the attack on the *'false face'* that had been made in the *Trinidad Spectator* as early as 1846.

That the new regime was unpopular is best expressed by a calypso, recalled by Lord Executor, condemning Chancellor's action:

King's Regulation, Government Contingent,
Cannot prevent our masquerade,

Governor Chancellor, *pas tay connet*,	Governor Chancellor did not know
Sassay fête granmama-moen.[31]	It was my grandmother's festival

The campaign to sustain a ban on masques and costumes began early in the *Port of Spain Gazette* in 1918. On 6 January it published a leader suggesting a formal appeal should be made to the public not to celebrate the festival. It also advised that the administration should announce regulations even more stringent than those introduced the year before. In the event, on 14 January the Governor issued a Proclamation containing the same stipulations as 1917 (no 7 of 1918).

In 1918, Shrove Monday and Tuesday were 11 and 12 February. True to its standpoint, during the week preceding, the *Gazette* published letters from the Mayors of Port of Spain and San Fernando, appealing to would-be masqueraders not to celebrate Carnival. These were accompanied by another editorial, on 10 February, appealing to 'Sound Patriotism And Good Sense' from those who might otherwise consider holding festivities.

Despite the confidence of some that bands would appear, the Carnival posed no threat to law and order (*Trinidad Guardian*, 12 February). On the Monday, the *Gazette* saw only 'a few solitary individuals parading in the streets in the afternoon ... screeching themselves hoarse'. Most masquers dressed in the 'Barbadian' style, and one or two were arrested. The *Guardian* also described the music:

The repertoires [*sic*] of the masqueraders was, as usual, a poor one, the only song being heard was one which had for its refrain the downfall of 'Kola.' Bamboo beating was very much in evidence, the string bands being located in the various dance halls which were open all day and late in the evening catering to those whose inclination lay in that direction.

'Kola', whose true name was Joseph Alexander, was a recently disgraced ruthless police officer.

Dance halls and dancing did not meet with wholesale approval. Just before Carnival they had been the subject of a clash in letters published in the *Port of Spain Gazette*. These were written by the Reverend C. G. Errey (who called for special regulation), and Lovey (who took Errey to task without damning his sentiment). He pointed out the difficulty of enforcing the regulations advocated by Revd Errey. Indirectly, this view was vindicated in the *Guardian*. It reported a 'certain amount of dancing about in the streets' on the evening of Shrove Tuesday. This was contrary to the Proclamation but tolerated by the police.

Dressing and near masquing did not receive the same degree of tolerance. The *Guardian* gave details of several court cases. An East Indian leader of 'a band of five bamboo-beaters', four 'Wild Indians', each with enormous head-dresses, and others with similar accoutrements were all fined. Eight men and women 'disguised as ranch boys and ranch girls', who sang 'When the War is Over', marching down the street, were treated in the same manner.

The report of the final day, in the *Gazette*, expressed satisfaction that 'as it began the Carnival season ended with unwonted quietness'. In confirmation the *Guardian's* editorial commented that 'the City was spared the infliction of those abominably senseless and tuneless compositions dignified by the name of song which prior to 1917, obtained in Port-of-Spain'. In this earlier era, the costumes of different bands changed little and 'versatility was emphasised in the songs of rival chantuelles'. In late 1918, following cessation of war and the two year prohibition of street masquing, new trends were to develop.

During this period, two popular wartime calypsos were composed by one of the chantwells who had risen to fame at the end of the nineteenth-century. Just before the signing of the Armistice with the Germans there was 'an impromptu Carnival celebration on a Sunday night in October, when it was prematurely reported that Germany had surrendered'. The *Argos*, Port of Spain's popular evening newspaper, was the subject of a song that was performed by Henry Forbes, the Senior Inventor. The chorus captured the imagination of the masquerade fraternity:

> *Argos* paper, latest telegram!
> *Argos* paper, latest telegram!
> Germans surrender under de British commander
> *Sans humanité.*

Two verses deal with the improbable 'possibility' of an invasion of Trinidad by the Germans, and the island's Contingents at the 'front':

> When de rumour went roun' de town
> Dat de Germans were coming to blow de town
> Some, like cowards, remained at home
> All de brave run down with stones
> Some run with bottles, some run with bricks
> Some run with bamboo, some run with sticks
> Old Lady Semper run down with she old big *po'chambe*
> *Sans Humanité.*

> Now listen to what I gotta say
> Trinidadian boys gotta rule the day
> Now listen to what I gotta say
> Trinidadian boys gotta rule the day
> Dey volunteered to fight fo' de King without anything
> But listen boys, we got all de rum we need in dis colony
> *Sans Humanité.*

The other song, *Run Your Run Kaiser William*, appears to have been composed in the same period. It may have been based on the song *Cheer boys cheer*, sung in Arima during the first Carnival following the Boer War. Similarly, *'Argos' Paper* was to feature in the first Carnival following the 1914–1918 confrontation.[32]

Keep The Carnival Down Town: the *Argos* vs. the *Trinidad Guardian* – 'Victory Carnival' 1919

The spontaneous reaction to the ending of the war was one of religious thanksgiving. Large crowds flocked to churches on 11 November 1918 when the news reached Port of Spain. An official 'Celebration of Peace' was held in the city on the 22nd and 23rd of the same month. There was illumination of public and municipal buildings and, on Saturday the 23rd, a parade of decorated motor cars from Marine Square to Government House. The procession almost certainly featured marching and singing by the populace. A letter from Walter Merrick published in the *Argos* (7 February 1919) recalled how 'during the recent peace demonstration I have ridden behind a band for a quarter of an hour during which time the popular refrain was "no more Kaiser again"'.

Performance of a war-time Carnival refrain suggests an expectation for renewal of the full festival at Shrovetide the next year. In January 1919, however, it became apparent to the pro-Carnival lobby that the Governor did not intend to lift the ban on masquing.

When Governor Keate had attempted to suppress masques in the late 1850s, it was the *Trinidad Sentinel* (a broadsheet run by black creoles) that had pronounced in favour of the festival. In 1919 the equivalent newspaper was the *Argos*. The publisher of this evening tabloid was of Chinese ancestry and his editor and staff were black creoles of liberal persuasion. They stood out for the festival against the city's two dailies. These were the conservative *Port of Spain Gazette* (whose editor had painted himself into the anti-masquing corner) and the *Trinidad Guardian* (whose editorial line was equivocal). The last named was a very new enterprise. Following the demise of the *Mirror*, in late 1916, the *Guardian*'s team had taken over the printing establishment and launched their newspaper in September 1917.

The *Guardian*'s owners, therefore, were looking to expand circulation and sought the main chance for self-publicity in the Carnival agitation. Awaiting the official line, the editor maintained a distance from the demands for a complete restoration of the festival. The *Gazette* sustained a regular commentary on the evils of the celebration. In these circumstances, it was the *Argos* that made the running in negotiations with the administration for renewal of the masquerade.

During January 1919, the *Argos* provides ample evidence for its activity. A successful petition was organised, its opponents attacked, and pro-Carnival articles published. By 26 January, it was able to announce the Governor had agreed to receive its deputation and petition at the same time. The meeting took place on 29 January and, after hearing its case, Sir John Chancellor told the delegates the matter would be decided by the Executive Council.

The next day the Governor recalled the deputation, explaining he would rather not rescind his ban but considering that 'the people had understood it as a war measure, and would regard it as a breach of faith and a trick upon his part, if he were to continue the restrictions ... he had decided not to prohibit masking'. The Carnival would be allowed on 3 and 4 March on the condition 'he would hold each member of the delegation personally responsible if any disorder occurred'.

It seems likely Chancellor tried to divide the delegation, both before, during and after the occasions he received them. At their meetings he attempted to overawe each member by close questioning. E. M. Lazare (one of the *Argos* team, but not present on 29 January) suggested the Carnival should be held on the Queen's Park Savannah (where the competition was held in 1902). This was devised as a fallback but appealed to the Governor.

After the decision to hold a true masquerade, the *Guardian* took up Lazare's proposal (perhaps with the Governor's connivance). Prior to this, it seems, the newspaper had floated the idea of a 'Victory Carnival' and this provided an ideal site.

Two competitions were launched. The *Argos* devoted its energies to organising an event in 'Down Town' Port of Spain, the traditional location for Carnival. The *Guardian* was more ambitious. It devised a rival tournament on the Queen's Park Savannah, and became associated with the Carnival in San Fernando.

In Port of Spain the actions of the *Guardian* were always ancillary to those of the *Argos*. As well as having the advantage of the usual location, the *Argos* cleverly used the slogan 'Keep The Carnival Down Town'. The *Guardian*'s scheme became associated with what was seen as unfriendly interference by the hierarchy. Its two day pageant proved a failure. In San Fernando, under the patronage of the mayor, the 'Victory Carnival' met with success.

The *Argos* referred to itself as the 'People's Paper' and in Port of Spain received popular and enthusiastic support.[33] Stipulations regarding disorder, however, led to a further attempt to change the masquerade and masquerade music.

Chancellor Paseo: tent admission charges and ballad calypso – Carnival 1919–1920

CHANCELLOR PASEO

Argos paper in this colony
For the Carnival victory

CHORUS:
Everybody hail, everybody hail
Everybody hail for Chancellor
Tout ronds paye là   [All around the country]

Words by Henry Julien [*sic*]
Air by George Johnson

Chancellor Paseo was published by the *Argos* on 24 February 1919 and the lyrics are almost certainly by Henry Julian (the Iron Duke). The traditional pattern of its verse and chorus stand as a symbol of the past; as do the 'topical' lyrics for '*Argos*' *Tango* (by 'Mr G. Marsello of the Madison Concert Co') printed at the same time. The dance rhythms in these titles were popular in Trinidad from the 1890s (Paseo) and by the 1910s (Tango).

The *Argos* printed a number of other songs before the Carnival. This was a result of Chancellor's insistence on good behaviour by the masqueraders and the paper's concern to 'improve' the standard of Carnival music. Commencing with lyrics to *March Boys March Along the Road to Berlin*, sent by 'Mr H. A. Gamble, News Agent, with the suggestion that it may be adopted to the tune of "Sailors Afloat" by Tuppe' (3 February), several of these attempted to change the way in which Carnival songs were performed. The words were usually panegyrics for the *Argos* (and Governor Chancellor) for reviving the Carnival, or in celebration of the end of the war.

Walter Merrick, the prominent black musician, whose ideas for parodies of contemporary British and North American popular songs were published by the *Argos* on 7 February, shrewdly observed such tunes were 'all very catchy and ... known by one and all'. Like others, he was unfamiliar with Tuppe's melody.

As early as the first decade of the century patriotic British (or French) themes had sometimes been featured by bands marching through the streets during Carnival. *Tipperary* was sung in 1915, and *Rule Britannia* became a regular fallback when patriotism was an issue. Yankee Minstrels had performed popular North American songs from the early 1900s, if not before.

Despite the recommendation of catchy airs (popular among white people), several songs printed in the *Argos* maintained traditional elements. Even a 'Kalenda' (in support of the 'Down Town Carnival') was published

MASKED CARNIVAL.

THE " ARGOS " COMPETITION.

Play Your Carnival as in the Good Old Days.

DOWN TOWN in and Around MARINE SQUARE.

That's where the " Argos " Masked Carnival Committee will hold its Competition.

Valuable CASH PRIZES Offered.

Bands singing best Patriotic Song, 1st prize $25. 2nd 15, 3rd 10.
Most Uniform & best dressed bands   „ $50, 2nd 30 3rd 20,
Best Fancy Dress bands,   ,. $25, 2nd 15,
Best Creole Song (Patois or English) „ $25, 2nd 15, 3rd 10,
Best band of Musicians   1st prize $40, 2nd 20.
3 best Individual Masqueraders $5 each.
4 Good Conduct Prizes $15 each.

Other Prizes to be Offered

NO NEED TO WEAR EXPENSIVE COSTUMES

Conditions :

Bands using bamboos and bottles will not be allowed in the competition.
Bands must consist of not less than TWENTY persons and must be accompanied by at least *Four Pieces of Music.*
Bands for the *Musical Competition* must consist of not less than EIGHT and members must be uniformly attired,
The Creole Song may be either in *Patois* or *English* and must be with leader (chantrel) and chorus,
The Fancy Dress Band is to be quite distinct from others, and may be for instance Minstrels (Yankees) Clowns ; Japanese , Sailors ; Pieriots ; etc.

KEEP YOUR EYES ON THIS SPACE FOR MORE PARTICULARS.

Keep The Carnival Down Town.

22 A successful petition to reinstate Carnival in 1919 resulted in the *Argos'* competition. This overwhelmed a rival event held by the *Trinidad Guardian*.

on 2 March, the day before the festival. Purportedly, this was set to the melody of Stephen Foster's *Poor Old Joe*. There was, in any case, a continuing differentiation between songs used by bands in parade and songs performed in the tents.

The circumstances of Carnival in 1919 meant that the organising committees paid visits to the tents of masquerade bands. Their aim was to ensure that the lyrics of songs did not jeopardise the conditions laid down for holding the celebration. This was also the purpose of the specially sponsored Carnival competitions.

In Port of Spain the *Argos* trod a fine line between so-called 'improvement' and the maintenance of traditional forms. This is exemplified by the four primary categories selected for competition: (i) Costume (ii) Music (iii) Conduct (iv), Special Prizes. In category (i) all bands had to 'consist of not less than TWENTY persons and [had to be] accompanied by at least *Four Pieces of Music*'. There were three sub-divisions: (a) Best Fancy Dress Band; (b) Best Wild Indian Band; (c) Three Best Individual Masqueraders. In the second category 'bands using bamboos and bottles' were not allowed. Again there were three sub-divisions: (a) Best Band of Musicians, each of which had to 'consist of not less than EIGHT' members and 'be uniformly attired'; (b) Best Creole Song, this to be sung 'either in *Patois* or English' and always 'with a leader (chantrel) and chorus'; (c) Best Patriotic Song.

There was variation in the categories chosen by the *Guardian* for their 'Victory Carnival' competition in Port of Spain. This was also the case for the Carnival in San Fernando. While objectives were similar, there were differences in emphasis. A principal aim was to 'improve' the presentation of the first day of Carnival and all the competitions were scheduled for Shrove Monday.

The *Argos* tournament, in Marine Square, commenced 'shortly after 12 noon [when] the competing bands began to put in their appearance'. The *Port of Spain Gazette* (supporting the *Argos*) reported 'the first on the spot' were 'the "Midnight Robbers"'. Their costume was 'fairly original', with the '*cap-a-pie* manner on which they were armed with revolvers, daggers and the like', adding 'to the gruesomeness of their jet black costumes'. The song 'they indulged in' was 'the suggestive and now monotonous refrain:

> *Argos* paper: latest telegram
> Germans surrender to British Commander.

The 'Roosters' were the next band and 'the burden of [their] song was to keep the Carnival "down town" as victory would surely be proclaimed from the limits of Marine Square'. This may have been a version of the 'Kalenda' published in the *Argos* on 2 March:

> Never mind if you smell horse dung
> So you keep the Carnival down-town
>
> If you go in the Savannah you will mash cow dung
> So keep the Carnival down-town
>
> Dr Masson say it is bad for the lung
> So keep it down-town
>
> The 'Argos' say we must play in town
> So keep it down-town
>
> Savannah side will be stale in a way
> So keep de Carnival down-town
>
> Razor-grass does cut creole foot
> So keep it down-town
>
> Caracas don't pen de Carnival
> So keep de Carnival down-town
>
> Tram and cab-horse all clear de way
> So keep it down-town
>
> To make room for Johony [*sic*] at the break a day
> So keep de Carnival down-town
>
> And they all join up and have the fun
> So keep de ting downtown
>
> Cold foot and hungry belly no nice
> So keep it downtown
> So keep de Carnival downtown

The song challenges and insults the *Guardian* in the form of a *picong* (as did the letter accompanying the lyrics).

This sums up the attitude of masquerade bands towards the *Guardian*'s arrangements. Once they had presented themselves in Marine Square, none made their way to the Queen's Park Savannah to compete for the other prizes. The 'Victory Carnival' had to postpone many of its arrangements in the hope of participants the day following.

The second day of the festival continued in much the same way. The bands kept themselves to Marine Square and refused to take part in the 'Victory' competition. Eventually, after representations, at about 3.00 p.m.

a few bands marched north and paraded before the Grand Stand on the Savannah. First to arrive were the Crapaud Syndicate. On positioning themselves 'several men rendered recitative songs the memorising of which was a remarkable feat in itself. The subject ... was the favourite of the day, the war and Kaiser William, and lustily the chorus joined in with an energetically sung refrain'. Their final verse was improvised: 'That they had come at the GUARDIAN's invitation with a composition to suit any competition.' The Crapauds were succeeded by the Robin Hobin Hood Band singing:

> Robin Hood forever
> Merry men in red and green
> It's the best band ever seen.

HM Loyal Convicts then appeared, followed by a pierrot, and the Old English Gentlemen. Only the pierrot did not receive a prize. HM Loyal Convicts won first prize for dress, while in the *Argos* competition they had come second in the same category. On that occasion their song was:

> Governor Chancellor say, Carnival we all must play
> Governor Chancellor say, Carnival we all must play
> The *Argos* paper, a champion advocator,
> Beg us to play in the very best manner
> Convicts shall gain the Victory.
> *Sans de humanité.*

In the musical contests run by the *Argos* prizes for 'best creole song' were awarded to Cavalry (1st), Tourist Social Union (2nd), and Red Cross Syndicate (3rd), while the 'best patriotic song' awards went to *Argos* Band (1st), Britannia (2nd) and Napoleon (3rd). The first prize for 'best band of musicians' was awarded to Headley's Band (a well known string aggregation), with 'Munroe's' Band in second place. (The last named was presumably run by Cyril Monrose).

It is unclear whether the admonitions to 'improve' the music of the Carnival bands had any real effect. The majority of songs probably remained traditional in format, although the lyrics may have been 'censored'. In Marine Square the 'Napoleon [band] ... marched past to the inspiring strains of the "Marseillaise"' and Britannia 'to the irresistible refrain of "Britannia Rules the Waves"' but neither tune created a precedent.

The music in San Fernando came under greater control. Performances of contemporary popular songs, *Good-by Broadway* and *Over There*, were required as bands marched along certain roads. In this, the Carnival Committee were well pleased with the results they achieved, as the *Guardian* reported on 5 March:

> a deputation of the members of the Committee visited the bands during their practices carrying out an educational campaign which bore splendid fruit, proof of which was afforded by the fact that there was less indecency in songs this Carnival than ever before. An amusing instance of the change that has been brought about is recorded by the following story. During the competition a member of the Committee went to a band and asked one of the leaders whether the band was taking part in the Calypso Competition, which was the next item on the programme.
>
> 'Oh! no,' she replied in a tone which showed her dignity was not a little wounded, 'we don't sing calypso, we sing rag-time'.
>
> The Committee man smiled for he knew that when the Committee made the bold venture of fixing 'Joan-of-Arc' as a song for the competition and stipulated that 'Good-by Broadway' should be sung along the route they came in for much criticism.

For the Musical Competition another contemporary popular piece, '*Liberty Bell* – a two step by W. K. Mohr', was required.

The San Fernando Committee appear to have believed they were in the process of engineering a complete break with tradition. Notwithstanding, a letter from a resident (*Guardian*, 9 March) indicates some bands had declined to participate or did not conform with the qualifications. The usual complaint about 'meaningless words set to musicless tunes' was reiterated. 'Even "Kaiser run away"', the correspondent wrote, 'was nowhere in comparison with "Goodbye Broadway, Hello France"'. This popular song, performed 'by one of the bands in perfect time and tune' had impressed, but appears to have been a temporary adoption in order to reinstate the full festival. The changes in Carnival music were more subtle.

On 23 February (just over a week before the festival), the *Guardian* published an edition devoted to the 'Victory Carnival'. Articles describing Carnivals in Venice, Rome and Caracas were featured, as well as two pieces on preparations in Port of Spain. The first, on 'The Makers Of Masks' is the only contemporary article on this subject. The second, on 'Carnival Bands At Practice' is similarly unique. It establishes the way in which masquerade band practices were centred around the performance of local music.

The *Guardian*'s reporter visited seven tents, one on the west side of Port of Spain (Woodbrook), two in the 'French Shores' (Princes Street and George Street), three in Belmont (Bedford Lane, St Francois Valley and Pelham Street), and one in John John (Plaisance Road). He described activities at four of these locations:

> At Cavalry, Woodford Street, there was a marked display of enthusiasm. A large benab covered over with coconut branches and liberally decorated with flags and paper balloons had been erected on a spot opposite the AME church. Inside the benab has been placed in neat rows along the sides several benches on which those who were privileged to gain admission were seated. A small charge of a couple of cents was exacted for entry, but this did not deter people from turning up in large numbers to listen to the airs which should prove exceedingly popular. Long before nine o'clock, the hour fixed for the proceedings to begin, spectators made their way to Woodford Street, so that when Mr E. Briggs and his musicians opened their programme with a lively composition, fully four hundred persons surrounded the benab. The musical instrument[s] of the band here consisted of four pieces – – –; a violin, flute, quatro and guitar, their blending, soft and low, being very good indeed. Several prominent numbers [*sic*] of the community who were present, expressed themselves as being quite pleased with what they had heard, the airs being principally patriotic. At George Street, w[h]ere the 'Bamboo Band' had also entrenched themselves under a coconut leaf covered hut, the crowd of spectators was not so large as in New Town, but what they lacked in members they made up for by their spirited approval of the tunes which were being rehearsed. Here the musical paraphernalia were confined to the popular 'instruments' of the proletariat which consisted of lengths of hollow reeds of bamboo, a small grater operated on by a musician with a stick, a 'schack-schack,' and the inevitable empty gin flask with a tin spoon as a beater.
>
> The rehearsals in Prince Street were also satisfactory, the efforts of the musicians to interpret aright the calypsos which had been composed for them by a local master of the art being enlivened by the one-stepping of some young girls whose dancing won the loud and unstinted applause of everybody, not excluding two policemen, who preserved order. At Belmont also the rehearsals went through without a hitch, the 'Wild Indian' band leading the way with a soul-stirring composition which is sure to attract attention on Carnival days.

(a)

(b)

23 Carnival characters depicted in 1919.

Unfortunately, in only two of the tents is there any detail of construction. Cavalry's tent was large (benab is derived from an Arawak word for a shelter made of a framework of poles covered with branches and leaves). The way in which it was decorated and the arrangement of the seating conform with the established pattern. Seats were placed around the edge with performers in the centre. This layout is also confirmed for the tent of a bamboo band described in a letter to the *Port of Spain Gazette* (26 February). The writer objected to a new entrance fee and bemoaned dancing to bamboo music by two dressed in disguise who 'wriggle[d] in the most immoral manner'. An admission charge is not mentioned in the description of the George Street tent, but two cents were taken by Cavalry at Woodford Street.

Lord Executor remembered Cavalry introduced a charge as early as 1906 but this appears to have been unusual and probably died out during the 1910s.

Atilla places the introduction of regular admission fees to 1919, 'when "King Fanto", hero of the country districts [San Fernando] visited Port of Spain' at the invitation of ' "King Dragon" (Clarence Lynch)'. To finance this, Lynch 'charged two cents for bamboo seats' at the tent of the Red Dragon Band, 46 George Street. Reports of charges add substance to Atilla's recollection. He also remembered that stick-players collected entrance fees for their bouts in yards where they now performed. Bamboo bands often provided percussive rhythm.

The instrumentation of the Bamboo Band in George Street appears to have been the regular complement. The string band led by E. Briggs at the Cavalry tent also played familiar musical instruments for the accompaniment of calypsos.

Music at these locations reflected the different classes of bands. None satisfied yet another correspondent in the *Port of Spain Gazette* (2 March). His letter complained that all practices amounted only to the production of 'some absurd doggerel consisting of half-a-dozen words of solo followed by a dozen words of chorus repeated over and over *ad nauseam*'. He referred, however, to songs performed by marching bands.

Traditional features were maintained in spite of the endeavours to change Carnival. Among the masques seen in the 'down town' competition in Port of Spain were dragons, a maypole (*sebucan*), pierrots, minstrels and wild Indians. There was at least one stilt walker (moko jumbie) and many of the fancily dressed bands who entered the *Argos* competition based their costumes on traditional concepts.

The change in emphasis was in presentation. Bamboo bands did not parade in the streets, but they maintained tents and played their regular music. Calypsos, although 'censored', were still performed (and, no doubt, methods were found of averting the 'censorship'). Even the so-called 'rag-time' pieces adopted in San Fernando met with resistance and were sung simply to secure the future of the festival. Some tunes were those that Walter Merrick advised should be taken up as parodies in Port of Spain. A bamboo band appeared in the San Fernando competition.

The major alteration was the introduction of regular admission charges for access to the tents. It is possible, however, that this consolidated a trend started to offset expenses during the previous two years when masquing was constrained.

Although differences between the pre-war and post-war Carnivals were less than they appear at first sight, they signalled the major changes that were to take place during the next decade. These included the introduction of more and more formal competitions, the separation of the singers from masquerade bands (groups of calypsonians ran tents of their own) and the development of a market for recordings of local music.

Lionel Belasco continued making records in New York annually from 1915 (he appears to have taken up residence in about 1917) but there were no other recordings by Trinidad musicians. During the Carnival of 1919 it was the 'Exclusive Victor Records of Carnival Music' by Henry Julian and Jules Sims, together with Lovey's recordings for Columbia, that were featured in press advertisements. To celebrate the end of the war and the return of Carnival, Dick and Wells also advertised the latest North American dance music available from Columbia.[34]

Prospective purchasers would not have been the average Carnival devotee, many of whom were having great difficulty in making a living. This abject poverty led to a revival of the Trinidad Workingmen's Association (dormant during the war) and a period of labour unrest. Strikes and disturbances began at about the same time as the Carnival, and the Governor's conditions may have been imposed because of the possibility of agitation. There is no evidence, however, of a direct link between the 1919 Carnival and the strikes.

The unrest, which took on a tone of racial antagonism, was paralleled by racial confrontations in Britain (and Italy). Even before the war had ended there was an incident involving disabled black soldiers of the British West Indies Regiment and disabled white soldiers in Liverpool. Then, on

6 December 1918, there was a serious revolt by black soldiers of the same Regiment in Taranto, Italy. The issue was discrimination by white soldiers. From the beginning of 1919, and especially in June, there were clashes in several British port-cities between black unemployed (usually seafarers) and the white population.

1919 was a period of demobilisation. The experience in Britain of the Trinidadian musician Al Jennings, explains something of the disillusionment of black people who had seen service in the war.

> In World War I, I was stationed at La Palice, and while there we got together a little band for our own amusement. After the war we gave a few concerts for wounded coloured soldiers in London before their repatriation. A war had just been fought; the West Indies had sent their sons then as they did in this last war [1939–45]. Those concerts were not a success because, as I learnt later, they were for unwanted coloured soldiers – men who were the remnants of thousands who would never see their homes and loved ones again.

Undoubtedly, this attitude represents the mood of soldiers of the Trinidad Contingent when they returned on the morning of 24 May. They were met by a large 'motley crowd' at St Vincent's Wharf, Port of Spain and disembarked to the accompaniment of the Constabulary band playing British wartime songs.

When they were all on land the band struck up *Cheer Boys Cheer* (or *Run Your Run Kaiser William*) 'which the crowd at once took up'. In formation, the soldiers marched to the Prince's Building. Here they were entertained to a 'Welcome Breakfast'. The *Gazette* (25 May) notes that: 'Lovey's band was in attendance and at once started some favourite selections and it was with difficulty that the boys could keep their seats.'

This mood of celebration was short-lived. The troops reached Trinidad bitter at the way they had been treated by British authorities, and to find there was no employment. The undercurrent of unrest was inflamed by this and news of race riots in Liverpool (4 to 10 June) and Cardiff (11 June). A few seamen willing to be repatriated from Cardiff left on 13 June and reached Trinidad on 17 July with first-hand descriptions of their discriminatory treatment. There had also been a race riot in Glasgow on 17 June and trouble in London one day earlier. Thus, when it came to the time of official Imperial Peace Celebrations, on 19 July, few black troops attended (although they had been asked to lead the Trinidad parade). There was racial violence in Trinidad, and in the same period disturbances in

Jamaica and British Honduras (Belize). In London, black soldiers had been insulted by not being allowed to take part in the procession.

One way by which news of these events was spread to black people in Britain, and in the English-speaking West Indies, was via the *African Telegraph*, organ of the Society of People of African Origin. This was edited in London by a Trinidadian, F. E. M. Hercules. Another source of information was the *Negro World* (newspaper of Marcus Garvey's Universal Negro Improvement Association, founded in Jamaica, but based in New York City, USA). In Trinidad the *Argos* printed news from these sources. From July 1919, Hercules spread his views in person in the English-speaking Caribbean.

With high unemployment and racial tension, the Trinidad Workingmen's Association became a focal point for dissent. By the end of August, Captain A. A. Cipriani (a creole of Corsican descent) had returned to Trinidad. Sickened by ' "the contempt, humiliation, insults and suffering heaped upon the men of the British West Indies" during the war', he immediately joined the TWA and encouraged others to do likewise. Membership increased rapidly and, with the backing of the Association, on 15 November stevedores in Port of Spain went on strike. After confrontations in early December the administration found it expedient to capitulate to the strikers.

Connie Williams records two songs associated with this strike. One, entitled *King Flecky*, called on Flecky Keezer 'to lead' the people 'in their strike'. It refers to Dardenell and Hill Sixty, 'both parts of the same hill in the Eastern section of Port of Spain, where the stevedores and poor people lived'. The other was based on the familiar wartime calypso *Run Your Run Kaiser William*:

> Raise your flag, ev'rybody, raise your flag!
> Fly your flag, ev'rybody, fly your flag!
> Hear what the stevedores say,
> Hear, boys, here!
> Two dawllars a day can't maintain our family.

> The English say we can live on two dawllars
> The English say we can live on two dawllars
> But listen to what we say
> Listen, boys, listen!
> Two dawllars a day can't maintain our family.

> Down with the flag, ev'rybody, down with the flag!
> Down with the flag, ev'rybody, down with the flag!
> Hear what we got to say, and
> Cheer, boys, cheer!
> [Two dawllars a day can't maintain our family].

In 1920, action taken by the executive was designed to minimise the effect of the surrender to the strikers. Several leaders of the TWA were arrested, imprisoned, and deported. Legislation was introduced, including the *Strikes and Lockout Ordinance* (no 1 of 1920) and the *Seditious Publications Ordinance* (no 10 of 1920). The latter banned the distribution of periodicals such as the *Negro World*. The *Argos* was eventually forced to cease publication.[35] These actions were taken both before and after the Carnival which was allowed to take place at Shrovetide (16 and 17 February).

Reports of the Carnival in 1920 make no reference to disturbed times. In this it seems Chancellor calculated it was politic not to intervene in a festival with a troubled history. There was no sponsorship in Port of Spain, although the San Fernando Committee remained in charge of the event in that city.

The *Guardian* (28 January) reported rehearsals in favourable terms noting that 'the masses of Port of Spain are already well advanced in their preparations for celebrating this event'. It described the activities in the tents after nightfall:

> In the camps scattered here and there in the area commonly known as 'The French Shores' enthusiastic crowds gather to listen to the bands practising their calypsoes and to join wholeheartedly in the refrains.

Complimenting the participants on their good behaviour they commented how there was:

> something fascinating in the rhythmic contortions and abandon of the feminine dancers at these practices which seem to have a peculiar attraction for strangers such as seaman and soldiers who are regular visitors to the camps.

There was other music such as 'the staccato sounds' of bamboo bands and the music of the dance halls where revellers in costume might 'be seen doing the modern jazz instead of the stately old quadrilles'.

A mix of past and contemporary musical trends is represented in this description. There is dancing to the singing of calypsos in the tents of masquerade bands (indicating a circular space remained in the centre); traditional bamboo music; and acceptance of the latest American (and European) fashion for jazz. Attendance by non-Trinidadians in the tents is mentioned for the first time.

The police in Port of Spain expected a revival of bamboo music in the streets and made preparations. They staged a special practice session to familiarise their horses with 'the *bamboo tamboo* that they might not be restive on Carnival days'. The event took place just after dawn, on 4 February and, the following day, the *Guardian* explained this and other unusual features. For example the column heading reads:

A CARNIVAL
PRACTICE.

FINE PERFORMANCE BY
POLICE BAND.

PREPARING FOR THE 16TH AT
ST JAMES.

CONSTABLES DISPLAY TALENT
WITH 'TAMBOO BAMBOO.'

The correspondent had been attracted by 'the loud but sonorous chantings of the "creole kalendar"' to the 'staccato sounds of the bamboo' coming from the direction of the Police Barracks in St James (to the west of the centre of Port of Spain). He was astonished at the early hour – a transgression of 'the unwritten canons of Masquerade law by holding a kalendar practise at 6.20 a.m.' – and to find that it was the police who were the performers. His observations provide one of the few extant descriptions of this type of music and also give an indication of the complexity of the development of black culture in Trinidad. The active participation of the police bamboo players represent a role reversal worthy of Carnival itself:

> The director was a tall pleasant faced individual in whom I recognised an old chant of the glorious carnivals of the late 90's. But what astonished me most was the fact that the band was composed chiefly of members of the Constabulary. Some of these had flamboyant flowers stuck in their hats, and were disguised in old bags, flags and sundry unmentionables which gave them a comic and outlandish appearance. I had not been on the scene more than half a minute when the music struck up. It began with the booming sound of the bass bamboo which

serves to regulate the time, and after a few beats, a number of the band who played the lighter reeds joined in. The 'cutting' (beating) of the finer reeds in rhythmic punctuation between the boom of the bass bamboo was really surprising. The shac shac players and the bottle and spoon operators completed the orchestra, and the music was furnished to the chanting of a 'single re' by the director in a high-pitched tenor, and then taken up in chorus by the other members of the band, not excluding the orchestra.

The crowd of onlookers attracted by these novel proceedings included children and an elderly woman who began moving in time to the music. A group of mounted police approached the performers and dispersed the band 'some of whose members were executing the most extraordinary capers with a grace which was born only of practice and good taste.' On completion of this exercise:

> the band reassembled this time beating a 'kalendar' in *lah minor*. As this favourite chord in creole music was touched, the chorus singers responded with a zest which shewed that they were going through the recitals whole-heartedly. Again the horses made their appearance and this time they were made to walk quietly through a lane which divided the band.

Unfortunately, the 'old chant of the glorious carnivals of the late 90's' is not identified (one is tempted to speculate it was Henry Julian). The system used by the singers to classify different musical motifs based on the tonic sol-fa is exemplified, as are the different lengths of bamboo that made up the consort.

This form of music went by two names: tamboo bamboo or bamboo tamboo. Its performance reflected the past. The lead singer employed by the police was associated with Carnivals from the last decade of the previous century. There was an innovation in the tents in 1920, however, that changed the way in which calypso was sung.

Walter Douglas also had the monikers Chieftain, Admiral and Railway. The latter was in recognition of his leadership of the Railroad Millionaires, a masquerade band he founded in 1921. Following his return from the First World War, he obtained employment as a ticket collector with the government railway company. Singing in the tents in 1920, Douglas 'introduced a new style known as the "Ballad" which was to remain popular until about 1927'. Lord Executor explained that 'the beat was slow, topics were more everyday, local parlance was employed, and many were sung in the Major Keys'. The song that established this pattern was *Doris*:

> Doris, you see what you do, you make a fool of you!
> Doris, you see what you do, you make a fool of you!
> You don't look too well before you leap
> But now you have to sit and weep
> You took six for a nine
> Better you put water in your wine.

Songs performed in Carnival parades reverted to favourites from before the war. This is the implication of a report in the *Port of Spain Gazette* (18 February) following the second day of the celebration. Covering the first day the *Guardian* (17 February) also indicates a restitution of traditional forms of masquing at *jouvert*:

> The customary old masks, arranged in odds and ends, chanting and bawling calypsos and other ditties, crept out from their homes and made for the heart of the city, infecting the workday world with the gay and joyous spirit of the Carnival.

Masqued characters included the customary Barbadian cooks, and representations of 'the underworld' such as beggars, burglars, crooks, highway robbers, pickpockets and railroad robbers. There were also those who depicted 'the limbs of the law' but 'unlike the real ones [they] conducted a successful business by extracting many "pounds" (pennies) from their good-natured victims'. In addition:

> To brisk or syncopated music, the maskers in bands paraded the streets swaying their bodies to the rhythm of tunes.

The report in the *Gazette* of the same day indicates that bands of different types of wild Indians were also present.

The *Gazette*'s account of the Carnival on 18 February emphasises the music had maintained pre-war values:

> in the matter of song, one was intensely bored with the meaningless ditties resurrected from the scrapheap of bygone years ... it must have been a complete shock to observe that months of so-called 'carnival practice' produced nothing more artistic than a two days monotonous refrain: 'We want a thousand gen-er-al, to follow de Kaiser funeral.' The weird reverberations of the 'bamboo' bands, with bottle accompaniment, monopolised the major part of the musical element; and it

was welcome relief when a Yankee troupe came along with string band
rendering of ever popular coon songs.

Music for the 'Carnival "Empire" Dance' at the Prince's Building on the
evening of *Lundi Gras* was by Headley's string band.

There was little or no trouble from the masqueraders, although on
Shrove Tuesday a bamboo band in San Fernando was involved in a fracas
with the police. The competition in that city seems to have followed the
pattern of the previous year. An innovation was the appearance of 'about
half a dozen pierrots' who delivered grandiloquent speeches.

The peaceful nature of Carnival was itself a masque for the underlying
current of disaffection. Evidence for this is provided by Patrick Jones (who,
circumstantial evidence indicates, performed calypsos under the name of
Oliver Cromwell, or the Lord Protector). He sang what he called the 'first
political cariso' in 1920. This contemporary commentary was entitled *Class
Legislation*:

> Class legislation is the order of this land
> We are ruled with an iron hand
> Class legislation is the order of this land
> We are ruled with an iron hand
> Britain boasts of equality
> Brotherly love and fraternity
> But British coloured subjects must be in perpetual misery
> In this colony.

Jones remembered that the *Guardian* published an editorial advising he
should be charged with sedition for this song. This may indicate it was
composed following the passing of the *Seditious Publications Ordinance* at the
end of March.

One method the British used to hold together their disparate Empire was
visits to Imperial territories by members of the Royal Family. Thus, on
16 September 1920, Edward Prince of Wales called at Trinidad returning
from a tour that had taken him to Australia. His successful stay lasted three
days and was consolidated by a grand ball at the Prince's Building. At this
Lovey's Band provided the music until the arrival of the Royal Party.[36]

In summary, the links with the Carnival of the late nineteenth century,
via the masquerade bands and their tents, can be seen to have been in a state
of flux by 1920. This is true especially for the top chantwells who, once
regular tent admission charges had been introduced, and the construction

and seating arrangements of the tents altered, formed themselves in to groups of competing singers. By the end of the decade, few calypsonians sang at the head of bands parading the streets. Most performed only in tents during the weeks leading up to Carnival. The themes adopted by these singers included political topics. Some of their songs began to be recorded commercially by visiting singers, or expatriates, in New York City, USA.

The appearance of bamboo bands is reported sporadically in Carnival after 1920, although this does not mean they did not participate regularly. Bamboo musicians almost certainly maintained their presence in yards where they sustained the singing of old-time *kalendas*. These tunes were also featured as road marches by bands whose presence in Carnival is more fully documented. Likewise, string bands such as Lovey's consistently took part in parades as well as continuing to provide music for festive dances. Instrumental music associated with Carnival was also recorded in New York but these developments lie outside the scope of this treatment.

5

Creole musical traditions: Africa, the Caribbean and beyond

Despite slavery, African-derived culture persisted in the Americas; a principal component being music associated with sacred and/or secular rituals.

While the drum and fiddle are the symbols of Africa and Europe respectively, this is not an exclusive division. Percussion instruments of European design and string instruments of African design were introduced by migrants from these continents and there was cross-cultural absorption. The symbol of the drum was modified to represent African and African-American culture in the Caribbean – a series of *creole* traditions that have evolved with respect to local geographical and/or political circumstances. Territorial proximity in the circum Caribbean, however, is a physical link between these different developments.

It is in the context of *creole* culture that music was sustained by African-Americans. In the historical record, drum dances are the most prominent, followed closely by dances accompanied by the fiddle. Both instruments featured in carnivalesque processions.

The social institutions that utilised music for these dances and processions also maintained other performance characteristics. For drum dances these were, principally, call and response singing, particular dance movements, and a circular arena for dancing, with the drums usually positioned at a point on the circumference. They might serve sacred and/or secular purposes – these distinctions are blurred in African and African-American culture. Activity appears to have been organised hierarchically and when these associations participated in processions, the same constitutional pattern was maintained. African 'tribal' groups took part in pre-Emancipation Jonkonnu in Jamaica and there were also occupational and territorial bands. Similar fellowships existed in Trinidad for the purpose of holding drum dances. Like the organisation of dances, therefore, the composition of Carnival bands had its foundation in societies into which enslaved Africans formed themselves in the Americas.

These units were not static. As people of African birth declined following the abolition of the slave trade, the direct link with that continent was broken. Sometimes societies died out, sometimes they shifted allegiance, and, post-Apprenticeship, they were sometimes rejuvenated by indentured labour from Africa.

Dances and parades performed by these groups can be divided into two contrasting modes of expression – those that emphasised refinement of style, and those designed to stress behaviour considered by some to be outlandish. Both might be used to effect compromise, or to resist circumstances outside the control of participants, and on occasion resistance would be violent.

Sometimes institutions were supported by all strata in a community, such as the Rose and Marguerite Societies in St Lucia. Described by Henry Breen in 1844, these owed allegiance to particular saints and sponsored dances with decorations and other accoutrements. Participants dressed in elaborate costumes and were accompanied by drumming and call and response singing. Societies represented rival points of view and, via patronage, were concerned with power.[1]

In time, organisations that maintained their equilibrium often absorbed outside influences while sustaining belief in their original objective. A good example is the Big Drum Dance of Carriacou. The most sacred part of this ritual, which opens proceedings, is devoted to African ancestry. The second phase comprises dances standardised before Emancipation, while the third allows for post-Emancipation creativity.[2]

The history of carnivalesque activities in the Caribbean can be divided in a similar progression. In Jamaican Jonkonnu, the introduction of Set Girls (*circa* 1775) is the first indication of a creole development. African nations participated in the pre-Set Girl and Set Girl eras (ending in 1837).[3] Early morning *j'ouvert* parades in Trinidad Carnival, were associated originally with paying respect to ancestors. Like 'nation' bands in Jamaica, therefore, they are a positive statement towards genealogy.

Similar statements regarding African integrity can be seen in contemporary drum rituals in the Caribbean. These confident expressions of descent are not static representations of the past but ideas modified by dynamics of time and social change. They represent, however, levels of cohesion in which African-Americans are least willing to compromise.

In general, drum dances feature call and response singing, with the lead singer improvising verses to a common chorus. The chantwell can be male or female, as may be the chorus, and the form is generally accepted as African in origin.

Ranging from sea shanties to communal self-help, such as *gayap* in Trinidad, manual labour gangs used call and response singing. Work songs were employed on plantations and in prison farms (in the United States) and other forms of occupation, or enslavement, where rhythmic work was necessary. Improvisation by a lead singer was usual in these collective songs with the chantwell's verses often being satirical or topical.

Similar songs are likely to have been performed by bands in carnival-esque parades during the nineteenth century, including slave Christmas waits. The latter have their own European tradition but a Christmas house-to-house visit witnessed by Sir William Young in St Vincent in 1791 was not European: it featured a Moko Jumbie. The African provenance of this masquerader on stilts can be traced, as well as its importance as a figure of sacred *and* secular ritual. Later in the day Young saw black creoles dancing the minuet to two fiddles and a tambourine, and newly arrived Africans performing their own steps to a balafo (an African instrument) – highlighting the creole process and experience before Emancipation.[4]

Adoption, adaptation and incorporation of European dances by black people in the Caribbean was not simply emulation (or flattery). It was a judgement against the elite's idealisation of Europe and disparagement of Africa. Reports (by white observers) often stress black people danced with a facility that Europeans were unable to surpass. It was not necessary to fully appreciate the satire to be aware of its results.

Before the ending of Apprenticeship, all these activities rested in planto-cracy patronage. This system appears to be a straightforward relationship between slave and master, in which the latter dispensed favours, but the reality was not so straightforward. For example, slave resistance altered the relationship. In Trinidad, the elite comprised French-speaking (Catholic) and English-speaking (Protestant) sectors. Groups of creole slaves were also divided linguistically. There were similar experiences in other territories. A profound cultural dispersal followed the slave uprising in San Domingo in 1791 that spread to places as far apart as Louisiana, Jamaica, and Trinidad –

(note the song said to have been composed by the leaders of the Shand Estate 'Revolt' in 1805).[5]

Participation by groups representing African ancestry was reported in Jamaican Jonkonnu by I. M. Belisario in 1837, singing accompanied by the gumbay drum, but their presence was rare. In Trinidad, in 1838, a 'savage Guinea song' was yelled out by a Carnival band that was 'nine tenths' *creole*. These indicate parallel changes in festivals at different points in the annual calendar, in islands over 1000 miles apart. At the same time, their history demonstrates differences in evolution.

In 1840 Jonkonnu became a focal point for radical politics in Kingston, Jamaica, and the mayor (a conservative) endeavoured to stamp out the elaborate festival. This battle continued in 1841 and resulted in bloodshed following which the ruling elite (administrators, plantocracy, and church-men) closed ranks and were able to stultify the celebration.[6]

In Trinidad, despite several attempts, it was never so easy to stamp out Carnival for the elite was never united. This was in part because of the alliance between black Americans and the French plantocracy. The latter was in competition with its British equivalent and, more often than not, the British administration. When threatened, the festival was stoutly defended by the African-American and French-American communities. Their alliance is best explained by the use of French Creole as a lingua franca by black people throughout the nineteenth century. When indentured Africans came to Trinidad, it was this language they adopted for everyday speech with their compatriots.

The period in which African indentured labour took place in the British West Indies was short lived. Direct African presence was maintained by troops recruited in West Africa who were members of the West India Regiment. An example of their cultural contribution is a Moko Jumbie performance in St Vincent, described by Charles William Day. Conversely, J. Kedjanyi reports a masquerade tradition introduced into a Ghanaian village by black Caribbean troops from the same Regiment.[7] Imperial trade also sustained contact between Africa and the West Indies. White colonial civil servants and military personnel moved between the two areas – the career of 'Captain' Baker (the Trinidad police chief in the 1870s–80s) is a case in point.

Call-and-response singing by Carnival bands was the tradition in Trinidad when calypso began to be sung regularly in English. Construction of Carnival tents, with a circle in the centre for performance, echoes folk buildings used for secular or sacred occasions. These might be recreational (a 'tent' housed the drummers involved in the dance that led to the Arouca riot), or religious (a similar construction is built for the African-derived cult of Shango).

Attention has been drawn to the link between drum dances and songs called *caliso*. Alongside the use of *kalenda* to signify activities of stickmen (their game/dance, and other aspects of the sport), it seems probable this was a post-Apprenticeship development. Stickfighting *kalenda* and *caliso* form part of the pattern of exotic 'new creole' dances introduced in this period. They also demonstrate movement of nomenclature from one activity to another. Stickfighting contestants adopted the name of an old creole dance (evolved prior to Emancipation), and the name of a novel drum dance was transferred to songs performed by leaders of Carnival bands. The African-American origin of these kinds of music, however, is unquestionable.

The Carnival in Trinidad represents a multiplicity of cross-cultural influences. Beginning in 1783, together with slaves of African and African-American ancestry, the population came to include Amerindian, Spanish, French, English, Chinese, Black North American (who fought for Britain in the US War of Independence), Venezuelan and free African peoples. Other settlers were from Martinique, Grenada, Tobago, Barbados, etc. Indentured labour from the Indian sub continent added to this complexity. This poses an almost insoluble problem of overall comprehension in the face of diversity.[8]

Trinidad Carnival, nevertheless, is the one calendar event in the English-speaking Caribbean for which reports are available from slavery to the present. Despite a one-sided bias, these accounts provide a unique opportunity to examine the way in which black culture was perceived. In general, music during the Carnival season mirrors the pattern of the festival's development.

Before Emancipation, fancy Carnival balls held by the Trinidad plantocracy almost certainly featured fashionable European dances accompanied by white musicians. Unlike Jamaica, there is no evidence for local compositions in these styles nor the equivalent of the 'negro tunes adapted for the piano-forte' by Philip Young, published as *West-India Melodies* in London, *circa* 1820–30.[9] Occasional reports of drum dances apart, and the lyrics to two songs (from 1805, and the 1820s), black music in Trinidad before Emancipation is little documented.

By the Carnival of 1845, however, the dichotomy of 'well played' and 'barbarous' music appears in print for the first time. Most later nineteenth-century reports single out drumming, lewd dancing, or ribald songs (all classed as barbaric). In 1871, when the 'barbarous *Cane-bouler* of the lower orders' was first specified in newspaper reports, this black Trinidad tradition was synonymous with social (and musical) discord. The term Canboulay, however, is not exclusive. Contemporary reports show that in the island of Carriacou it is a Shrove Sunday evening family feast, while in St Lucia it is 'a dance mime of cane cutting in slave times' accompanied by '*shâtwél*' and chorus. There may also be a link with *Danses de la canne à sucre*, accompanied by drums, performed in Guadeloupe and Martinique.[10]

Charles William Day found black musicians playing for European dances a feature of Trinidad social life in the late 1840s. They picked and chose their clientele, as Day noted to his disgust. Alongside drummers, dancers and singers, these musicians represent the different black creole approaches to music: compromise or confrontation with the values of the elite. Within these categories there was scope for variation and improvisation.

Sometimes, a change in musical direction can be attributed to economic and social circumstances. This appears to be the case during the '*jamette* Carnival' (1870s to 1890s). Such distinctions are probably too facile. If a report in the *Chronicle* in 1882 is accurate, at the same time as drumming and drum dances predominated, some young black musicians were taking up the fiddle, and clarinet. Both instruments were featured, together with drums, in the Maribone stickband for the Carnival of 1877.

Canboulay was a significant component in Carnival until the ban on drums in 1884. From that time, a slow compromise began in the way the festival was celebrated. By 1898 it was clarinets and fiddles that accompanied 'indecent ballads in patois'. The next year, when 'calipso' in English became acceptable, it was reported customary 'for songs to be specially composed for the season'. This tradition was at least as old as the 'ribald' song performed at Shrovetide in 1851. The topic on that occasion was personal misfortune. In 1899, the song that captured the imagination was a political outcry on the abolition of the Port of Spain Borough Council. The use of English to articulate this complaint was symbolic on account of its direct message (no translation was needed). African-Americans found it less and less useful to resist British rule by using French Creole as a means of communication.

Initial patronage for the Fancy Bands that began singing English 'calipso' in 1900, was supplied by Ignacio Bodu. A man of French Creole descent and former Borough Councillor, he had supported stickbands in the 1870s and '80s. Like the masqueraders, despite abolition of the Borough Council he modified his attitude towards British colonial rule. Imperial patriotism was the theme of the Carnival of 1900.

From the 1870s, a particular criticism of the festival was corruption of children by 'lascivious' dances and 'obscene' songs. Schools run by the British colonial establishment were against the Carnival but educated songsters maintained links with the French Creole hierarchy and generally opposed the administration. Criticism as well as praise was evident in their topical calypsos, and the few lyrics that have survived from 1900 to the 1920s sustain this interpretation. In addition there were calypsos on other themes (including ribaldry), and songs from different islands continued to be absorbed into the mainstream of Carnival music.

The singing of 'calipso' in English, and adoption of string and woodwind instruments for its accompaniment, is indicative of a coming together of two aspects of black musical tradition in Trinidad. Respectable music (denoting a Venezuelan influence) accompanied a vocal style evolved from defiant nonconformity for competitions, or *picongs*, between songsters and stand-offs between masquerade bands as they paraded. Forms of confrontation often went hand in hand with patronage and might represent territorial or occupational allegiance.

Fancy Band chantwells were store clerks and the like, with a level of education confirmed by the intellectual content of their songs. Membership of these groups was from the same social strata and costumes were financed individually, but music, drink and food paid for communally. When Fancy Bands met in the street they would confront one another in song, but not physically. When a stickband passed, both groups would ignore each other; *batonnier* bands were seeking other fighters. Membership of stickbands, whose reappearance in the festival in 1903 caused consternation, was generally tinkers, fishermen and groups of similar occupation. There were no absolute rules – 'gentlemen' stickfighters were called *lom kamisol* (jacket men). Knowledge of stickfighting techniques was also necessary as a means of self defence.[11]

String bands also appeared on their own account. The earliest reference to a co-ordinated unit is the bogus police band that took part in the Carnival of 1899 and the following year the Excelsior String Band (led by Mr Martinez) marched in parade. Repertoire was usually dance music, the paseos and Spanish Waltzes (*castilians*) from Venezuela, as well as European rhythms. Lovey's String Band featured the former on its pioneering trip to the United States.

This American tour was not only significant in establishing a reputation for Trinidad musicians in person and on gramophone records, but also because of its encouragement by visitors from the United States. Tourists had begun to pay regular visits to the Carnival from the end of the nineteenth century and were personified by a masquerade band as early as 1899.

String band music symbolises creole compromise in the context of African-American culture. Calypso represents part compromise and part defiance towards European perceptions, and stickfighting *kalenda* no compromise at all. Recordings of Trinidad Carnival music obtained by the Victor Talking Machine Company in 1914 denote this cross-section of attitudes; dispositions present in Carnival from the turn of the century to First World War restrictions in 1917.

The Carnival of 1919, despite the failure of the *Guardian*'s event in Port of Spain, represents another significant move towards compromise by the masquerades. The discipline of 'official competition' began to be accepted as a norm that was gradually imposed on the annual celebration until 1942, when the Carnival was banned during the Second World War.

Creole musical performance maintained its three-pronged approach. String bands continued to play their repertoire of 'Spanish' influenced music in parades and at dances. From 1919, however, songsters began to separate from Carnival bands. There was a fashion for ballad calypsos. Old-style defiance was reflected in the music of tamboo bamboo bands (successors to the stickbands). 'Leggos', performed by other masquerade bands, sometimes represented nonconformity and sometimes denoted compromise.

The relationship between black masqueraders and the police was hostile until the end of the nineteenth century. Songs were disliked but difficult to stop being performed in the streets. There were good relations on all sides during the early 1900s when Fancy Bands held sway. Following the Water Riot in 1903, a careful path was trodden to re-establish accord with the majority of Carnival devotees, a policy that continued until 1917.

The likely distribution of local music between islands by black troops stands alongside the similar transfer of songs from one place to another by migrant labour. Martiniquians introduced their songs into the mainstream of black Trinidad folk music during the nineteenth century. Atilla the Hun has also noted the contribution of ships' crews in the spread of songs from island to island.

D. P., writing in the *Sunday Guardian* (Trinidad) on 23 February 1941, believed there were links between 'improvised *picong*' and similar songs performed in Latin America. He also saw parallels with calypso and 'certain South American ditties – especially those of the working people of Venezuela and Central America'. These influences on Trinidad music stand alongside a corollary made regularly that places the origin of calypso in songs of twelfth-century French troubadours.[12] There are other analogues, such as parallels between African troubadour traditions and those of the Trinidad songsters. Morton Marks argues certain forms of ritual black American music are characterised by 'switching between European and African forms, from "order" to making "noise"'. This observation is consistent with the evolution of Trinidad Carnival and its associated refrains. In essence, the masquerade was a point in the calendar when power was brokered between different sectors of the community.[13]

From the first reliable reports in the nineteenth century, Carnival music retained a variety of styles; from the gentile to the disruptive. The songs of black creoles included commentaries, panegyrics and protestations (sometimes ribald or insulting). There were also the pugilistic and self reflective songs of the stickfighting bands. All these components came together at the turn of the century under the collective name of 'calipso'. As the century progressed, calypsonians upheld this broad base of styles in their Carnival tent performances and, from the late-1920s, via the gramophone record – a continuity sustained by the colonial environment in which musicians performed. Songsters maintained a sense of purpose that, by the end of the Second World War, was to achieve popular appeal for their music both in the United States and in other areas of the English-speaking world.

Notes

1 Background to West Indian music

1 Lewis O. Inniss, 'Carnival in The Old Days (from 1858)', *Beacon*, vol. 1, no. 12 (1932), p. 12; PRO CO 884/4/40

2 J. S. Handler, 'The History Of Arrowroot And The Origin Of Peasantries In The British West Indies', *Journal of Caribbean History*, vol. 2 (1971), pp. 46–93.

3 J. H. Parry and P. M. Sherlock, *A Short History Of The West Indies*, 3rd edn (London, 1971), pp. 59, 171.

4 Sidney W. Mintz and Richard Price, 'An Anthropological Approach To The Afro-American Past: A Caribbean Perspective', *Occasional Papers In Social Change*, no. 2 (Philadelphia, 1976); Edward Brathwaite, *The Development of Creole Society in Jamaica, 1770–1820* (Oxford, 1971); Sidney W. Mintz, *Caribbean Transformations* (Baltimore, 1984); Magnus Mörner, *Race Mixture In The History Of Latin America* (Boston, 1967).

5 47 Geo. III c. 36; Parry and Sherlock, *Short History*, pp. 173, 180.

6 3 and 4 Gulielmi IV c. 73; 1 and 2 Victoriae c. 19; William A. Green, *British Slave Emancipation: The Sugar Colonies and the Great Experiment* (Oxford, 1976), pp. 156–61.

7 John Houlston Cowley, 'Music and Migration: Aspects of Black Music in the British Caribbean, the United States, and Britain, before the Independence of Jamaica and Trinidad and Tobago', unpublished PhD thesis, University of Warwick, 1992, p. 5.

8 Ibid., pp. 6–7.

9 Cowley, 'Music and Migration', appendix 5 (drum legislation in Trinidad). For the eighteenth century in the West Indies – Elsa V. Goveia, 'The West

237

Indian Slave Laws of the Eighteenth Century', in Laura Foner and Eugene D. Genovese, eds., *Slavery in the New World: A Reader in Comparative History* (Englewood Cliffs, 1969), pp. 120–21.

10 Dena J. Epstein, *Sinful Tunes And Spirituals: Black Folk Music To the Civil War* (Urbana, 1978), pp. 52–3 (contrasts the open playing of drums in the West Indies with secret playing in the United States); Cowley, 'Music and Migration', p. 18.

11 Cowley, 'Music and Migration', appendix 3 has one sample of this complex phenomenon.

12 An example, from St Vincent, is in Sir William Young, 'A Tour Through Several Islands . . .' in Bryan Edwards, *The History Civil and Commercial Of The British Colonies In The West Indies*, vol. III (London, 1801), p. 276.

13 See, for instance, the description of 'the barbarous music of that dark season' (night) in Charles William Day, *Five Years' Residence In The West Indies*, vol. II (London, 1852), p. 90.

14 John Cowley, 'Carnival and other Seasonal Festivals in the West Indies, USA, and Britain: a selected bibliographical index', *Bibliographies In Ethnic Relations*, no. 10 (Coventry, 1991).

15 Cowley, 'Carnival and other seasonal Festivals'; Fernando Ortiz, trans. Jean Stubbs, 'The Afro-Cuban Festival "Day of the Kings"', in Judith Bettelheim, ed., *Cuban Festivals: An Illustrated Anthology* (New York, 1993), pp. 3–47.

16 Andrew Pearse, 'Music in Caribbean Popular Culture', *Revista Inter-Americana*, vol. 8, no. 4 (1978), pp. 629–39.

17 Bridget Brereton, *A History Of Modern Trinidad 1783–1962* (London, 1981), pp. 10–47; Jean F. Dauxion Lavaysse (ed. E. B.), *A Statistical, Commercial, And Political Description of Venezuela, Trinidad, Margarita, and Tobago* (London, 1820), pp. 321–40; Linda A. Newson, *Aboriginal and Spanish Colonial Trinidad: A Study in Culture Contact* (London, 1976), pp. 177–224; Parry and Sherlock, *Short History*, pp. 170–2; Eric Williams, *History of the People of Trinidad and Tobago* (London, 1964), pp. 40–50; 65–85.

18 Pierre-Gustave-Louis Borde, trans. A. S. Mavrogordato, *The History of Trinidad under the Spanish Government, Second Part (1622–1797)* (Trinidad, 1982), p. 311; B. W. Higman, 'African and Creole Slave Family Patterns in Trinidad', in Margaret E. Crahan and Franklin W. Knight, eds., *Africa And The Caribbean: The Legacies Of A Link* (Baltimore, 1979), p. 62; L. M. Fraser, 'History of the origin of the Carnival', 16 March 1881: PRO CO 295/289/81.

19 Andrew Pearse, 'Carnival in Nineteenth Century Trinidad', *Caribbean Quarterly*, vol. 4, nos. 3–4 (1956), pp. 175–93.

2 'Pain nous ka mangé'

1 Borde, *History*, p. 306, 308–9; Pearse, 'Carnival', p. 177; Henry A. Kmen, *Music in New Orleans: The Formative Years, 1791–1841* (Baton Rouge, 1966), pp. 3–55 Epstein, *Sinful Tunes*, p. 92, p. 84.
2 Pearse, 'Carnival', p. 179.
3 'Martial Law For Christmas', from *Trinidad Gazette*, 29/12/1824, reprinted *Port of Spain Gazette*, 21/9/1925, p. 4.
4 E. L. Joseph, *History of Trinidad* (Trinidad, 1838), pp. 229–30; *Barbados Mercury and Bridgetown Gazette*, 1/2/1806, p. 3; Lionel Mordaunt Fraser, *History of Trinidad (First Period) From 1781 to 1813*, vol. I (Trinidad, 1891), pp. 268–70; Brereton, *History*, pp. 48–9; Anthony de Verteuil, *A History Of Diego Martin 1784–1884* (Trinidad, 1987), pp. 71–3 and the plates III, following p. 94, no. 7 'Slave Revolt'; Michael Mullin, *Africa in America; Slave Acculturation and Resistance in the American South and the British Caribbean 1736–1831* (Urbana, 1992), pp. 223–6.
5 Borde, *History*, p. 313.
6 De Verteuil, *Diego Martin*, p. 11 and the plates II, following p. 67, no. 6 'Begorrat The King'.
7 Cowley, 'Music and Migration', appendix 5.
8 Pearse, 'Carnival', p. 178.
9 *General Index* (to the laws of Trinidad, passed between 1797 and 1850 (*sic* – 1830)), p. 14; *The Trinidad Almanac for the year 1824* (Trinidad, *c.* 1823), p. 88; Joseph, *History*, pp. 106–7; Lionel Mordaunt Fraser, *History of Trinidad (Second Period), From 1814 to 1839*, vol. II (Trinidad, 1896), pp. 53–4.
10 *Trinidad Gazette*, 23/12/1820, p. 2; 10/1/1821, p. 2; 13/1/1821, p. 2; Pearse, 'Carnival', pp. 179–80.
11 'Martial Law For Christmas', *POSG* 21/9/1925, p. 4.
12 Mrs (A. C.) Carmichael, *Domestic Manners and Social Conditions of the White, Coloured and Negro Population of the West Indies*, vol. II (London, 1833), pp. 288–97.
13 De Verteuil, *Diego Martin*, the plates IV, following p. 125, no. 5, 'Slave Revolt Commission'; Daniel J. Crowley, 'La Rose and La Marguerite Societies In St Lucia', *Journal of American Folklore*, vol. 71, no. 282 (1958), p. 550.
14 Carmichael, *Domestic*, vol. II, pp. 301–2.
15 X, 'The Origin of Canne Boulee', *POSG* (Supplement), 26/3/1881, p. 1; Censor, 'The Origin Of Canboulay And The Old Way Of Playing It', *Trinidad Chronicle*, 16/3/1881, p. 3; Richard S. Dunn, *Sugar And Slaves: The Rise of the Planter Class in the English West Indies, 1624–1713* (New York, 1973), p. 191; J. N. Brierley, *Trinidad Then And Now* (Trinidad, 1912), p. 319.

16 Cowley, 'Music and Migration', p. 185; PRO CO 295/289/81. Contemporary Carnival reports – *Trinidad Gazette*, 20/2/1822, p. 2; below, note 18 (1827); *POSG*, 4/3/1829, p. 3; 24/2/1830, p. 2.

17 X, 'The Origin of Canne Boulee'; Censor, 'The Origin'; X, 'The Origin of the Cannes Boulees' (in French), *POSG*, 19/3/1881, p. 3.

18 Kmen, *Music*, pp. 21–3, 32–5; *POSG*, 1/2/1826, pp. 2–3; Pearse, 'Carnival', p. 181; Lieutenant Colonel Capadose, *Sixteen Years In The West Indies*, vol. I (London, 1845), pp. 151–3; *Trinidad Guardian*, 16/2/1827 p. 1; *POSG*, 14/2/1827, p. 2; 4/4/1827, p. 2; Ignacio Jordan de Asso y del Rio, and Miguel de Manuel y Rodriguez, trans. Lewis F. C. Johnston, *Institutes of the Civil Law of Spain* (6th edn, materially corrected, Madrid, 1805) (London, 1825), p. 278; F. W. N. Bayley, *Four Years' Residence In The West Indies* (London, 1833), p. 214; *TG*, 17/4/1827, p. 2.

19 *Trinidad Sentinel*, 2/2/1860, p. 3 (under heading 'San Fernando', quoting '*Guardian*, January 27'); Bayley, *Four Years'*, p. 215; Carmichael, *Domestic*, vol. II, p. 53, Capadose, *Sixteen Years*, vol. I, pp. 155–6.

20 *POSG*, 5/2/1831, p. 2; 9/2/1831, p. 2; 12/2/1831, p. 2; 16/2/1831, p. 3; Anthony de Verteuil, *The Years Of Revolt: Trinidad 1881–1888* (Trinidad, 1984), p. 57.

21 *POSG*, 22/1/1833, p. 2; 25/1/1833, p. 1.

22 Pearse, 'Carnival', pp. 183–4; *POSG*, 13/2/1834, p. 2.

23 *POSG*, 2/8/1833, reprinted 21/9/1925, p. 6; Joseph, *History*, pp. 105–8; Carmichael, *Domestic*, vol. II, pp. 75–6; Capadose, *Sixteen Years*, vol. I, pp. 149–51.

24 Joseph, *History*, pp. 258–9; *POSG*, 5/8/1834, p. 3; Capadose, *Sixteen Years*, vol. I, pp. 156–64.

25 The term beau stick (or 'bow-'tick') meaning a club or heavy stick may have been used widely in the Caribbean. See, for example, the words to 'a genuine St Kitts negro song by Sam Matthews' printed by Day: *Five Years'*, vol. II, pp. 121–2; Cowley, 'Music and Migration': appendix 5 (order by the Cabildo); pp. 84–91 (stickfighting).

26 *Trinidad Royal Gazette*, 31/1/1834, p. 1; 27/1/1835, p. 1; 9/2/1836, p. 4; 27/1/1837, p. 1; 23/2/1838, p. 1.

27 Cowley, 'Music and Migration', appendix 5. The 'banjee drum' – *POSG*, 25/11/1845, p. 3 (African Dances); *Trinidad Spectator*, 27/12/1845, p. 2 (Christmas); *POSG*, 20/2/1849, p. 2 (Carnival – 'banjee' only is used); *POSG*, 12/11/1853, p. 2 (Congo dances/wakes).

28 *POSG*, 2/3/1838, pp. 2–3.

29 Donald Wood, *Trinidad In Transition* (London, 1968), p. 39 – other suggestions – Crowley, 'La Rose', p. 550 (Damas); Roger D. Abrahams and John F. Szwed, *After Africa: Extracts From British Travel Accounts and Journals of the Seventeenth, Eighteenth, and Nineteenth Centuries concerning the Slaves, their Manners and*

Customs in the British West Indies (New Haven, 1983), pp. 242–3 (Jamaica); p. 263 (St Lucia); *POSG*, 9/6/1900, p. 4.

30 1 and 2 Victoriae c. 19; Green, *British Slave Emancipation*, pp. 154–8; *POSG*, 3/8/1838, p. 2; Bridget Brereton, 'The Birthday of Our Race: A Social History of Emancipation Day in Trinidad, 1838–88' in B. W. Higman, ed., *Trade, Government And Society In Caribbean History 1700–1920* (London, 1983), p. 73.

31 PRO CO 295/289/81; X, 'The Origin of Canne Boulee'.

32 *TRG*, 5/2/1839, p. 4.

33 *Trinidad Standard*, 7/2/1842, p. 3; *POSG*, 8/2/1842, p. 3; *POSG*, 6/2/1844, p. 1.

34 *POSG*, 23/2/1844, p. 3; Wood, *Trinidad*, pp. 243–4 (from *Trinidad Standard*, 5/2/1845).

35 *Trinidad Spectator*, 27/12/1845, p. 2; *POSG*, 25/11/1845, p. 3.

36 *TRG*, vol. 6, c. 17/2/1846, p. 20; *POSG*, 17/2/1846, p. 3; *Trinidad Standard*, 19/2/1846, p. 3; *POSG*, 20/2/1846, p. 3; *Trinidad Standard*, 23/2/1846, p. 3; *Trinidad Spectator*, 25/2/1846, p. 2.

37 Day, *Five Years'*, vol. i, pp. 313–16 – 7 March was a Sunday in 1847.

38 Ibid., pp. 288–9. Day notes Christmas Day was a Saturday, as was the case in 1847.

39 *Trinidad Spectator*, 8/3/1848, p. 3; *POSG*, 20/2/1849, p. 2.

40 *Fair Play and Trinidad News*, 6/3/1879, p. 2.

41 *FP&TN*, 6/3/1879, p. 2; Wood, *Trinidad*, p. 244 (from *Trinidad Standard*, 5/2/1845); Day, *Five Years'*, vol. i, pp. 288–9; Pearse, 'Carnival' p. 186; *POSG*, 20/2/1849, p. 2; *POSG*, 3/8/1838, p. 2.

42 Migrants – Wood, *Trinidad*; Brereton, *History*. Martinique dancing/St Rose Society – *POSG*, 17/3/1846, p. 2. Prison riot – Wood, *Trinidad*, pp. 175–7; David Vincent Trottman, *Crime In Trinidad: Conflict And Control In A Plantation Society 1838–1900* (Knoxville, 1986), pp. 62–3; *POSG*, 2/10/1849, pp. 2–3; 5/10/1849, p. 2.

43 *POSG*, 13/3/1838, p. 2; 'Belé – from Martinique', *Trinidad Sentinel*, 1/4/1841 (Pearse Papers); José M. Bodu, comp., *Trinidadiana: Being a Chronological Review of Events which have occurred in the island from the conquest to the Present Day, with brief notices of the careers of some Eminent Colonists* (Trinidad, 1890), pp. 15–16.

44 J. J. Thomas, *The Theory and Practice of Creole Grammar* (reprinted London, 1969), (original ed.) p. v.; *FP&TN*, 1/3/1883, pp. 2–3; Andrew Pearse, 'Aspects Of Change In Caribbean Folk Music', *Journal of the International Folk Music Council*, vol. 7 (1955) p. 30; Day, *Five Years'*, vol. i, pp. 294–6.

45 Day, *Five Years'* vol. i, p. 289; vol. ii, p. 55; vol. i, pp. 260–1; vol. ii, p. 90.

46 *Trinidad Spectator*, 20/1/1847, p. 2; Pearse, 'Aspects' p. 31; *POSG*, 3/10/1848, p. 3; Cowley, 'Music and Migration', appendix 5. Day discusses 'Methodist wakes' in *Five Years'*, vol. ii, pp. 54–5.

47 *POSG*, 12/11/1853, p. 2.

48 Cowley, 'Music and Migration', appendix 5; *POSG*, 7/3/1851, p. 3.
49 *POSG*, 30/1/1856, p. 3; 6/2/1856, p. 3; *TC*, 5/3/1881, p. 2.
50 *POSG*, 7/2/1857, p. 3.
51 PRO CO 295/289/81; *POSG*, 11/2/1899, p. 7 (this places Keate's suppression incorrectly); *Trinidad Sentinel*, 25/2/1858, p. 2; *POSG*, 3/2/1858, p. 2; 27/2/1858, p. 2; Pearse, 'Carnival', p. 187; *Trinidad Sentinel*, 4/3/1858, pp. 2–3; Charles S. Espinet and Harry Pitts, *Land Of The Calypso: The Origin And Development Of Trinidad's Folk Song* (Trinidad, 1944), p. 61.
52 PRO CO 295/289/81; *POSG*, 19/3/1859, p. 3; *Trinidad Sentinel*, 10/3/1859, p. 3; *POSG*, 11/2/1899, p. 7; Kelvin Singh, *Bloodstained Tombs: The Muharram Massacre 1884* (London, 1988).
53 PRO CO 295/289/81; Inniss, 'Carnival,' p. 12; *POSG*, 11/2/1899, p. 7; Wood, *Trinidad*, p. 246; *Trinidad Sentinel*, 2/2/1860, p. 2; 23/2/1860, p. 3.
54 *POSG*, 13/2/1861, p. 3.
55 *Star of the West*, 7/2/1868, p. 3.
56 *POSG*, 21/2/1863, p. 3.
57 *POSG*, 10/2/1864, p. 3; *TC*, 3/10/1865, p. 2.
58 *POSG*, 17/2/1866, p. 3; *SOTW*, 15/2/1866, p. 3.
59 *SOTW*, 7/2/1868, p. 3; *TC*, 16/6/1868, p. 3; 19/6/1868, p. 3; 23/12/1864, p. 3; *POSG*, 11/1/1865, pp. 1–2; Trottman, *Crime*, pp. 180–1; *POSG*, 10/3/1846, p. 2. Compare discussions on crime in the two editions of L. A. A. de Verteuil, *Trinidad: Its Geography, Natural Resources, Administration, Present Condition and Prospects* (London, 1858), pp. 197–200; and (London, 1884), pp. 179–85.
60 *TC*, 3/10/1865, p. 2; PRO CO 295/289/81; *POSG*, 11/2/1899, p. 7.
61 *SOTW*, 11/2/1869, p. 3; *POSG*, 2/3/1838, p. 2; 20/1/1846, p. 2; L. A. Dunn, 'Carnival Through The Years', pt 2, *Evening News* (Trinidad), 26/2/1952, p. 2; *Trinidad Sentinel*, 3/8/1858 (Pearse Papers); Brereton, 'Birthday', p. 75; Bodu, *Trinidadiana*, p. 21; p. 23.
62 Charles Kingsley, *At Last: A Christmas In The West Indies*, 2 vols. (London, 1871).
63 Capadose, *Sixteen Years*, vol. I, p. 151; all quotations from Kingsley's *At Last* are taken from the one-volume edition (London, 1877) – horse races, pp. 366–7; music and dancing, pp. 369–70; Edward Bean Underhill, *The West Indies: Their Social and Religious Condition* (London, 1862), p. 24; Andrew T. Carr, 'A Rada Community in Trinidad', *Caribbean Quarterly*, vol. 3, no. 1 (1953), pp. 35–6, 48.
64 Day, *Five Years'*, vol. I, pp. 250–1; Kingsley, *At Last*, p. 124.

3 'Not A Cent To Buy Rice'

1 *POSG*, 9/3/1870, p. 3.
2 Wood, *Trinidad*, pp. 251–2; Lewis Osborn Inniss, *Trinidad And Trinidadians: A*

Collection Of Papers, Historical, Social And Descriptive About Trinidad And Its People (Trinidad, 1910), pp. 87–8 (reports only two were involved in the attack); Raymond Quevedo, *Atilla's Kaiso: A Short History of Trinidad Calypso* (Trinidad, 1983), p. 10, 165; De Verteuil, *Diego Martin,* pp. 134–55; Andrew Pearse, 'Mitto Sampson on Calypso Legends of the Nineteenth Century', *Caribbean Quarterly,* vol. 2, nos. 3–4 (1956), pp. 259–60. (Cedric) le Blanc's composition of *Not A Cent To Buy Rice* – Patrick Jones, 'Patrick Jones tells of calypso, chants songs of ancient calypsonians', in *Calypso Lore And Legend,* Cook Road Recordings (LP) 5016 (Stamford, n.d.).

3 *TC,* 14/2/1871, p. 4; *Echo,* 18/2/1871, p. 2; 25/2/1871, p. 3; *TC,* 21/2/1871, p. 3; 9/2/1877, p. 3; *New Era,* 6/3/1871, p. 3; *SOTW,* 23/2/1871, p. 3; Daniel J. Crowley, 'The Traditional Masques of Carnival', *Caribbean Quarterly,* vol. 4, nos. 3–4 (1956), pp. 215–16; *POSG,* 25/2/1871, p. 3.

4 Pearse, 'Carnival', p. 192; Crowley, 'Toward A Definition of Calypso', pt 1, *Ethnomusicology,* vol. 3, no. 2 (1959), p. 61; Wood, *Trinidad,* p. 241; *NE,* 20/10/1873, pp. 2–3; *POSG,* 14/2/1874, p. 3; *TC,* 17/2/1874, p. 3; *POSG,* 21/2/1874, p. 3; Bridget Brereton, *Race Relations In Colonial Trinidad 1870–1900* (Cambridge, 1979), p. 124; *FP&TN,* 18/2/1875, p. 3; *POSG,* 17/4/1875, p. 3; *TC,* 29/2/1876, p. 3; 3/3/1876, p. 2; 7/3/1876, p. 3; Pearse, 'Carnival', p. 189.

5 De Verteuil, *Trinidad,* 1884, pp. 182–5; Trottman, *Crime,* p. 12, 92, 311, 96.

6 Trottman, *Crime,* p. 92, 311; C. 4366, p. 50; *POSG,* 3/2/1877, p. 3; *Trinidad Palladium,* 3/2/1877, p. 2.

7 *TC,* 9/2/1877, p. 3.

8 Chapter 2 above and *TC,* 13/2/1877, p. 3; 26/2/1879, p. 3; *POSG,* 11/2/1880, p. 3; *TC,* 2/3/1881, p. 3; *POSG,* 12/1/1884, p. 4; PRO CO 295/301/56 – Freeling to Derby, 19/3/1884. Canboulay in country districts – Abbé Armand Massé, trans. M. L. de Verteuil, *The Diaries of Abbé Armand Massé 1878–1883,* vol. 4 (Trinidad, 1988), pp. 146–7; Inniss, 'Carnival', pp. 12–13 *Argos,* 17/2/1918, p. 7; Retired Warrior, 'Old Time Carnival: The Days Of The Stick Fighters; Ferocious Battles Recalled; A Retired Warrior's Memoirs', *TG,* 2/3/1919, p. 7; Shull, 'Pierrots A Feature Of Carnival In '90s', *Sunday Guardian* (Trinidad), 3/3/1946, p. 6; H. Neale Fahey, 'Divergence of Opinion on Recent Carnival Explained', *EN,* 12/3/1952, p. 3; Pearse 'Carnival' pp. 188–93; Pearse 'Mitto Sampson' pp. 256–62; Crowley, 'Traditional Masques', pp. 194–5; Andrew T. Carr, 'Pierrot Grenade', *Caribbean Quarterly,* vol. 4, nos. 3–4 (1956), pp. 281–3.

9 *TP,* 10/2/1877, p. 3; *TC,* 13/2/1877, p. 3; *Fair Play and Trinidad and Venezuela News,* 15/2/1877, p. 3; *POSG,* 17/2/1877, p. 3; *TP,* 7/4/1877, p. 2.

10 *FP&TN,* 5/3/1878, p. 2; *POSG,* 9/3/1878, p. 3. *TC,* 26/2/1879, p. 3 – indicates a 'Hosay procession' in 1878.

11 *TC,* 26/2/1879, p. 3; *FP&TN,* 27/2/1879, p. 3; *POSG,* 1/3/1879, p. 3.

12 *POSG*, 11/2/1880, p. 3; *FP&TN*, 12/2/1880, p. 2.

13 PRO CO 884/4/40; *TC*, 26/2/1879, p. 3; *NE*, 7/3/1881, p. 2; letter from 'Anti-Causist', *TC*, 30/3/1881, p. 3.

14 PRO CO 884/4/40; *NE*, 7/3/1881, pp. 2–3; *TC*, 2/3/1881, p. 3; 12/3/1881, p. 3; Bodu, *Trinidadiana*, pp. 43–4; Eugene Francis Chalamelle, *Some Reflections on the Carnival of Trinidad* (Trinidad, 1901), pp. 14–15; 'Canne Brule Riot 1881: Eye-witness account of Frances Richard (96) of 11 Rudin St, Belmont, as it was related on 4th July 1953 to J. D. Elder', Pearse Papers; Brierley, *Trinidad*, pp. 322–30; Inniss, *Trinidad*, pp. 82, 91–2; *POSG*, 21/9/1925, p. 13 (reprints articles on first lighting of streets, and Canboulay Riot); PRO CO 295/289/93 (25 March 1881) – has slightly different wording for the 'Notice' of 14 February and contradictory accounts from Freeling and Baker; PRO CO 295/289/66 (8 March); *TC*, 5/3/1881, p. 3; PRO CO 295/289/69 (9 March); PRO CO 295/289/70 (9 March); PRO CO 295/289/62 (7 March); PRO CO 295/289/63 (7 March). Carnival effigy burning in Martinique – Lafcadio Hearn, 'La Verette and the Carnival in St Pierre, Martinique', *Harper's Monthly Magazine*, vol. 77, no. 461 (1888), p. 741; and in St Lucia: Harold F. C. Simmons, 'Terre Bois Bois', *Caribbean Quarterly*, vol. 6, no. 4 (1960), pp. 282–5.

15 Bridget Brereton, 'Trinidad Carnival 1870–1900', *Savacou*, nos. 11–12 (1975), pp. 28–31; *POSG*, 21/9/1925, p. 13; PRO CO 884/4/40; *POSG*, 22/10/1881, p. 3; Pearse, 'Carnival', pp. 189–90. A contemporary retrospective on the riot – *TC*, 4/3/1882, p. 3.

16 *POSG*, 5/11/1881, p. 3; *FP&TN*, 9/11/1881, p. 2; *POSG*, 11/2/1882, p. 3; *FP&TN*, 9/2/1882, p. 3 (reprinted in *POSG*, 25/2/1882, p. 3, without naming the bands); *FP&TN*, 23/2/1882, p. 3; *TP*, 25/2/1881, p. 4; *TC*, 4/3/1882, p. 3; *FP&TN*, 9/3/1882, p. 3; Brereton, 'Trinidad Carnival', p. 19; Cowley, 'Music and Migration', appendix 5; Brereton, 'Birthday', p. 76.

17 *TRG*, 10/1/1883, p. 11; *POSG*, 13/1/1883, p. 4; *TP*, 10/2/1883, p. 3; *FP&TN*, 22/2/1883, pp. 2–3; 15/2/1883, p. 3; 14/2/1884, p. 2; *TC*, 7/2/1883, p. 2; *POSG*, 10/2/1883, p. 4; *TRG*, 7/3/1883, pp. 224–5.

18 *POSG*, 10/2/1883, pp. 3–4; *TC*, 14/2/1883, p. 2; *FP&TN*, 1/3/1883, pp. 2–3; *TC*, 3/3/1883, p. 2; Inniss, *Trinidad*, p. 97; Brereton, *Race Relations*, p. 161; Cowley, 'Music and Migration,' appendix 5.

19 *TC*, 2/3/1881, p. 3; *FP&TN*, 1/3/1883, pp. 3–4; Inniss – *Trinidad*, p. 97, and 'Carnival' p. 13; *NE*, 20/10/1873, p. 2; *Trinidad Review*, 9/8/1883, pp. 12–14; Massé, *Diaries*, vol. 4, p. 148; Crowley, 'Toward', part 1, pp. 59–60; Harry Pitts, 'Calypso: From Patois To Its Present Form', *SG*, Independence Supplement, 26/8/1962, p. 41; Massé, *Diaries*, vol. 4, p. 165, 261; *TC*, 10/11/1880, p. 3; *TC*, 4/2/1882, p. 3; *POSG*, 10/2/1883, pp. 3–4; De Verteuil, *Trinidad*, 1884, pp. 182–5; PRO 884/4/40; Retired Warrior, 'Old Time Carnival', p. 7; (Canboulay stickbands) – excerpt from letter sent by Edric Connor to Lennox Pierre,

21 February 1949, collected by J. D. Elder, 21 June 1953 (Pearse Papers); *TC*, 9/2/1877, p. 3; *TRG*, 7/3/1883, pp. 224–5.

20 *POSG*, 12/1/1884, p. 4; *TRG*, 23/1/1884, pp. 69–70; *POSG*, 26/1/1884, p. 4; *TRG*, 30/1/1884, pp. 87–9; *POSG*, 12/4/1884, p. 5; *TR*, 31/1/1884, p. 2; *POSG*, 2/2/1884, in Gordon Rohlehr, *Calypso and Society In Pre-Independence Trinidad* (Trinidad, 1990), p. 31; *TR*, 7/2/1884, p. 2; Cowley, 'Music and Migration', appendix 5; *TR*, 14/2/1884, p. 2; *FP&TN*, 14/2/1884, pp. 2–3 (reprints many of the legal documents); *POSG*, 1/3/1884, p. 3; 23/2/1884, p. 4; *FP&TN*, 6/3/1884, p. 2; PRO CO 295/301/56 (8 March); *TR*, 28/2/1884, p. 2; *TRG*, 12/3/1884, p. 237.

21 *POSG*, 1/3/1884, p. 3; C. 4366; Singh, *Bloodstained Tombs*, pp. 3–4. PRO CO 884/9/47.

22 *POSG*, 31/1/1885, p. 4; *NE*, 23/2/1885, pp. 2–3; *TC*, 18/2/1885, p. 2; *POSG*, 21/2/1885, p. 4; PRO CO 295/305/53 (26 February). *POSG*, 13/3/1886, pp. 3–4. J. H. Collens, *A Guide To Trinidad*, 2nd edn (London, 1888), p. 50.

23 L. O. Inniss, *Reminiscences Of Old Trinidad* (Trinidad, 1932), pp. 14–15; *An Ordinance for amending and consolidating the Law with regard to the constitution of the Medical Board, the Practice of Medicine and Surgery and the Selling of Drugs*, no. 6 of 1887 (8 March); Stewart H. Holbrook, *The Golden Age Of Quackery* (New York, 1959).

24 John Urich, 'Bamboula' *West Indian Melodies*, no. 2 (London, n.d.) and *West Indian Melodies*, 2 nos. (London, n.d.) – both were part of the 'Alliance Musicale' (1887).

25 Collens, *Guide*, pp. 46–7; *POSG*, 15/2/1888, p. 3.

26 *POSG*, 15/2/1888, p. 3; Bodu, *Trinidadiana*, p. 79; Brereton, 'Trinidad Carnival', p. 48; *POSG*, 13/1/1883, pp. 4–5; *Illustrated London News*, 5/5/1888, p. 475, 496–497; Bodu, *Trinidadiana*, p. 78. Hearn, 'La Verette', pp. 738–42; Anca Bertrand, 'Carnival a Saint-Pierre', *Parallèles*, no. 4 (1965), p. 7. *Lajables* legend – Hearn, 'La Verette', p. 740: for Trinidad – L.O. In(n)iss, 'Folk Lore and Popular Superstition', in T. B. Jackson, ed., *The Book Of Trinidad* (Trinidad, 1904), pp. 114–16. Henry Edward Krehbiel, *Afro-American Folk Songs: A Study In Racial and National Music* (New York, 1914), pp. 125–6, 147–50. Lafcadio Hearn, *Two Years In The French West Indies* (New York, 1890), pp. 424–38.

27 Brereton, 'Birthday', pp. 77–80; *Public Opinion*, 7/8/1888, p. 5; 24/8/1888, p. 5; 10/8/1888, p. 4; E. M. Encinas, 'Emancipation Day', in Alfred Richards, comp., *Discovery Day Celebration 1927; Souvenir* (Trinidad, 1927), p. 77.

28 Doug Seroff, 'The Fisk Jubilee Singers in Britain', in Rainer Lotz and Ian Pegg, eds., *Under The Imperial Carpet: Essays In Black History* (Crawley, 1986), pp. 42–54; Hans Nathan, *Dan Emmett and the Rise of Early Negro Minstrelsy* (Norman, 1962). Henry Henricksen, 'Black Patti', *Record Research*: (1979), nos. 165–6, (pt 1), pp. 4–8; nos. 167–8, (pt 2), pp. 4–8; *Freeman* (Indianapolis),

13/7/1889; Bodu, *Trinidadiana*, p. 93; *POSG*, 5/12/1888, p. 5; Roger D. Abrahams, ed. *Afro-American Folktales: Stories from Black Traditions in the New World* (New York, 1985), pp. 11–13.

29 *POSG*, 29/12/1888, p. 5.

30 *POSG*, 23/1/1889, p. 5; Bodu, *Trinidadiana*, p. 106; *POSG*, 6/2/1889, p. 4; Thomas, *Theory*, p. 4; Espinet and Pitts, *Land*, pp. 36, 63; Raymond Quevedo (Atilla the Hun), 'Calypso' in booklet notes to, *Calypsos: by Wilmoth Houdini and his Royal Calypso Orchestra* (US) Decca Album no. 78 (New York, 1939), p. 3; Roger D. Abrahams, *Singing The Master: The Emergence of African American Culture in the Plantation South* (New York, 1993); *NE*, 13/9/1889, p. 3; *POSG*, 31/1/1885, p. 4; *NE*, 8/11/1889, p. 2; Pitts, 'Calypso', p. 41.

31 Inniss, *Trinidad*, p. 89; *NE*, 8/11/1889, p. 2; Victor Coridun, *Carnival de St-Pierre (Martinique)* (reprinted, Fort-de-France, 1980) – Chansons 20: *Colby*; Bodu, *Trinidadiana*, p. 102; *POSG*, 13/11/1889, p. 5; Patrick Jones, 'Patrick Jones'; a Paris recording – *Colby* (Vieil air de St Pierre, Martinique) by 'Madame Maïotte Almaby et son Orchestre des Isles', made on 25 November 1937 (Odeon 281.229).

32 Quevedo, *Atilla's*, pp. 14–15; John Cowley, '*L' Année Passée*: Selected Repertoire in English-Speaking West Indian Music', *Keskidee*, no. 3 (1993), pp. 28–30; Espinet and Pitts, *Land*, pp. 28–30; A. L. Lloyd and Isabel Aretz de Ramón y Rivera, eds., *Folk Songs Of The Americas* (New York, 1966), p. 170.

33 *POSG*, 9/2/1889, p. 4; 16/2/1889, p. 4; 20/2/1889, p. 4; Bodu, *Trinidadiana*, p. 98; Trottman, *Crime*, pp. 92–3, 130. *NE*, 21/2/1890, pp. 2–3. Cowley, 'Music and Migration', appendix 5. *POSG*, 10/2/1891, p. 4, 6; Bridget Brereton, 'Sir John Gorrie: A Radical Chief Justice Of Trinidad (1885–1892)', *Journal of Caribbean History*, vol. 13 (1980), p. 65; *POSG*, 13/2/1891, p. 4; 17/2/1891, p. 6; Collens, *Guide*, pp. 40–1; Inniss, 'Folk Lore', pp. 115–16; *POSG*, 23/1/1889, p. 7.

34 *POSG*, 1/4/1891, p. 6; 7/4/1891, pp. 4–5; *NE*, 8/4/1891, p. 3; *POSG*, 14/4/1891, pp. 4–5; *TRG*, 15/4/1891, pp. 587–90; *POSG*, 17/4/1891, pp. 4–5; 21/4/1891, pp. 5–6; 28/4/1891, p. 4; 16/6/1891, pp. 3–4, 6–7; *NE*, 17/6/1891, pp. 2–3; Anastasia Coombs, interview by J. D. Elder, Santa Cruz, 30 June 1951, and other unpublished items in Pearse Papers.

35 Tennessee Jubilee Singers – Doug Seroff, ed., '100 Years From Today: Selected Items Of Musical Matters Drawn From The Black Community', *78 Quarterly*, vol. 1, no. 5 (1990), pp. 56–62; Doug Seroff, ed., '100 Years From Today: A Survey Of Afro-American Music In 1890 As Recorded In The Black Community Press', *78 Quarterly*, vol. 1, no. 6 (1991), pp. 52–63; *NE*, 11/2/1891, p. 3; 1/4/1891, p. 3; 8/4/1891, p. 3; *POSG*, 1/5/1891, p. 4; 22/5/1891, p. 4; 16/6/1891, p. 4. Spanish Waltzes – *POSG*, 1/12/1891, p. 4. Venezuelan Ball – *POSG*, 8/12/1891, p. 4. Carnival in 1890s – George H. Masson, 'Progress of Health Conditions in Trinidad and Tobago', Richards, *Discovery Day*, p. 40. Carnival Songs – Chalamelle, *Reflections*, pp. 21–2. *Louis Camille* – Massie Patterson and

Lionel Belasco, with free transcription by Maurice Baron, *Calypso Songs of the West Indies* (New York, 1943), pp. 8–9; the murder of Eligon – *POSG*, 7/7/1891, p. 4; 24/7/1891, p. 4; 25/8/1891, pp. 5–6. *Capitan Gabar bas* ... – Quevedo, 'Calypso', p. 3.

36 *TRG*, 17/2/1892, p. 221; *POSG*, 23/2/1892, p. 3; Shull, 'Pierrots'; Fahey, 'Divergence'; *POSG*, 1/3/1892, p. 4; Inniss, *Trinidad*, pp. 97–8; Brereton, 'Sir John Gorrie'.

37 *POSG*, 1/12/1891, p. 4; Retired Warrior, 'Old Time Carnival'; Joseph Clarke and Anthony, interview, Pearse Papers; *POSG*, 14/2/1893, pp. 2–3; 15/2/1893, p. 3; 16/2/1893, p. 2; Brereton, 'Carnival', p. 47.

38 Robert C. Toll, *Blacking Up: The Minstrel Show in Nineteenth-Century America* (New York, 1974), pp. 37–8; *FP&TN*, 14/2/1884, p. 3; William W. Austin, *'Susanna', 'Jeanie', And 'The Old Folks At Home': The Songs of Stephen C. Foster from His time to Ours*, 2nd edn. (Urbana, 1987), pp. 234–5; *POSG*, 14/2/1893, p. 3; 20/1/1894, p. 3; 22/1/1894, p. 2; *TRG*, 10/1/1894, p. 31, 33–4; Chalamelle, *Reflections*, p. 10; *POSG*, 23/1/1894, p. 3; 25/1/1894, p. 3; 7/2/1895, p. 3; Crowley, 'Traditional Masques', p. 196; Charles Jones, *Calypso and Carnival Of Long Ago And Today* (Trinidad, 1947), p. 25; *POSG*, 30/1/1894, p. 3; 7/2/1894, p. 3; 6/2/1894, p. 2.

39 Brereton, *Race Relations*, p. 157; *POSG*, 2/3/1895, p. 3; 27/2/1895, p. 3; 28/2/1895, p. 3; 7/2/1895, p. 3; *Mirror* (Trinidad), 28/2/1900, p. 10 (in their banner for 1902, White Rose stated they were established in 1896: *M*, 12/2/1902, p. 10). Clarke and Anthony, Pearse Papers; Shull, 'Pierrots'; Neal Fahey, 'Divergence'; Crowley, 'Traditional Masques', pp. 197–8; Errol Hill, *The Trinidad Carnival: Mandate For A National Theatre* (Austin, 1972), p. 93; Clarke and Anthony, Pearse Papers; *POSG*, 18/2/1896, p. 5; 19/2/1896, p. 5.

40 Pearse, 'Carnival', p. 190.

4 'Iron Duke In The Land'

1 Further references can be found in Cowley 'Music and Migration,' and previous chapters. Specifically – Anthony de Verteuil, *The Years Before* (Trinidad, 1981), pp. 219–21. Pearse, 'Carnival', pp. 190–3, defines the folk society.

2 Pitts, 'Calypso', p. 41; Charles Jones, *Calypso*, p. 13, 17; Clarke and Anthony, Pearse Papers; Mask, 'Carnival of Yore', *SG*, 19/2/1933, p. 18; Owen Rutter, *If Crab No Walk: A Traveller In The West Indies* (London, 1933), p. 104. 'Dame Lorraine' – Charles Jones, *Calypso*, p. 21; L. A. Dunn, '"Dame Lorine" – Lady of Midnight To Dawn', *SG*, 4/2/1951, p. 3; Clarke and Anthony, Pearse Papers; Crowley, 'Traditional Masques', pp. 195–6; Patrick Jones, 'Jour Ouvert', *Humming Bird*, Carnival no. (1957), p. 19; Raymond Quevedo, 'Dame Lorraine', *Humming Bird*, Carnival no. (1961), p. 4. 'Jour Ouvert' – Charles Jones, *Calypso*, pp. 21, 25, 27; Crowley, 'Traditional Masques', pp. 222–3; Patrick Jones,

'Jour Ouvert', Fancy Bands – Charles Jones, *Calypso*, pp. 27, 31, 33, 39, 41; A. H. Maloney, *Amber Gold: An Adventure In Autobiography* (Boston, 1946), pp. 227–8; Clarke and Anthony, Pearse Papers; Crowley, 'Traditional Masques', pp. 197–8. Early calypso and calypsonians – Wenzell Brown, *Angry Men – Laughing Men: the Caribbean Cauldron* (New York, 1947), p. 258; Espinet and Pitts, *Land*, pp. 30–31; Clarke and Anthony, Pearse Papers. Musical definitions: *calenda* – *POSG*, 26/2/1898, p. 5; Cowley, 'Music and Migration', pp. 71–94; *double tone calipso* – *POSG*, 20/1/1900, p. 5; Paul Bowles, 'Calypso – Music of the Antilles', *Modern Music*, vol. 17, no. 3 (1940), p. 157; St Denis Preston, 'Calypso: the jazz of the West Indies', *Melody Maker*, 25/2/1950, p. 3; Clarke and Anthony, Pearse Papers; Quevedo, *Atilla's Kaiso*, pp. 2, 20; *lavways – POSG*, 25/2/1908, p. 7; music by *nègres jardins – M*, 27/2/1906, p. 10; *single tone calipso* – Paul Bowles, 'Calypso'; Charles Jones, *Calypso*, p. 17; St Denis Preston, 'Calypso – jazz'; Clarke and Anthony, Pearse Papers; Quevedo, *Atilla's*, p. 2, 21.

3 *POSG*, 3/3/1897, p. 3; 2/3/1897, p. 4; 4/3/1897, p. 3; Chalamelle, *Reflections*, pp. 23–5.

4 *M*, 15/2/1898, p. 2; 19/2/1898, p. 6; *POSG*, 17/2/1898, p. 3; 20/2/1898, p. 7; 22/2/1898, p. 5; *M*, 22/2/1898, p. 5; 23/2/1898, p. 3; *POSG*, 26/2/1898, p. 7; *M*, 23/2/1898, p. 3; *POSG*, 23/2/1898, p. 7; 26/2/1898, p. 5.

5 Brereton, *History*, pp. 146–8; *POSG*, 21/9/1925, p. 20 – reprints contemporary newspaper reports.

6 *POSG*, 20/1/1899, p. 3; 1/2/1899, p. 3; 7/2/1899, p. 6; 8/2/1899, p. 4; 11/2/1899, p. 7; *M*, 14/2/1899, p. 8. On the importance of *Governor Jerningham* – Quevedo, 'Calypso', and *Atilla's*, pp. 10–11; Patrick Jones, 'Patrick Jones' (which includes a performance of the song). Le Blanc's sobriquet as Persecutor – Clarke and Anthony, Pearse Papers. *M*, 14/2/1899, pp. 7–9; 15/2/1899, p. 7; *POSG*, 14/2/1899, p. 4; 15/2/1899, pp. 4–5; 17/2/1899, p. 7; Espinet and Pitts, *Land*, p. 31.

7 *POSG*, 20/1/1900, p. 5; Patrick Jones, 'Patrick Jones'; *POSG*, 27/1/1900, p. 5; 7/2/1900, p. 4; Pitts, 'Calypso', p. 41; *POSG*, 7/2/1900, p. 7; *M*, 12/2/1900, p. 9; 23/2/1900, p. 10; *POSG*, 27/2/1900, p. 6; 1/3/1900, p. 4; *M*, 27/2/1900, p. 10; *POSG*, 27/2/1900, p. 5. White Rose: Charles Jones, *Calypso*, p. 17, 33 (he refers to Frederick rather than Henry Julian); Clarke and Anthony, Pearse Papers; 'Ballad Singer Calypso', Pearse Papers; Patrick Jones, 'Patrick Jones'; Crowley, 'Traditional Masques', pp. 197–8, 200; Pitts, 'Calypso', p. 41. *POSG*, 1/3/1900, pp. 4–5; *M*, 28/2/1900, pp. 10–11; *POSG*, 21/3/1900, p. 5; 2/3/1900, p. 5; Clarke and Anthony, Pearse Papers; S. L. C., 'Calypso Memories That Will Never Die', *TG*, 20/2/1945, p. 4. *POSG*, 1/3/1900, pp. 5, 7; *M*, 1/3/1900, p. 7; Dave Russell, *Popular Music in England 1840–1914: A social history* (Manchester, 1987), pp. 116–27; *POSG*, 13/6/1900, pp. 4–6. Boer War – Thomas Packenham, *The Boer War* (London, 1979).

8 'Russell & Coy' advertisements – *POSG*, 13/1/1901, p. 5, 20/1/1901, p. 5. *M*, 23/1/1901, p. 7; *POSG*, 24/1/1901, p. 5; *M*, 25/1/1901, p. 7; *POSG*, 7/2/1901, p. 5. The propriety of holding Carnival – *M*, 26/1/1901, p. 3; *POSG*, 27/1/1901, p. 7; *M*, 28/1/1901, pp. 9–10, 12; 29/1/1901, p. 7; 30/1/1901, pp. 2–3; *POSG*, 30/1/1901, p. 4, 7; *M*, 31/1/1901, p. 13; *POSG*, 31/1/1901, p. 5; *M*, 1/2/1901, pp. 13–14 (names the band leaders (which included Henry Julian) – apparently, they had approached Bodu in the first instance); *POSG*, 1/2/1901, p. 4 (letter from Julian, Director, White Rose Social Union). *POSG*, 8/2/1901, p. 5; 10/2/1901, p. 5; 19/2/1901, p. 4; 20/2/1901, p. 4; *M*, 20/2/1901, p. 9; *POSG*, 23/2/1901, p. 5; Clarke and Anthony, Pearse Papers; *POSG*, 21/2/1901, p. 3, 5; 22/2/1901, p. 3.

9 *POSG*, 25/1/1902, p. 14; 31/1/1902, p. 4. Bernard is identified as Pharaoh in a letter from E. M. Lazare (the radical black lawyer) – *M*, 13/2/1902, p. 8. Formation of (Sweet) Evening Bells – 'Ballad Singer Calypso'; and Pitts, 'Calypso', p. 41. *POSG*, 31/1/1902, p. 4, Algernon E. Aspinall, *The British West Indies: Their History, Resources and Progress* (London, 1912), pp. 155–7; *M*, 13/2/1902, p. 7. *POSG*, 5/2/1902, p. 3; 12/2/1902, p. 5; 11/2/1902, p. 3; 12/2/1902, p. 5; 13/2/1902, p. 4; *M*, 13/2/1902, pp. 7–9; *POSG*, 14/2/1902, p. 4; 10/8/1902, p. 3.

10 *POSG*, 22/1/1903, p. 5; 23/1/1903, p. 5; 30/1/1903, p. 3; 1/2/1903, p. 6; 15/2/1903, p. 5 (Arima and Maracas); 7/2/1903, p. 6 (San Fernando); 17/2/1903, p. 2 and 20/2/1903, p. 4 (Port of Spain); 12/2/1903, p. 5 (St Joseph); 20/2/1903, p. 5 (Tacarigua and Tumpuna); 8/2/1902, p. 4; *M*, 12/2/1902, p. 11; Patrick Jones, 'Patrick Jones'; Pitts, 'Calypso', pp. 41, 43; *POSG*, 25/2/1903, p. 4; *M*, 27/2/1903, p. 11; *POSG*, 26/2/1903, p. 5. Competition reports/results: Arima – 26/2/1903, p. 5; Maracas – 27/2/1903, p. 5; Princes Town – *M*, 26/2/1903, p. 11 *POSG*, 26/2/1903, p. 5, 27/2/1903, p. 5; San Fernando – 24/2/1903, p. 3; *M*, 26/2/1903, pp. 10–11, *POSG*, 26/2/1903, p. 5; St Joseph – 26/2/1903, p. 5; Tacarigua – 27/2/1903, p. 5; Tunapuna – 26/2/1903, p. 5, *M*, 26/2/1903, p. 11. (There are no reports of competitions having taken place in Port of Spain). *POSG*, 25/2/1903, p. 4; Patrick Jones, 'Patrick Jones', *POSG*, 24/2/1903, p. 3, Crowley, 'Traditional Masques', pp. 196–7. *M*, 27/2/1903, p. 11; *POSG*, 11/2/1902, p. 3.

11 Brereton, *History*, pp. 149–51.

12 Ibid. Contemporary newspaper extracts – *POSG*, 21/1/1925, pp. 26–7; Quevedo, *Atilla's*, p. 22; Clarke and Anthony, Pearse Papers (for this version of the song). Other sources – Cd. 1661; Cd. 1662; Cd. 1988; K. O. Laurence, ed., 'The Trinidad Water Riot of 1903: Reflections of an Eyewitness', *Caribbean Quarterly*, vol. 15, no. 4 (1969), pp. 5–22; and Henry C. Alexis, 'The Water Riots of 1903', in Reinhard W. Sander, ed., *From Trinidad: An Anthology of West Indian Writing* (London, 1978), pp. 244–52; Eric Williams, *History*, pp. 179–88. This version of Fijonel's song (Raymond Quevedo) Atilla the Hun, 'Calypsoes From 1908–1958', *Trinidad Calypso Book* (Trinidad, *c.* 1959),

p. 13. *POSG*, 10/2/1904, p. 7. Holder: Quevedo, *Atilla's*, pp. 11–12, 167; Cd. 1988; *POSG*, 18/2/1904, p. 5; 19/2/1904, p. 5. Carnival reports – *M*, 16/2/1904, p. 9; *POSG*, 16/2/1904, p. 4; *M*, 17/2/1904, p. 8; *POSG*, 17/2/1904, p. 4. Venezuelan blockade: contemporary newspaper extracts – *POSG*, 21/9/1925, p. 26; Miriam Hood, *Gunboat Diplomacy: Great Power Pressure in Venezuela* (London, 1975), pp. 163–94; *POSG*, 17/2/1903, p. 4; 13/2/1904, p. 4; Patrick Jones, 'Patrick Jones'. Carnival references (the case of mistaken police identity took place on the Saturday before Carnival), Patrick Jones, 'Patrick Jones'; *M*, 15/2/1904, p. 9; *POSG*, 16/8/1916, p. 8; 18/2/1904, p. 4; 16/8/1916, p. 8.

13 Joseph Belgrave, 'Reflections on Carnival', *Beacon*, vol. 2, no. 1 (1932), p. 16; *POSG*, 25/2/1908, p. 7; *Argos*, 20/1/1919, p. 5; *POSG*, 10/2/1904, p. 7; *M*, 16/8/1916, p. 5; *POSG*, 16/8/1916, p. 8; 7/3/1905, p. 4.

14 *POSG*, 7/2/1905, p. 3; 14/2/1905, p. 2; 23/2/1905, p. 4; 24/2/1905, p. 7. On Sophie Mattaloney's status as a caliso singer – Atilla's recording: *History Of Carnival*, Decca 17253 (New York City, 15 March 1935); and his 'Calypsoes', p. 11. *M*, 7/3/1905, p. 13; *POSG*, 7/3/1905, p. 4; *M*, 8/3/1905, p. 11; *POSG*, 8/3/1905, p. 5; 'Evolution of Steel Band (Notes taken at a discussion with Hon. R. Quevedo and Len. Pierre on 30/6/53)', Pearse Papers; Charles Jones, *Calypso*, p. 43. The Myler case – *POSG*, 10/3/1905, p. 7, 14/3/1905, p. 7; 16/3/1905, p. 4; 23/3/1905, p. 5; 25/3/1905, p. 6 (he was discharged with a caution). *POSG*, 8/3/1905, p. 5; 9/3/1905, p. 4; 8/3/1905, p. 3; 10/3/1905, p. 2; 9/3/1905, p. 7; 12/3/1905, p. 3.

15 *Penny Cuts*, 17/2/1906, p. 3; Patrick Jones, 'Patrick Jones'; Bruce Procope, 'The Dragon Band or Devil Band', *Caribbean Quarterly*, vol. 4, nos. 3, and 4 (1956), p. 275; *M*, 28/2/1906, p. 8; *POSG*, 28/2/1906, p. 7; *M*, 27/2/1906, p. 10; *POSG*, 1/3/1906, p. 2; Jose Ramon Fortuné, 'The Days When Stick-Fighting Was A Major Trinidad Sport', *SG*, 7/3/1954, p. 4a (sport); Alexander Bynoe, '"Freddie Manga" Dead: Old Carnival Stick Fighter', *TG*, 7/2/1933, p. 4; Quevedo, *Atilla's*, p. 15, 169.

16 *POSG*, 6/2/1907, p. 2, 4; *M*, 23/2/1909, p. 6; *POSG*, 12/2/1907, p. 5; *M*, 12/2/1907, p. 2; *POSG*, 13/2/1907, pp. 4–5; *M*, 13/2/1907, p. 12; Clarke and Anthony, Pearse Papers; *POSG*, 14/2/1907, p. 7; *POSG*, 27/12/1907, p. 4.

17 Brake's last entry – *Colonial Office List For 1907* (London, 1907), p. 367; Swain first confirmed in post – *Colonial Office List For 1908* (London, 1908), p. 381. Bonanza competition – *POSG*, 7/2/1908, p. 4. Carnival – *POSG*, 1/3/1908, p. 7; *M*, 3/3/1908, p. 15; 4/3/1908, p. 14; *POSG*, 3/3/1908, p. 4; 4/3/1908, p. 5; 16/8/1916, p. 8.

18 Charles Jones, *Calypso*, p. 31, 33; Clarke and Anthony, Pearse Papers; *M*, 24/2/1909, p. 2; 8/2/1910, p. 7; Atilla, 'Calypsoes', pp. 13, 15; Quevedo, *Atilla's*, p. 24.

19 *M*, 23/2/1909, p. 6; Hearn, 'La Verette', p. 740; Charles Jones, *Calypso*, p. 21,

25, 27; *POSG*, 24/2/1909, p. 4; *M*, 24/2/1909, p. 2; *POSG*, 23/2/1909, p. 4; 25/2/1909, p. 7; 23/2/1909, p. 4; 24/2/1909, p. 5; Atilla, 'Calypsoes', p. 13.

20 *POSG*, 8/2/1910, p. 3; *M*, 8/2/1910, p. 7; *Argos*, 16/2/1919, p. 6 (on Blackwood Wright); *M*, 9/2/1910, p. 3; *POSG*, 9/2/1910, p. 5; Quevedo, *Atilla's*, p. 24; Atilla, 'Calypsoes', p. 15; Quevedo, *Atilla's*, p. 18, 173–4.

21 *M*, 28/2/1911, p. 7; *POSG*, 28/2/1911, p. 9. Beginner's recollections – Michael Anthony, *Glimpses of Trinidad and Tobago, with a glance at the West Indies* (Trinidad, 1974), pp. 59, 62. Charlie Phair – *POSG*, 15/2/1911, p. 5. Carnival competitions – *POSG*, 1/3/1911, p. 5. Court cases – *POSG*, 2/3/1911, p. 3 (Chin Tambi was recalled by Charles Jones, *Calypso*, p. 43 and, one of Andrew Pearse's informants); Houdini's reminiscences – Errol Hill, 'The gypsy calypso king wants to return', *SG*, 11/2/1968, p. 12.

22 References are in previous chapters. A composer credit to 'J. A. Coggin' in a 1914 recording by Lovey's Band suggests J. and Albert Coggins may be the same person – Richard Spottswood comp., 'A Discography of West Indian Recordings (1912–1945),' unpublished MS. Eclipse String Band – *POSG*, 25/2/1902, p. 4 (pre-Carnival dance); 12/2/1902, p. 5 (Carnival). String bands led by Mr Martinez (Excelsior, in Carnival) – *POSG*, 27/2/1900, p. 6: *M*, 27/2/1903, p. 11 (Carnival); 8/3/1905, p. 11 (pre Carnival ball in Princes Town). Belasco's String Orchestra – *POSG*, 4/2/1903, p. 7 (Fête Champetre); 18/2/1904, p. 4 (Carnival ball); 18/2/1905, p. 5 (Agricultural show); 3/2/1907, p. 4 (pre-Carnival ball in Princes Town). Denis Walton String Band – *POSG*, 6/2/1907, p. 4 (pre-Carnival ball). Trinidad Banjo, Mandoline And Guitar Orchestra – *West India Committee Circular*, vol. 24, no. 355 (7 May 1912), pp. 236–7.

23 *Argos*, 15/2/1912, p. 6; Charles Jones, *Calypso*, pp. 13, 17; *M*, 20/2/1912, p. 6; *POSG*, 20/2/1912, p. 7; *M*, 21/2/1912, p. 3; *POSG*, 21/2/1912, p. 4.

24 *POSG*, 28/4/1912, p. 11; 7/2/1899, p. 6; 1/5/1912, p. 8; 5/5/1912, p. 10; *M*, 6/5/1912, p. 7; 8/5/1912, p. 9; *POSG*, 8/5/1912, p. 9; *Lloyds List*, 22/5/1912, col. 28; Spottswood, 'A Discography'; *Victor Records Spanish American Catalogue*, *c.* 1922, pp. 127–8 (Trinidad), 129–30 (Venezuela). Columbia catalogue illustration – Donald R. Hill, *Calypso Calaloo: Early Carnival Music in Trinidad* (Gainesville, 1993), p. 118. Richard K. Spottswood, comp. *Ethnic Music on Records: A Discography of Ethnic Recordings Produced in the United States 1893 to 1942* (Urbana, 1990), vol. 1, pp. xxvii–xlvi. Quevedo, *Atilla's*, pp. 15, 169. Advertisements – *POSG*, 17/8/1912, pp. 7–8; 20/8/1912, p. 7; 29/8/1912, p. 7; 31/8/1912, p. 7.

25 *M*, 28/1/1913, p. 8; *POSG*, 2/2/1913, p. 11; *Argos*, 22/2/1912, p. 4. Diametre costume – Crowley, 'Traditional Masques', pp. 196–7; *POSG*, 4/2/1913, p. 9; *M*, 4/2/1913, p. 6; *POSG*, 5/2/1913, p. 7; *M*, 5/2/1913, p. 6. Executor's song – Lord Executor: St Francois Valley–interview notes, 10 February 1952

(Pearse Papers). Pointer's arrival in Trinidad – *POSG*, 1/10/1912, p. 2; his visit
– Brereton, *History*, pp. 152–3; Brinsley Samaroo, 'The Trinidad Workingmen's Association And The Origins Of Popular Protest In A Crown Colony',
Social and Economic Studies, vol. 21, no. 2 (1972), pp. 208–9; the song –
Quevedo, *Atilla's*, p. 25; this text is from Mitto Sampson, 'Old And New Calypsoes Compared: Was "Netty Netty" Catchy As "Letter For Thelma"?', *TG*,
30/1/1954, p. 6.

26 *TRG*, 22/1/1914, p. 107; *POSG*, 14/2/1914, p. 5; 25/2/1914, p. 3; *M*, 24/2/1914,
p. 6; 25/2/1914, p. 2, 6.

27 Spottswood, 'A Discography'; *POSG*, 28/8/1914, pp. 7–8; *M*, 28/8/1914, p. 7.
Po' Me One – Connie Williams, *12 Songs From Trinidad* (San Francisco, 1959),
p. 12. *Saylor Boy* – *POSG*, 13/2/1907, p. 4; *M*, 24/2/1909, p. 2, 28/2/1911, p. 7.
Papa Gorrie – *POSG*, 13/2/1891, p. 4. *Nobody's Business* – Paul Oliver, *Songsters
And Saints: Vocal Traditions On Race Records* (Cambridge, 1984), p. 67 (com-
mercial recordings in US); Jamaica: early 1950s – a recording by Boysie Grant –
MRS 06; West Africa – a recording from the same period – *Nobody's Business
But My Own* by Calender and his Maringar Band – Decca WA 2506 (Sierra
Leone). Monrose's relationship to Belasco – 78 F. Supp. 686. *Buddy Abraham* –
Connie Williams *12 Songs*, p. 13. *Little Brown Boy* – Patterson and Belasco
Calypso Songs, pp. 10–11 (origin and local title, confirmed – *POSG*, 19/2/1950,
p. 4). *My Little Man's Gone Down De Main* – verse from a performance by
'Anthony' in a field recording by Andrew Pearse. Advertisements for the
'Calipsos' and 'Kalendas' – *POSG*, 13/2/1915, p. 5; 16/2/1915, p. 3; 2/3/1916,
p. 5; *TG*, 2/3/1919, p. 4. *Belle Marie Coolie* – Thomas W. Talley, *Negro Folk
Rhymes* (New York, 1922), pp. 225–6 (source given incorrectly as Venezuela).
Iron Duke In The Land – text transcribed from *Calypso Pioneers*, Rounder
Records CD 1039. *Ringing A Bell* – *M*, 8/2/1915, p. 9. *Bayonet Charge …* –
Patrick Jones, 'Patrick Jones'. *Bagai sala que pocheray moin* – lyrics partially
transcribed in booklet to *Trinidad Loves To Play Carnival*, Matchbox MBCD
302–2.

28 *POSG*, 5/9/1914, p. 5, etc.. Random sample of advertisements – *POSG*,
5/2/1902, p. 3 (Davidson and Todd); *M*, 27/2/1903, p. 10 (H. Strong); *POSG*,
16/2/1904, p. 5 (H. Strong); 19/2/1904, p. 5 (H. Strong); 24/2/1906, p. 2 (Pedro
Prada); 6/2/1907, p. 2 (Wilsons); 12/2/1911, p. 4 (Wilsons); 4/2/1913, p. 9
(Strong's).

29 *M*, 8/2/1915, p. 9; 13/2/1915, p. 3. Selected advertisements – Victor: *POSG*,
13/2/1915, p. 5 (H. Strong – Just In Time For Carnival); 16/2/1915, p. 3 (Smith
Bros. – New Creole Victor Records); p. 5 (H. Strong – Just In Time For
Carnival) – (unlike Strong, Smith Bros. (The Bonanza) included the East Indian
selections); – Columbia: *POSG*, 28/1/1915, p. 11 (Muir, Marshall – Lovey); *M*,
13/2/1915, p. 4 (Muir, Marshall – Lovey); *POSG*, 14/2/1915, p. 7 (Muir,

Marshall – Lovey, 38 Records). Anthony, *Glimpses*, p. 60; *M*, 16/2/1915, p. 3; 13/2/1915, p. 4; 17/2/1915, p. 7; *POSG*, 17/2/1915, pp. 2–3; *M*, 17/2/1915, p. 3; Daniel J. Crowley, 'The Midnight Robbers', *Caribbean Quarterly*, vol. 4, Nos. 3, and 4 (1956), p. 263.

30 *POSG*, 2/3/1916, p. 5; *M*, 7/3/1916, p. 7; 8/3/1916, p. 2. Brown, *Angry Men*, p. 262. 'Leggos' – Bowles, 'Calypso', p. 157; Espinet and Pitts, *Land*, p. 31; Lion, 'How Leggo and La Vouez Were Born', *EN*, 2/6/1981; Lion, 'Kalinda-Stick Man Chant: Leggo and La Vouez Part Two', *EN*, 26/6/1981. Trinidad Contingents – *POSG*, 21/9/1925, p. 29; C. L. Joseph, 'The British West Indies Regiment 1914–1918', *Journal of Caribbean History*, vol. 2 (1971), pp. 94–124; *POSG*, 8/3/1916, p. 11. Theodore Roosevelt, 'Where the Steady Trade-Winds Blow', *Scribner's Magazine*, vol. 61, no. 2 (1917), p. 185. Singers – *TG*, 30/1/1936, p. 8 (letter from Raymond Quevedo); *POSG*, 6/1/1918, p. 7 (letter from Citizen). Sam Manning – *Gleaner*, 1/5/29, p. 10. Swain's retirement – *M*, 16/8/1916, p. 5; *POSG*, 16/8/1916, p. 8. Chancellor's appointment – *Colonial Office List For 1917* (London, 1917), p. 394.

31 *M*, 16/8/1916, p. 5; *Gazette Extraordinary* (*TRG*), 12/1/1917, pp. 103–4; *TRG*, 1/2/1917, p. 201; *POSG*, 20/2/1917, p. 3; 21/2/1917, p. 4; 21/2/1917, p. 11; *Trinidad Spectator*, 25/2/1846, p. 2; Pitts, 'Calypso', p. 41.

32 *POSG*, 6/1/1918, p. 6; *Argos*, 16/1/1918, pp. 1, 7 (contrary attitude); Trinidad and Tobago: *Proclamation*, no. 7 of 1918 (14 January); *POSG*, 8/2/1918, p. 3 (Port of Spain appeal); 10/2/1918, p. 3 (San Fernando appeal), p. 11 (Sound Patriotism And Good Sense); 12/2/1918, p. 3; *TG*, 12/2/1918, p. 6; *Argos*, 12/2/1918, p. 7. Kola – *POSG*, 14/8/1915, p. 2; *Argos*, 28/2/1919, p. 5. Dance hall letters – *POSG*, 9/2/1918, p. 3 (Revd Errey); 10/2/1918, p. 8 (Lovey). Carnival – *TG*, 13/2/1918, p. 6; *POSG*, 13/2/1918, p. 3; 'Evolution of Steel Band', Pearse Papers; '*Argos' Paper*: Arthur F. Raymond, 'Origin of the Savannah Carnival and the Development of the Down Town Celebrations', *Humming Bird*, Carnival no. (1960), p. 9; *POSG*, 4/3/1919, p. 9; Atilla, 'Calypsoes', p. 15; Williams, *12 Songs*, p. 15; Quevedo, *Atilla's*, p. 25, 181. *Run Your Run Kaiser William* – Edric Connor, coll. and ed., *Songs From Trinidad* (London, 1958), p. 25; Atilla, 'Calypsoes', p. 15; J. D. Elder, 'Colour, Music And Conflict: A Study of Aggression in Trinidad with Reference to the Role of Traditional Music', *Ethnomusicology*, vol. 8, no. 2 (1964), p. 132; Quevedo, *Atilla's*, p. 25, 182.

33 Armistice and 'Celebration of Peace' in Port of Spain – *POSG*, 21/9/1925, p. 30; *Argos*, 7/2/1919, p. 5. Ownership of *Argos*, – Tony Martin, 'Revolutionary Upheavals In Trinidad, 1919: Views From British And American Sources, *Journal of Negro History*, vol. 58, no. 3 (1973), p. 316. Restoration of the masqued Carnival: the *Argos* team – 11/1/1919, p. 2; 16/1/1919, p. 5; 19/1/1919, p. 2; 20/1/1919, p. 5; 23/1/1919, p. 7; 26/1/1919, p. 3; 29/1/1919,

p. 7; 30/1/1919, p. 5; 16/2/1919, p. 7; 19/2/1919, p. 7; *TG*, 23/2/1919, p. 12; 4/3/1919, p. 6; 5/3/1919, p. 7; Raymond, 'Origin', pp. 8–10; Rohlehr, *Calypso and Society*, pp. 87–103

34 *Argos*, 24/2/1919, p. 9; 3/2/1919, p. 2. Other songs – *Argos*, 4/2/1919, p. 10; 14/2/1919, p. 2; 28/2/1919, p. 3, supplement, p. ii (between pp. 3–4); 1/3/1919, supplement, p. i (between pp. 6–7); 2/3/1919, p. 4. Merrick's letter – 4/2/1919, p. 5. Kalenda – 2/3/1919, p. 5. Tents – 3/2/1919, p. 5 (or 6); Rohlehr, *Calypso and Society*, p. 95; Raymond, 'Origin', p. 9. *Argos* competition – *Argos*, 3/2/1919, p. 2; 16/2/1919, p. 7; *POSG*, 6/3/1919, p. 7. *Guardian* competition – *TG*, 23/2/1919, p. 6, p. 12; 4/3/1919, p. 6; 5/3/1919, p. 7. San Fernando competition – *TG*, 2/3/1919, p. 10; 4/3/1919, p. 6; 5/3/1919, p. 7. Carnival – *POSG*, 4/3/1919, p. 9; *Argos*, 2/3/1919, p. 5; *TG*, 4/3/1919, p. 6; *POSG*, 5/3/1919, p. 8; *TG*, 5/3/1919, p. 7; Raymond, 'Origin', pp. 9–10. Song by HM Loyal Convicts performed by 'Anthony' in a field recording by Andrew Pearse. *POSG*, 6/3/1919, p. 7. Headley's String Band performed for a pre-Carnival dance in 1914 – *POSG*, 14/2/1914, p. 4. *TG*, 9/3/1919, p. 8. 'The Makers Of Masks: A Little-known Industry in Port Of Spain,' 23/2/1919, p. 4; 'Carnival Bands At Practice; Keen Interest Displayed; Preparations In Full Swing', 23/2/1919, pp. 4–5. *POSG*, 26/2/1919, p. 4; Pitts, 'Calypso', p. 43; 'Evolution of Steel Band', Pearse Papers; Quevedo, *Atilla's*, p. 36; *POSG*, 2/3/1919, p. 7; moko jumbie photograph – *Trinidad Carnival* (Trinidad, 1988), between pp. 132–3. Belasco's New York recordings – Spottswood, *Ethnic Music*, vol. 5, pp. 2889–92; biographical particulars – *POSG*, 17/1/1933, p. 7. Sample of advertisements placed during Victory Carnival – H. Strong (Victor Carnival Records): *POSG*, 25/2/1919, p. 7; *TG*, 28/2/1919, p. 9; 2/3/1919, p. 4; *POSG*, 2/3/1919, p. 7; – Muir, Marshall (Lovey's Columbia Records): *TG*, 23/2/1919, p. 2; 26/2/1919, p. 1; 2/3/1919, p. 2. Advertisements by Dick and Wells – *POSG*, 4/3/1919, p. 9; 6/3/1919, p. 7.

35 Strikes in Trinidad, disturbances in Britain (and elsewhere) and the Contingents – Brereton, *History*, pp. 160–4; 'Electric Tram Car Strike' *POSG*, 21/9/1925, p. 30 (extract from 6/4/1919); W. F. Elkins, 'Black Power In The British West Indies: The Trinidad Longshoremen's Strike', *Science and Society*, vol. 33 (1969), pp. 71–5; W. F. Elkins, 'A Source Of Black Nationalism In The Caribbean: The Revolt of the British West Indies Regiment at Taranto, Italy', *Science and Society*, vol. 34 (1970), pp. 99–103; W. F. Elkins, 'Hercules And The Society Of Peoples Of African Origin', *Caribbean Studies*, vol. 11, no. 4 (1972), pp. 47–59; Neil Evans, 'Regulating the Reserve Army: Arabs, Blacks and the Local State in Cardiff', in Kenneth Lunn, ed., *Race And Labour In Twentieth-Century Britain* (London, 1985), pp. 68–115; Peter Fryer, *Staying Power: The History of Black People in Britian* (London, 1984) pp. 298–316; Jacquelin Jenkinson, 'The Glasgow Race Disturbances of 1919', in Kenneth Lunn, ed., ibid., pp. 43–67; Al Jennings, 'Colour Bar', *MM*, 7/2/1946, p. 5; Joseph, 'British

West Indies Regiment'; Martin, 'Revolutionary Upheaval'; Tony Martin, *The Pan-African Connection: From Slavery to Garvey and Beyond* (Dover, Mass., 1983), pp. 63–93; Roy May and Robin Cohen, 'The Inter-relation between Race and Colonialism: A Case Study of the Liverpool Race Riots of 1919', *Race and Class*, vol. 16, no. 2 (1974), pp. 111–26. Ron Ramdin, *From Chattel Slave to Wage Earner: A History of Trade Unionism in Trinidad and Tobago* (London, 1982), pp. 54–63; 'Return Of Trinidad Contingent' – *POSG*, 21/9/1925, p. 30 (extract from 25/5/1919); Samaroo, 'Trinidad Workingmen's Association'; 'The Stevedore's Strike' – *POSG*, 21/9/1925, p. 30 (extracts from 2/12/1919; 5/12/1919); Williams, *12 Songs*, pp. 5–6.

36 San Fernando competitions – *TG*, 15/2/1920, p. 14; rehearsals – 28/1/1920, p. 8; police 'tamboo bamboo' practice – 5/2/1920, p. 9; Douglas – Hill, *Trinidad Carnival*, p. 65; Pitts, 'Calypso', p. 43; Carnival – *TG*, 17/2/1920, p. 8; *POSG*, 17/2/1920, p. 3; 18/2/1920, p. 9; *TG*, 18/2/1920, p. 14; 19/2/1920, p. 9, 12; *Class Legislation* – Patrick Jones, 'Patrick Jones', and Rohlehr *Calypso and Society*, p. 105, 546; Prince of Wales/Lovey's band – *POSG*, 19/9/1920, p. 17; 31/1/1937, p. 8.

5 Creole musical traditions: Africa, the Caribbean and beyond

1 Henry H. Breen, *St Lucia: Historical, Statistical and Descriptive* (London, 1884 – reprinted, 1970), pp. 190–230; Crowley, 'La Rose and La Marguerite'.
2 Cowley, 'Music and Migration,' pp. 95–7.
3 Ibid., pp. 138–52.
4 Young, 'A Tour', pp. 275–6.
5 Louisiana – Thomas Fiehrer, 'From quadrille to stomp: the Creole origins of jazz', *Popular Music*, vol. 10, no. 1 (1991), pp. 24–5. Jamaica – Brathwaite, *Creole Society*, p. 89.
6 Cowley, 'Music and Migration', p. 575; pp. 153–5; Swithin Wilmot, 'The Politics Of Protest In Free Jamaica – The Kingston John Canoe Christmas Riots, 1840 and 1841', *Caribbean Quarterly*, vol. 36, nos. 3–4 (1990), pp. 65–75.
7 J. Kedjanyi, 'Masquerade Societies In Ghana', *Research Review*, vol. 3, no. 2 (1967), pp. 51–7; Day, *Five Years'*, vol. I, p. 260.
8 Kevin A. Yelvington, 'Introduction: Trinidad Ethnicity', in Yelvington, ed., *Trinidad Ethnicity* (London, 1993), pp. 1–32.
9 Francis Egan, *The Slow March, Quick Step and Waltzes of the Kingston Regiment of Militia* (London, c. 1823); Francis Egan, *West Indian Pot Pourri* (London, c. 1820s). Young's publication is discussed in Robert Stevenson, *A Guide To Caribbean Music History* (Lima, 1975), p. 66.
10 *Echo*, 25/2/1871, p. 3; Donald R. Hill, 'The Impact of Migration on the Metropolitan and Folk Society of Carriacou, Grenada', *Anthropological Papers of the American Museum of Natural History*, vol. 54, pt. 2 (1977), pp. 119–20; Wilfred

256 *Notes to pages 234–6*

A. Redhead, *A City On A Hill* (Barbados, 1985), p. 378; Daniel J. Crowley, 'Kinds of Folk Music Differentiated According to Social Institution', *Caribbean Society And Culture Notes*, vol. 1, no. 2 (1955), p. 9; Anca Bertrand, 'Notes pour une definition du folklore antillais', *Parallès*, no. 28 (1968), p. 15.

11 Clarke and Anthony, Pearse Papers (and other interviews in Pearse Papers).

12 D. P., 'Carnival Is Here Again', *SG*, 23/2/1941, p. 15. S. M. E. 'Our Local Troubadours Sing – And Trinidadians Take Up The Refrain', *SG*, 21/1/1940, p. 17; Lion, *Calypso: From France to Trinidad, 800 Years of History* (Trinidad, *c.* 1987).

13 Morton Marks, 'Uncovering Ritual Structures in Afro-American Music', in Irving I. Zaretsky and Mark P. Leone, eds., *Religious Movements In Contemporary America* (Princeton, 1974), p. 110; Denis-Constant Martin, 'Filiation or Innovation?: Some Hypotheses to Overcome the Dilemma of Afro-American Music's Origins', *Black Music Research Journal*, vol. 11, no. 1 (1991), pp. 19–38.

Bibliography

Books, pamphlets, articles

Abrahams, Roger D., ed., *Afro-American Folktales: Stories from Black Traditions in the New World* (New York, 1985)

Abrahams, Roger D., *Singing The Master: The Emergence of African-American Culture in the Plantation South* (New York, 1993)

Abrahams, Roger D., and John F. Szwed, eds., *After Africa: Extracts from British Travel Accounts and Journals of the Seventeenth, Eighteenth, and Nineteenth Centuries concerning the Slaves, their Manners, and Customs in the British West Indies* (New Haven, 1983)

Alexis, Henry C., 'The Water Riots of 1903', in Reinhard W. Sander, ed., *From Trinidad: An Anthology of West Indian Writing* (London, 1978), pp. 244–252

Anthony, Michael, *Glimpses of Trinidad and Tobago, with a glance at the West Indies* (Trinidad, 1974)

Aspinall, Algernon, E., *The British West Indies: Their History, Resources and Progress* (London, 1912)

'Atilla the Hun' – see Raymond Quevedo

Austin, William W., *'Susanna', 'Jeanie', And 'The Old Folks At Home': The Songs of Stephen C. Foster from His time to Ours*, 2nd edn (Urbana, 1987)

Bayley, F. W. N., *Four Years' Residence In The West Indies* (London, 1833)

Belgrave, Joseph, 'Reflections on Carnival', *Beacon*, vol. 2, no. 1 (1932), pp. 16–17

Bertrand, Anca, 'Carnaval a Saint-Pierre', *Parallès*, no. 4 (1965), pp. 7–11
'Notes pour une definition du folklore antillais', *Parallès*, no. 28 (1968), pp. 4–19
Bettelheim, Judith, ed., *Cuban Festivals; An Illustrated Anthology* (New York, 1993)
Bodu, José M., *Trinidadiana: Being a Chronological Review of Events which have occurred in the island from the Conquest to the Present Day, with brief notices of the careers of some Eminent Colonists* (Trinidad, 1890)
Borde, Pierre-Gustave-Louis, trans. A. S. Mavrogordato, *The History of Trinidad under the Spanish Government, Second Part (1622–1797)* (Trinidad, 1982) (first published, Paris, 1883)
Bowles, Paul, 'Calypso – Music of the Antilles', *Modern Music*, vol. 17, no. 3 (1940), pp. 154–9
Brathwaite, Edward, *The Development of Creole Society in Jamaica 1770–1820* (Oxford, 1971)
Breen, Henry H., *St Lucia: Historical, Statistical and Descriptive* (London, 1970) (first published, London, 1844)
Brereton, Bridget, 'The Trinidad Carnival 1870–1900', *Savacou*, nos. 11–12 (1975), pp. 46–57
   Race Relations In Colonial Trinidad 1870–1900, (Cambridge, 1979)
   'Sir John Gorrie: A Radical Chief Justice Of Trinidad (1885–1892)', *Journal of Caribbean History*, vol. 13 (1980), pp. 44–72
   A History of Modern Trinidad 1783–1962 (London, 1981)
   'The Birthday of Our Race: A Social History of Emancipation Day in Trinidad 1833–88', in B. W. Higman ed., *Trade, Government And Society In Caribbean History 1700–1920* (London, 1983), pp. 69–83
Bridgens, R., *West India Scenery* (London, c. 1830s–40s)
Brierley, J. N., *Trinidad Then And Now* (Trinidad, 1912)
Brown, Wenzell, *Angry Men – Laughing Men: The Caribbean Cauldron* (New York, 1947)
Bynoe, Alexander, '"Freddy Manga" Dead: Old Carnival Stick Fighter', *Trindad Guardian*, 7 February 1933, p. 4
C., S. L., 'Calypso Memories That Will Never Die', *Trinidad Guardian*, 20 February 1945, p. 4
Capadose, Lieutenant Colonel (Henry), *Sixteen Years In The West Indies*, 2 vols. (London, 1845)
Carmichael, Mrs (A. C.), *Domestic Manners and Social Conditions of the White,*

Coloured, and Negro Population of the West Indies, 2 vols. (London, 1833)

'Carnival Bands At Practice; Keen Interest Displayed; Preparations In Full Swing', *Trinidad Guardian*, 23 February 1919, pp. 4–5

Carr, Andrew T., 'A Rada Community in Trinidad', *Caribbean Quarterly*, vol. 3, no. 1 (1953), pp. 35–54

'Pierrot Grenade', *Caribbean Quarterly*, vol. 4, nos. 3–4 (1956), pp. 281–314

Censor, 'The Origin Of Canboulay And The Old Way Of Playing It', *Trinidad Chronicle*, 16 March 1881, p. 3

Chalamelle, Eugene Francis, *Some Reflections on the Carnival of Trinidad* (Port of Spain, 1901)

Collens, J. H., *A Guide To Trinidad*, 2nd edn (London, 1888)

Colonial Office List For 1907 (London, 1907)

Colonial Office List For 1908 (London, 1908)

Colonial Office List For 1917 (London, 1917)

Connor, Edric, coll. and ed., *Songs From Trinidad* (London, 1958)

Coridun, Victor, *Carnival de St.-Pierre (Martinique)* (Fort-de-France, 1980) (first published, 1930)

Cowley, John, 'Carnival and other Seasonal Festivals in the West Indies, USA and Britain: a selected bibliographical index', *Bibliographies in Ethnic Relations*, no. 10 (Coventry, 1991)

'*L' Année Passée*: Selected repertoire in English-speaking West Indian Music', *Keskidee*, no. 3 (1993), pp. 2–42

Crahan, Margaret E., and Franklin W. Knight, eds., *Africa And The Caribbean: The Legacies Of A Link* (Baltimore, 1979)

Crowley, Daniel J., 'Kinds of Folk Music Differentiated According To Social Institution: St Lucia', *Caribbean Society And Culture Notes*, vol 1, no. 2 (1955), pp. 8–9

'The Traditional Masques of Carnival', *Caribbean Quarterly*, vol. 4, nos. 3–4 (1956), pp. 194–223

'The Midnight Robbers', *Caribbean Quarterly*, vol. 4, nos. 3–4 (1956), pp. 263–74

'La Rose and La Marguerite Societies in St Lucia', *Journal of American Folklore*, vol. 71, no. 282 (1958), pp. 541–52

'Toward A Definition Of Calypso', pt 1, *Ethnomusicology*, vol. 3, no. 2 (1959), pp. 57–66; pt 2, no. 3 (1959), pp. 117–24

Day, Charles William, *Five Years' Residence In The West Indies*, 2 vols. (London, 1852)

De Asso y del Rio, Ignacio Jordan, and Miguel de Manuel y Rodriguez, trans. Lewis F. C. Johnston, *Institutes of the Civil Law of Spain* (6th ed., materially corrected, Madrid, 1805) (London, 1825)

De Verteuil, Anthony, *The Years Before* (Trinidad, 1981)
   The Years Of Revolt: Trinidad 1881–1888 (Trinidad, 1984)
   A History of Diego Martin 1784–1884 (Trinidad, 1987)

De Verteuil, Louis A. A., *Trinidad: Its Geography, Natural Resources, Administration, Present Conditions and Prospects* (London, 1858)
   Trinidad: Its Geography, Natural Resources, Administration, Present Conditions and Prospects, 2nd edn (London, 1884)

Dunn, L. A., '"Dame Lorine" – Lady Of Midnight To Dawn', *Sunday Guardian* (Trinidad), 4 February 1951, p. 3
   'Carnival Through The Years', *Evening News* (Trinidad): pt 1, 25 February 1952, p. 11; pt 2, 26 February 1952, pp. 2, 11

Dunn, Richard S., *Sugar And Slaves: The Rise of the Planter Class in the English West Indies, 1624–1713* (New York, 1973)

E., S. M., 'Our Local Troubadours Sing – And Trinidadians Take Up The Refrain', *Sunday Guardian* (Trinidad), 21 January 1940, p. 17

Edwards, Bryan, *The History, Civil And Commercial of the British Colonies in the West Indies*, 3 vols. (London, 1801)

Egan, Francis, *West Indian Pot Pourri* (London, *c.* 1820s)
   The Slow March, Quick Step and Waltzes of the Kingston Regiment of Militia (London, *c.* 1823)

Elder, J. D., 'Colour, Music, And Conflict: A Study of Agression in Trinidad with Reference to the Role of Traditional Music', *Ethnomusicology*, vol. 8, no. 2 (1964), pp. 128–36

Elkins, W. F., 'Black Power In The British West Indies: The Trinidad Longshoremen's Strike of 1919', *Science and Society*, vol. 33 (1969), pp. 71–5
   'A Source Of Black Nationalism In The Caribbean: The Revolt Of The British West Indies Regiment At Taranto, Italy', *Science and Society*, vol. 34 (1970), pp. 99–103
   'Hercules And The Society Of Peoples Of African Origin', *Caribbean Studies*, vol. 11, no. 4 (1972), pp. 47–59

Encinas, E. M., 'Emancipation Day', in Alfred Richards, comp. , *Discovery Day Celebration 1927: Souvenir* (Trinidad, 1927), p. 72

Epstein, Dena J., *Sinful Tunes And Spirituals: Black Folk Music to the Civil War* (Urbana, 1978)

Espinet, Charles, and Harry Pitts, *Land of the Calypso: The Origin And Development Of Trinidad's Folk Song* (Trinidad, 1944)

Evans, Neil, 'Regulating the Reserve Army: Arabs, Blacks and the Local State in Cardiff, 1919–45', in Kenneth Lunn, ed., *Race And Labour In Twentieth-Century Britain* (London, 1985), pp. 68–115

Eversley, T. Fitz-Evan, comp., *The Trinidad Reviewer for the Year 1900* (London, *c.* 1899)

Fahey, H. Neale, 'Divergence Of Opinion On Recent Carnival Explained', *Evening News* (Trinidad), 12 March 1952, p. 3

Fiehrer, Thomas, 'From quadrille to stomp: the Creole origins of jazz', *Popular Music*, vol. 10, no. 1 (1991), pp. 21–38

Foner, Laura and Eugene D. Genovese, eds., *Slavery in the New World: A Reader in Comparative History* (Englewood Cliffs, 1969)

Fortuné, Jose Ramon, 'The Days When Stick-Fighting was a Major Trinidad Sport', *Sunday Guardian* (Trinidad), 7 March 1954, p. 4a (Sport)

Fraser, Lionel Mordaunt, *History of Trinidad (First Period), From 1781 to 1813* (vol. 1) (Trindad, 1891)

History of Trinidad (Second Period), From 1814 to 1839 (vol. 2) (Trindad, 1896)

Fryer, Peter, *Staying Power: The History of Black People in Britain* (London, 1984)

Goveia, Elsa V., 'The West Indian Slave Laws of the Eighteenth Century', in Laura Foner and Eugene D. Genovese, eds., *Slavery in the New World: A Reader in Comparative History* (Englewood Cliffs, 1969) pp. 113–37

Green, William A., *British Slave Emancipation: The Sugar Colonies and the Great Experiment* (Oxford, 1976)

Handler, J. S., 'The History Of Arrowroot And The Origin Of Peasantries In The British West Indies', *Journal Of Caribbean History*, vol. 2 (1971), pp. 46–93

Hearn, Lafcadio, 'La Verette and the Carnival in St Pierre, Martinique', *Harper's Monthly Magazine*, vol. 77, no. 461 (1888), pp. 737–48

Two Years In The French West Indies (New York, 1890)

Henricksen, Henry, 'Black Patti', *Record Research*: (1979), nos. 165–6, (pt 1), pp. 4–8; nos. 167–8, (pt 2), pp. 4–8; (1980), nos. 171–2, (pt 3), pp. 4–5, 24; nos. 173–4, (pt 4), p. 9; nos. 177–8, (pt 5), p. 8; (1981), nos. 181–2, (pt 6), p. 10; nos. 183–4, (pt 7), p. 9; nos. 185–6, (pt 8), p. 8; nos. 187–8, (pt 9), p. 8

Higman, B. W., 'African and Creole Slave Family Patterns in Trinidad', in Margaret E. Crahan and Franklin W. Knight, eds., *Africa And The Caribbean: The Legacies Of A Link* (Baltimore, 1979), pp. 41–64

Higman, B. W., ed., *Trade, Government And Society In Caribbean History 1700–1920* (London, 1983)

Hill, Donald R., 'The Impact of Migration on the Metropolitan and Folk Society of Carriacou, Grenada', *Anthropological Papers of the American Museum of Natural History*, vol. 54, pt. 2 (1977), pp. 189–392

Calypso Calaloo: Early Carnival Music In Trinidad (Gainesville, 1993)

Hill, Errol, 'The gypsy calypso king wants to return', *Sunday Guardian* (Trinidad), 11 February 1968, pp. 12–13

The Trinidad Carnival: Mandate For A National Theatre (Austin, 1972)

Holbrook, Stewart H., *The Golden Age Of Quackery* (New York, 1959)

Hood, Miriam, *Gunboat Diplomact 1895–1905: Great Power Pressure in Venezuela* (London, 1975)

Inniss, Lewis Osborn, 'Folk Lore and Popular Superstition', in T. B. Jackson, ed. *The Book Of Trinidad* (Trinidad, 1904), pp. 111–24

Trinidad And Trinidadians: A Collection Of Papers, Historical, Social And Descriptive About Trinidad And Its People (Trinidad, 1910)

'Carnival In The Old Days (from 1858)', *Beacon*, vol. 1, no. 12 (1932), pp. 12–13

Reminiscences Of Old Trinidad (Trinidad, 1932)

Jackson, T. B., ed., *The Book Of Trinidad* (Trinidad, 1904)

Jenkinson, Jacqueline, 'The Glasgow Race Disturbances Of 1919', in Kenneth Lunn, ed., *Race And Labour In Twentieth-Century Britain* (London, 1985), pp. 43–67

Jennings, Al, 'Colour Bar', *Melody Maker*, 7 December 1946, p. 5

Jones, Charles ('Duke of Albany'), *Calypso and Carnival Of Long Ago And Today* (Trindad, 1947)

Jones, Patrick, 'Jour Ouvert', *Humming Bird*, Carnival no. (1957), p. 19

'Patrick Jones tells of calypso, chants songs of ancient calypsonians', in the LP *Calypso Lore And Legend*, Cook Road Recordings 5016 (Stamford, n.d.)

Joseph, C. L., 'The British West Indies Regiment 1914–1918', *Journal of Caribbean History*, vol. 2 (1971), pp. 94–124

Joseph, E. L., *History Of Trinidad* (London, 1970) (first published London, 1838)

Kedjanyi, J., 'Masquerade Societies In Ghana', *Research Review*, vol. 3, no. 2 (1967), pp. 51–7

Kingsley, Charles, *At Last: A Christmas In The West Indies* (London, 1877) (first published (in two vols.), London, 1871)

Kmen, Henry, *Music In New Orleans: The Formative Years 1791–1841* (Baton Rouge, 1966)

Krehbiel, Henry Edward, *Afro-American Folksongs: A Study in Racial and National Music* (New York, 1914)

Laurence, K. O., ed., 'The Trinidad Water Riot of 1903: Reflections of an Eyewitness', *Caribbean Quarterly*, vol. 15, no. 4 (1969), pp. 5–22

Lavaysse, Jean F. Dauxion (ed. E. B.), *A Statistical, Commercial, And Political Description of Venezuela, Trinidad, Margarita and Tobago* (London, 1820)

Lion, The (Roaring) (Hubert Raphael Charles/Rafael de Leon), 'How Leggo And La Vouez Were Born', *Evening News* (Trinidad), 2 June 1981

 'Kalinda – Stick Man Chant And La Vouez: Part Two', *Evening News* (Trinidad), 26 June 1981

 Calypso: From France to Trinidad, 800 Years of History (Trinidad, *c.* 1987)

Lloyd, A. L., and Isabel Aretz de Ramón y Rivera, eds., *Folk Songs Of The Americas* (New York, 1966)

Lotz, Rainer and Ian Pegg, eds., *Under The Imperial Carpet: Essays in Black History* (Crawley, 1986)

Lunn, Kenneth, ed., *Race And Labour In Twentieth-Century Britain* (London, 1985)

'The Makers of Masks: A Little-known Industry in Port Of Spain', *Trinidad Guardian*, 23 February 1919, p. 4

Maloney, A. H., *Amber Gold: An Adventure In Autobiography* (Boston, 1946)

Marks, Morton, 'Uncovering Ritual Structure in Afro-American Music', in Irving I. Zaretsky and Mark P. Leone, eds., *Religious Movements in Contemporary America* (Princeton, 1974)

Martin, Denis-Constant, 'Filiation or Innovation?: Some Hypotheses to Overcome the Dilemma of Afro-American Music's Origins', *Black Music Research Journal*, vol. 11, no. 1 (1991), pp. 19–38

Martin, Tony, 'Revolutionary Upheaval In Trinidad, 1919: Views From British And American Sources', *Journal of Negro History*, vol. 58, no. 3 (1973), pp. 313–26

 The Pan-African Connection: From Slavery to Garvey and Beyond (Dover, Mass., 1983)

Mask, 'Carnival of Yore: Canboulay and Stick Fights were once Carnival joys', *Sunday Guardian* (Trinidad), 19 February 1933, p. 18

Massé, Abbé Armand, trans. M. L. de Verteuil, *The Diaries of Abbé Armand Massé 1878–1883*, 4 vols. (Trinidad, 1988)

Masson, George H., 'Progress of Health Conditions in Trinidad and Tobago', in Alfred Richards, comp. , *Discovery Day Celebration 1927: Souvenir* (Trinidad, 1927), pp. 40–3

May, Roy and Robin Cohen, 'The Inter-relation between Race and Colonialism: A Case Study of the Liverpool Race Riots of 1919', *Race and Class*, vol. 16, no. 2 (1974), pp. 111–26

Mills's Trinidad Almanac and Pocket Register for the Year of Our Lord 1840 (Trinidad, *c.* 1839)

Mintz, Sidney W., *Caribbean Transformations* (Baltimore, 1984)

Mintz, Sidney W., and Richard Price, 'An Anthropological Approach To The Afro-American Past: A Caribbean Perspective', *Occasional Papers in Social Change*, no. 2 (Philadelphia, 1976)

Mörner, Magnus, *Race Mixture In The History Of Latin America* (Boston, 1967)

Mullin, Michael, *Africa in America: Slave Acculturation and Resistance in the American South and The British Caribbean 1736–1831* (Urbana, 1992)

Nathan, Hans, *Dan Emmett and the Rise of Early Negro Minstrelsy* (Norman, 1962)

Newson, Linda A., *Aboriginal and Spanish Colonial Trinidad: A Study in Culture Contact* (London,1976)

Oliver, Paul, *Songsters And Saints: Vocal Traditions On Race Records* (Cambridge, 1984)

Ortiz, Fernando, trans. Jean Stubbs, 'The Afro-Cuban Festival "Day of the Kings"', in Judith Bettelheim, ed., *Cuban Festivals; An Illustrated Anthology* (New York, 1993), pp. 3–47

P., D., 'Carnival Is Here Again', *Sunday Guardian* (Trinidad), 23 February 1941, p. 15

Packenham, Thomas, *The Boer War* (London, 1979)

Parry, J. H. and P. M. Sherlock, *A Short History of the West Indies*, 3rd. edn (London, 1971)

Patterson, Massie and Lionel Belasco, with free transcription by Maurice Baron, *Calypso Songs of the West Indies* (New York, 1943)

Pearse, Andrew, 'Aspects Of Change In Caribbean Folk Music', *Journal of the International Folk Music Council*, vol. 7 (1955), pp. 29–36

'Carnival in Nineteenth Century Trinidad', *Caribbean Quarterly*, vol. 4, nos. 3–4 (1956), pp. 175–93

'Mitto Sampson on Calypso Legends of the Nineteenth Century', *Caribbean Quarterly*, vol. 4, nos. 3–4 (1956), pp. 250–62

'Music in Caribbean Popular Culture', *Revista/Review Interamericana*, vol. 8, No. 4 (1978), pp. 629–39

Pitts, Harry, 'Calypso: From Patois To Its Present Form', *Sunday Guardian* (Trinidad), Independence Supplement, 26 August 1962, pp. 41, 43

Preston, St Denis, 'Calypso: the jazz of the West Indies', *Melody Maker*, 25 February 1950, p. 3

Procope, Bruce, 'The Dragon Band or Devil Band', *Caribbean Quarterly*, vol. 4, nos. 3–4 (1956), pp. 275–80

Quevedo, Raymond (Atilla the Hun), 'Calypso;' in booklet notes to the 78rpm record album *Calypsos: by Wilmoth Houdini and his Royal Calypso Orchestra* (US) Decca Album no. A78 (New York, 1939), pp. 3–4

'Calypsoes From 1908–1958', in *Trinidad Calypso Book* (Trinidad, c. 1959), pp. 11, 13, 15, 18–19, 21, 23, 56

'Dame Lorraine', *Humming Bird*, Carnival no. (1961), p. 4

Atilla's Kaiso: A Short History of Trinidad Calypso (Trinidad, 1983)

Ramdin, Ron, *From Chattel Slave to Wage Earner: A History Of Trade Unionism In Trinidad And Tobago* (London, 1982)

Raymond, Arthur F., 'Origin of the Savannah Carnival and the Development of the Down Town Celebrations', *Humming Bird*, Carnival no. (1960), pp. 8–10

Redhead, Wilfred A., *A City On A Hill* (Barbados, 1985)

(Retired Warrior), 'Old Time Carnival: The Days Of The Stick Fighters; Ferocious Battles Recalled; A Retired Warrior's Memoirs', *Trinidad Guardian*, 2 March 1919, p. 7

Richards, Alfred, comp., *Discovery Day Celebration 1927: Souvenir* (Trinidad, 1927)

Rohlehr, Gordon, *Calypso and Society In Pre-Independence Trinidad* (Trinidad, 1990)

Roosevelt (Colonel) Theodore, 'Where the Steady Trade-Winds Blow', *Scribner's Magazine*, vol. 116, no. 2 (1917), pp. 169–88

Russell, Dave, *Popular muisc in England 1840–1914: A social history* (Manchester, 1987)

Rutter, Owen, *If Crab No Walk: A Traveller in the West Indies* (London, 1933)

Samaroo, Brinsley, 'The Trinidad Workingmen's Association And The Origin Of Popular Protest In A Crown Colony', *Social and Economic Studies*, vol. 21, no. 2 (1972), pp. 205–22

Sampson, Mitto, 'Old And New Calypsoes Compared: Was "Netty Netty" Catchy As "Letter For Thelma"?', *Trindad Guardian*, 30 January 1954, p. 6

Sander, Reinhard W., ed., *From Trinidad: An Anthology of West Indian Writing* (London, 1978)

Seroff, Doug, 'The Fisk Jubilee Singers in Britain', in Rainer Lotz and Ian Pegg, eds., *Under The Imperial Carpet: Essays in Black History* (Crawley, 1986), pp. 42–54

'100 Years From Today: Selected Items Of Musical Matters Drawn From The Black Community', *78 Quarterly*, vol. 1, no. 5 (1990), pp. 56–62

'100 Years From Today: A Survey Of Afro-American Music In 1890 As Recorded In The Black Community Press', *78 Quarterly*, vol. 1, no. 6 (1991), pp. 52–63

Shull, 'Pierrots A Feature Of Carnival In '90s', *Sunday Guardian* (Trinidad), 3 March 1946, p. 6

Simmons, Harold F. C., 'Terre Bois Bois', *Caribbean Quarterly*, vol. 6, no. 4 (1960), pp. 282–5

Singh, Kelvin, *Bloodstained Tombs: The Muharram Massacre 1884* (London, 1988)

Spottswood, Richard K., comp., *Ethnic Music on Records: A Discography of Ethnic Recordings Produced in the United States, 1893 to 1942*, 7 vols. (Urbana, 1990)

Stevenson, Robert, *A Guide To Caribbean Music* (Lima, 1975)

Talley, Thomas W., *Negro Folk Rhymes* (New York, 1922)

Thomas, J. J., *The Theory and Practice of Creole Grammar* (London, 1969) (first published, Trinidad, 1869)

Toll, Robert C., *Blacking Up: The Minstrel Show in Nineteenth Century America* (New York, 1974)

The Trinidad Almanac for the Year 1824 (Trinidad, *c.* 1823)

(Trindad Banjo, Mandoline And Guitar Orchestra), *West India Committee Circular*, vol. 24, no. 355 (7 May 1912), pp. 236–7

Trindad Carnival (Trinidad, 1988) (a slightly edited version of *Caribbean Quarterly*, vol. 4, nos. 3–4 (1956))

Trottman, David Vincent, *Crime in Trinidad: Conflict And Control In A Plantation Society 1838–1900* (Knoxville, 1986)

Underhill, Edward Bean, *The West Indies: Their Social and Religious Condition* (London, 1862)

Urich, John, *West Indian Melodies* (2 nos., Orchestral and P. F. parts) (London (1887)) (part of the 'Alliance Musicale')

West Indian Melodies, no. 2, *Bamboula* (P. F.) (London (1887)) (part of the 'Alliance Musicale Album Bijou')

(*Victor Records Spanish American Catalogue, c.* 1922 – title page, etc. missing in copy held by author)

Williams, Connie, *12 Songs From Trinidad* (San Francisco, 1959)

Williams, Eric, *History of the People of Trinidad and Tobago* (London, 1964)

Wilmot, Swithin, 'The Politics Of Protest In Free Jamaica – The Kingston John Canoe Christmas Riots, 1840 and 1841', *Caribbean Quarterly*, vol. 36, nos. 3–4 (1990), pp. 65–75

Wood, Donald, *Trinidad In Transition* (London, 1968)

'X', 'The Origin of the Cannes Boulees' (in French), *Port of Spain Gazette*, 19 March 1881, p. 3

'The Origin of Cannes Boulee' (English translation), *Port of Spain Gazette*, Supplement, 26 March 1881, p. 1

Yelvington, Kevin A., 'Introduction: Trinidad Ethnicity', in Kevin (A.) Yelvington, ed., *Trinidad Ethnicity* (London, 1993), pp. 1–32

ed., *Trinidad Ethnicity* (London, 1993)

Young, Philip, *West-India Melodies; or Negro Tunes. Adapted for the Piano-Forte. As Performed by the Negroes in the West-Indies, with Regular Negro Beat (Imitated as made by the various African Instruments they use) which commences on the weak part of the measure; now first Collected and Arranged by Philip Young (late Pupil of Dr. Crotch;) resident in Jamaica* (London (1822?))

Young, Sir William, 'A Tour Through Several Islands of Barbadoes, St Vincent, Antiguia, Tobago and Grenada in the Years 1791, and 1792', in, Bryan Edwards, *The History, Civil And Commercial of the British Colonies in the West Indies*, vol. 3 (London, 1801), pp. 261–301

Zaretsky, Irving I., and Mark P. Leone, eds., *Religious Movements in Contemporary America* (Princeton, 1974)

Legal and Official Documents

1. British Legislation and Government Sources

A: ACTS OF PARLIAMENT

47 Geo. III c. 36 – *An Act for the Abolition of the Slave Trade* (25 March 1807)

3 and 4 Gueliemi IV c. 73 – *An Act for the Abolition of Slavery throughout the* British *Colonies; for promoting the Industry of the manumitted Slaves; and for compensating the Persons hitherto entitled to the Services of such Slaves* (28 August 1833)

1 and 2 Victoriae c. 19 – *An Act to amend the Act for the Abolition of Slavery in the* British *Colonies* (11 April 1838)

B: COLONIAL OFFICE CORRESPONDENCE (Public Record Office)

CO 295/289/62: Sir S. Freeling to the Earl of Kimberly (7 March 1881)

CO 295/289/63: Sir S. Freeling to the Earl of Kimberly (7 March 1881)

CO 295/289/66: Sir S. Freeling to the Earl of Kimberly (8 March 1881)

CO 295/289/69: Sir S. Freeling to the Earl of Kimberly (9 March 1881)

CO 295/289/70: Sir S. Freeling to the Earl of Kimberly (9 March 1881)

CO 295/289/81: L. M. Fraser, 'History of the origin of the Carnival' (16 March 1881)

CO 295/289/93: Sir S. Freeling to the Earl of Kimberly (25 March 1881)

CO 295/301/56: Sir S. Freeling to the Earl of Derby (8 March 1884)

CO 295/305/53: Sir A. E. Havelock to the Earl of Derby (26 February 1885)

C: COLONIAL OFFICE REPORTS (Public Record Office)

CO 884/4/40: *Mr Hamilton's Report on the Causes of the Disturbances in Connection with the Carnival in Trinidad*, 13 June 1881 (Confidential Print, September 1881)

CO 884/9/147: *Notes On West Indian Riots* (March 1905)

D: PARLIAMENTARY REPORTS

C. 4366: *Correspondence respecting the recent Coolie Disturbances in Trinidad at the Mohurrum Festival, with the Report thereon by Sir H. W. Norman, KCB, CIE.* (March 1885)

Cd. 1661: *Papers Relating To The Recent Disturbances At Port Of Spain Trinidad* (July 1903)

Cd. 1662 : *Report Of The Commission Of Enquiry Into The Recent Disturbances At Port Of Spain Trinidad* (July 1903)
Cd. 1988 : *Further Papers Relating To The Disturbances At Port of Spain, Trinidad, In March, 1903* (April, 1904)

2. *Trinidad Legislation and Government Sources (Library of Foreign and Commonwealth Office)*

General Index (to the laws of Trinidad, passed between 1797 and 1850 (*sic* – 1830)) – selected entries (chronologically):
'Prohibition of Negro dances in Town. Order of Government, 4*th January*, 1801'. (POLICE: 1st vol. p. 139), p. 15
'Permission to people of colour to hold Balls and Assemblies, subject to a donation for paupers of 16 Dollars. – Minutes of Council, 15*th August*, 1807'. (FREE COLOURED PEOPLE: 1st vol. p. 564), p. 9
'Police Regulations of the 30th May, 1797, re-published. – 25*th November*, 1808'. (POLICE: 1st vol. p. 624), p. 15
'General Regulations for the Police of Port of Spain. – 25*th November*, 1808'. (POLICE: 1st vol. p. 630), p. 15
'Negroes are forbidden to carry bludgeons or other weapons, on pain of a month's imprisonment and being worked in the chain gang, Ord.(er by the Cabildo) 12*th September*, 1810'. (POLICE: 1st vol. p. 829), p. 15
An Ordinance for establishing an effective system of Police within the Town of Port of Spain , no. 4 of 1835 (7 September)
An Ordinance for improving the Police in and near the Town of Port of Spain, no. 11 of 1837 (30 December)
An Ordinance to consolidate and amend the Laws relative to the Police, no. 6 of 1849 (3 July)
An Ordinance for rendering certain Offences punishable on Summary Conviction (*Summary Convictions*), no. 6 of 1868 (7 April)
An Ordinance for Regulating the Festivals of Immigrants, no. 9 of 1882 (1 July)
An Ordinance to amend the Ordinance no. 6 of 1868 intituled 'An Ordinance for rendering certain Offences "Punishable on Summary Conviction"' (*Summary Convictions (amendment)*), no. 11 of 1883 (10 July)
An Ordinance for the better preservation of the Peace (*Peace Preservation*), no. 1 of 1884 (25 January)
An Ordinance to amend the Ordinance no. 6 of 1868 intituled 'An Ordinance for

rendering certain Offences "Punishable on Summary Conviction"'
(*Summary Convictions (amendment)*), no. 2 of 1884 (1 February)
An Ordinance to amend the Law relating to premises Licenced for the retail of intoxicating Liquor (*Licencing Amendment*), no. (?) of 1884 (1 February)
An Ordinance for amending and consolidating the Law with regard to the constitution of the Medical Board, the Practice of Medicine and Surgery and the selling of Drugs, no. 6 of 1887 (8 March)
An Ordinance for the suppression of certain practices during Carnival, no. 2 of 1891 (2 February)
Trinidad and Tobago: *Proclamation* no. 7 of 1918 (14 January 1918)
Strikes and Lockout Ordinance, no. 1 of 1920
Seditious Publications Ordinance, no. 10 of 1920

3. US Legal Documents

78 F. Supp. 686 (Baron v. Leo Feist Inc. et. al. – 14 June 1948)

Newspapers (&c)

Argos (Trinidad)
Barbados Mercury and Bridgetown Gazette (Barbados)
The Echo of Trinidad (Trinidad)
Evening News (Trinidad)
Fair Play and Trinidad News and *Fair Play and Trinidad and Venezuelan News* (Trinidad)
Freeman (Indianapolis, USA)
Gleaner (Jamaica)
Illustrated London News (Britain)
Lloyds List (Britain)
Melody Maker (Britain)
Mirror (Trinidad)
New Era (Trinidad)
Penny Cuts (Trinidad)
Port of Spain Gazette (Trinidad)
Public Opinion (Trinidad)
Star of the West (Trinidad)

Sunday Guardian (Trinidad)
Trinidad Chronicle (Trinidad)
Trinidad Gazette (Trinidad)
Trinidad Guardian (Trinidad, 1827) – (Public Record Office, Britain)
Trinidad Guardian (Trinidad, from 1918)
Trinidad Palladium (Trinidad)
Trinidad Review (Trinidad)
Trinidad Royal Gazette (Trinidad) – (Public Record Office, Britain)
Trinidad Sentinel (Trinidad)
Trinidad Spectator (Trinidad)
Trinidad Standard (Trinidad)
West India Committee Circular (Britain)

Unpublished Works

John Houlston Cowley, 'Music and Migration: Aspects of Black Music in
    the British Caribbean, the United States, and Britain, before the
    Independence of Jamaica and Trinidad and Tobago', unpublished
    PhD thesis, University of Warwick, 1992
Spottswood, Richard, comp. 'A Discography of West Indian Recordings
    (1912–1945)'

Andrew Pearse Papers (University of the West Indies, St Augustine, Trinidad
    and Tobago)

'Ballad Singer Calypso'
'*Belé* – from Martinique', (*Trinidad Sentinel*, 1 April 1841)
Clarke, Joseph and Anthony – interview, October 1953
(Connor, Edric) – excerpt from letter sent by Edric Connor to Lennox
    Pierre, 21 February 1949, regarding the formation of Canboulay stick-
    bands; collected by J. D. Elder, 21 June 1953
Coombs, Anastasia – interview by J. D. Elder, Santa Cruz, 30 June 1951
(Garcia, Philip) Lord Executor: St Francios Valley – interview notes (by
    J. D. Elder), 10 February 1952
(Quevedo, Raymond and Lennox Pierre) 'Evolution of Steel Band' (Notes
    taken at a discussion wtih Hon. R. Quevedo and Len. Pierre on
    30 June 1953)

(Richard, Frances) 'Canne Brule Riot 1881: Eye-witness account of Frances Richard (96) of 11 Rudin St., Belmont, as it was related on 4th July 1953 to J. D. Elder'

West Indian Committee Collection (Institute of Commonwealth Studies, University of London

Views of Trinidad (album of photographs, 1870s–80s)

Discography

Calypso Pioneers 1912–1937, Rounder Records CD 1039 – (includes *Iron Duke In The Land* by J. Resigna (Iron Duke/Julian White Rose))

Calypso Lore And Legend, Cook Road Recordings (LP) 5016 – (includes 'Patrick Jones tells of calypso, chants songs of ancient calypsonians'.)

Calypsos: Sung by Wilmoth Houdini with his Royal Calypso Orchestra, Decca Album A78 – (an album of 78rpm records released in the USA in 1939; includes booklet with article on 'Calypso' by Raymond Quevedo)

History Of Carnival: Christmas, Carnival Calenda and Calypso from Trinidad 1929–1939, Matchbox MBCD 301-2 – (includes *History of Carnival* by Atilla the Hun)

Trinidad Loves To Play Carnival: Carnival Calenda and Calypso from Trinidad 1914–1939, Matchbox MBCD 302-2 – (includes *Bagai Sala que Pocheray Moin* by Jules Sims)

Orchestra créoles: Quand Paris biginait 1930–1940, Music Memoria (CD) 30876 – (includes *Colby* by Maïotte Almaby)

273

Index

274

Second World War 220, 235, 236
secular 6–8, 50, 136, 228, 230, 232
Seditious Publications Ordinance 222, 226
See My Little Brown Boy (or *He Is A Dude*) 178, 193
Senior Inventor *see* Henry Forbes
Set Girls (Jamaican Jonkonnu bands) 42, 229
Shand Estate Revolt (Trinidad) 12–15, 231
Shango (religion) 232
shanties *see* chanties
shâtwél see chant(er)
Shine's Pasture, Port of Spain 106, 119
shoe blacks *see* boot blacks
Shortest (Abraham Ravin – stickman) 129
Shrove Monday 24, 34, 52, 55, 59, 68, 88, 89, 100, 102, 110, 120, 130, 132, 140, 143, 145, 149, 157, 160, 161, 167, 170, 171, 177, 199, 204, 205, 212, 226
Shrove Saturday 101, 128
Shrove Sunday 2, 24, 30, 31, 34, 39, 41, 52, 53, 67, 69, 80, 89–92, 94, 99, 102, 127, 137 (*Dimanche Swa* – evening), 139, 233
Shrove Tuesday 11, 24, 54, 55, 68, 74, 81, 88, 89, 91, 92, 102, 108, 125, 127, 130, 138, 141, 145, 149, 154, 157, 158, 161, 167, 169–71, 173–5, 178, 200, 203, 205, 206, 213, 226
Shrovetide 1, 8, 12, 22, 23, 32, 36, 37, 40, 53, 59, 99, 120, 137, 139, 153, 208, 222, 233
Simeron (John Jacob – stickman) 122, 123
Simmons, Elizabeth (queen, Dahlias *diametre* band) 60
Sims, Jules (chantwell) 192, 194, 197, 202, 219
singer(s) and singing 2, 8, 17, 18, 21, 29, 52, 72, 75, 80, 102, 114–15, 117, 118, 127, 130, 135–7, 140–2, 145, 150–2, 155, 157–60, 162, 174–6, 178, 180, 182, 188, 191, 200, 203, 207, 219, 227, 229, 231, 233
'Singing Gloria' 176
single tone, or tome (form of calypso) 138, 162, 193, 194, *202*
Sissieretta Jones *see* Black Patti
66th Regiment (British) 77
slave dancing societies, *Convois* or *Regiments* (Trinidad) 13, 14, 15, 18, 131, 134
slave insurrection (Trinidad) 18, 19, 29
slaves and slavery 1, 3, 4–18, 20–2, 25, 26, 28–30, 33, 39, 43, 44, 52, 53, 61, 80, 83, 87, 104, 121, 131, 134–6, 184, 228–30, 232
snake charmers (masque) 142, 199
snake dance 113
Society of People of African Origin 221
Society of St Rose *see* Rose Society

soldiers (masque) 174
Solicitor General (masque) 71
songster(s) 131, 136, 137, 138, 140, 144, 151, 153, 160, 162, 174, 182, 191, 234, 235, 236
Sonny Bo, or Sonny Broken (stickman) 124
Sons of Evil (devil band) 191
Sorzanoville, or Sorzansville, Port of Spain 85, 100, *146*
Soucatau, or Soucantan (Henry Jacob – stickman) 123
Soucouyan legend 121
'Sound the bugle the Kaiser cried' 201
South Africa 152
South America 1, 9, 40, 62, 71, 193, 236
South American Indian warriors (band) 40, 42, 83, 134
souveniers de la vie africaine see custom(s) and tradition(s)
Sovereign pair of England (masque) 40
Spain, Spanish 4, 9, 11, 25, 43, 232
Spanish (band) 35, 42
Spanish (language) 4, 9, 32, 43, 71, 132, 134, 135, 186, 196
Spanish airs 149
Spanish Grandee (masque) 87
Spanish law 15, 22
Spanish Main *see* South America
Spanish morris dancers *see* Venzuelan may-pole dancers
Spanish peons (from South America) 40, 43, 98, 134, 135
Spanish Valses or Waltzes 124, 128, 156, 184, 185, 186, 192, 193, 202, 235
speeches 81, 87 (bombastic), 126 (verbal exchanges), 132 (patriotic), 137 (verbal contests), 174 (eloquent), 198 (high sounding words), 226 (grandiloquent)
spirit of Carnival 88
spirituals 114
sponsorship *see* patronage
spoons *see* bottle and spoon
St Ann's, Port of Spain 20, 35, 64, 78
St Ann's River (Dry River, Port of Spain) 34, 78, 136, 146
St Christopher (St Kitts) 8, 44
St Croix 13
St George (slave dancing society) 13
St James (stickband) 171
St James, Port of Spain 95–6, 99, 100, 141, 171, 189, 223
St Joseph, Trinidad 23, 61, 100, 160
St Lucia 8, 32, 229, 233
St Marguerite (St Margaret Mary Alocoque – patron saint) 229